THE WHICH? GUIDE TO
YORKSHIRE AND
THE PEAK DISTRICT

THE WHICH? GUIDE TO

YORKSHIRE
AND THE
PEAK DISTRICT

MARTIN WAINWRIGHT
AND TIM LOCKE

Published by Consumers' Association
and Hodder & Stoughton

Which? Books are commissioned and researched by The Association for
Consumer Research and published by Consumers' Association,
2 Marylebone Road, London NW1 4DF, and Hodder & Stoughton,
47 Bedford Square, London WC1B 3DP

Editor for *Holiday Which?*: Polly Phillimore
Additional verification: Penny Cartledge

Typographic design and cover design by Paul Saunders
Cover illustration by Charles Penny
Line illustrations by Sally Maltby
Maps by David Perrott Cartographics
Maps for the walking chapter by Tim Locke
Index by Marie Lorimer

First published September 1992
Copyright © 1992 Consumers' Association Ltd

British Library Cataloguing in Publication Data
The Which? Guide to Yorkshire and the Peak District
914.28
ISBN 0-340-55035-X

Thanks for choosing this book...
If you find it useful, we'd like to hear from you. Even if it
doesn't do the job you were expecting, we'd still like to know.
Then we can take your comments into account when preparing
similar titles or, indeed, the next edition of the book. Address
your letter to the Publishing Manager at Consumers' Association,
FREEPOST, 2 Marylebone Road, London NW1 4DF. We look
forward to hearing from you.

Typeset by Saxon Printing Limited, Derby
Printed and bound in Great Britain by Richard Clay Ltd, Bungay,
Suffolk

CONTENTS

ABOUT THIS GUIDE

This Guide is one of a series of guidebooks produced by *Holiday Which?* It is unusual among guides to Yorkshire in that it covers not only the much visited Dales, Moors and Vale of York, but the industrial south and west of Yorkshire and the former East Riding, too. It aims to combine the best in travel-writing with advice and recommendations based on thorough research of the areas.

The eight chapters that follow a brief introduction to Yorkshire and the Peak District report on the sights, towns and villages, with a section of recommendations for accommodation and places to eat at the end of each chapter. In Chapter 9, 'Walking', Tim Locke gives a useful summary of the best walks in the area; some suggestions for walks are dealt with briefly because the routes are well signed and easy to follow, others are covered in more detail in the *Holiday Which? Good Walks Guide*. Twelve circular walks that range from gentle strolls to energetic rambles are described in detail.

The final section gives telephone numbers for tourist information offices and general information on accommodation, transport, markets and some suggestions for entertainment.

WHERE TO STAY

The hotels and B&Bs have all been inspected and selected by the *Holiday Which?* team; they are described in more detail in *The Which? Hotel Guide 1993* published by Consumers' Association and Hodder & Stoughton. The price categories of our recommended hotels are based on the cost, per night, of a double or twin-bedded room in 1992, including VAT and breakfast. Tariffs quoted by hotels sometimes include dinner – check when you book. You can expect to pay £9 to £15 for a set meal in a simple hotel, and up to £35 in a luxury one. A further selection of places to stay in the area is available in the third edition of *The Good Bed and Breakfast Guide*, published by Consumers' Association and Hodder & Stoughton.

- **£** – under £70 per room per night
- **££** – £70 to £110 per room per night
- **£££** – over £110 per room per night

WHERE TO EAT

Our recommendations for places to eat were complied with the help of *The Good Food Guide* and most are featured in the 1993 edition, published by Consumers' Association and Hodder & Stoughton. Hotels featured in this section are recommended primarily for their food. A ★ marks a place that is particularly good value.

OPENING TIMES

Opening days and times of the sights were only available for 1992. Some may change so it's best to double-check, particularly if you intend to visit early or late in the season. Where days and times are erratic we give a contact telephone number. The local tourist offices (see end section) have up-to-date details of all the attractions in their areas.

A note about the authors

MARTIN WAINWRIGHT

Martin Wainwright was born and brought up in Leeds where he now works as *The Guardian*'s Northern correspondent. He also broadcasts on BBC TV and Radio 4 and has published local histories of Leeds and Bath. He is 42, married to Penny and they have two sons, Thomas and Oliver.

TIM LOCKE

Tim Locke is an experienced travel writer, with an interest in walking, and has travelled extensively in Britain, Europe and the Far East. His published works include *The Holiday Which? Good Walks Guide*, and *The Holiday Which? Town and Country Walks Guide*, as well as guides to the Lake District and the West Country, all published by Consumers' Association.

INTRODUCTION

Yorkshire goes on and on. The county's ancient borders stretch from the Tees to the Trent and reach within eight defiantly Lancastrian miles of the Irish Sea. Within this immense boundary, the variety of life and landscape, the warp and woof of West Riding textile terminology, is remarkable.

Much of the rolling broad acreage is very well-known: the lovely Dales carved out of the Pennines by the tumbling waters of the Swale, Ure, Nidd, Wharfe and Aire; the wind-soughed heather of the Brontë moors; the seabirds' redoubt on the Flamborough cliffs. Another landscape, too, is engraved on the nation's psyche: the chimneys and redbrick terrace-house grids of the great industrial cities and towns.

The people are comparably large and boldly-drawn in character. Yorkshiremen and women have furnished the country, again and again, with dominant figures in every hard-working sphere; statesmen, writers, clergy and villains have shared, for all their different callings, that obstinate determination which is the county's special hallmark.

'There be such a company of wilful gentlemen in Yorkshire as there be not in all England beside,' wrote the exasperated Abbot of York in 1556, and his generalisation is proudly nurtured to this day. Fencing with local people, trying to better their masterful use of monosyllabic 'ayes' or even complete silence when addressed, is one of the joys of a Yorkshire holiday. Keeping a register of examples of extreme bluntness (never allow this to offend you; you've lost the game if you do), is another.

Yorkshire would like its boundaries to embrace the whole world; biologists at its five universities have been known to claim marine specimens from the Dogger Bank, 60 miles offshore, as part of the 'Yorkshire' list. But the borders had to stop somewhere. And in 1974, amid much furore, they were drastically shortened for administrative purposes, parts of geographical Yorkshire being ceded to town halls in Lancashire, Durham and the new counties of Cleveland, Humberside and Greater Manchester. Further revisions are likely to replace the northern half of hapless, endlessly derided Humberside with a new East Yorkshire. Meanwhile, famous Yorkshire institutions, like the county cricket club, stick to the ancient, maximum boundaries.

Thus, any author of a guidebook to Yorkshire faces the boundary dilemma. We have included all the places in the area we think the visitor would like to see, crossing the borders of North, South and West Yorkshire, and, disregarding boundaries old or new, included the east coast and the towns, villages and countryside down to the mouth of the River Humber.

The Peak District, first of Britain's National Parks and a wild and wonderful wilderness, is an essential part of the hinterland of Sheffield and the wide, recreational spaces of the South Pennines. Borders mean little to the rambler or naturalist on Bleaklow or Kinder Scout.

Most visitors to Yorkshire and the Peak District, especially those coming for the first time, will seek out the major attractions, such as the city of York, the Dales, Chatsworth, the North York Moors and the coast. Tourism is very long-standing in these 'blue-chip' areas and visitors' facilities, from books and maps to cafés and souvenirs, are consequently sophisticated and comprehensive. With such advantages, however, come irritations like traffic jams, high prices and sometimes, understandably, local weariness with visitors. The rewarding Jekyll face far outweighs the grumpy Hyde one, but it is as well to go prepared.

A similarly mild caution should also be heeded by visitors to the region's relatively new tourist attractions. Industrial centres such as Leeds, Sheffield and, above all, Bradford have been immensely successful at marketing their gritty charms in the last decade. The National Museum of Film, Photography and Television at Bradford now receives 1,000,000 visitors a year, and the tramp of crocodiles of Japanese tourists can be heard on J B Priestley's streets. The industrial, and especially Victorian, legacy of the cities, and their smaller neighbours of Huddersfield and Halifax, has been excellently preserved and provides enormous interest. But these centres are all busy, workaday places too, and if you find yourself at 5pm on a rainy day in one of the many, uniform-looking suburbs, you may find the temptation to flee to Harrogate, Whitby or Buxton irresistible.

Yorkshire also has plenty of *terra incognita* to attract the exploring tourist. There is the 'secret' countryside surrounding Barnsley and Doncaster, glimpsed from the rushing M1: the grazing deer and Palladian columns may be mistakenly dismissed as mirages by the passing traveller. And the peace of Holderness, far to the east, with its immense skies and soaring church spires, is not yet savoured by many outsiders. Some of the most rewarding moments of a visit to the region will be spent in such places.

An eye for detail on the broad Yorkshire canvas can bring the same lasting satisfaction. Can you find (and coincide with

the rare open days of) the hermitage in the rock at Pontefract?
Will you track down the gritstone miniature-chimney
tombstone to a family of steeplejacks in Beckett Street
cemetery, Leeds? In all these acres you should come across
something to claim, like a nineteenth-century explorer, as
your very own. Set in the context of famous and never-
disappointing landscapes like Fountains Abbey, Gordale Scar
or Robin Hood's Bay, it will sum up the appeal of the greatest
county in England.

KEY MAP

1 West Yorkshire
2 The Yorkshire Dales
3 Harrogate, Ripon and The North
4 North York Moors
5 East Yorkshire
6 York and around
7 South Yorkshire
8 The Peak District

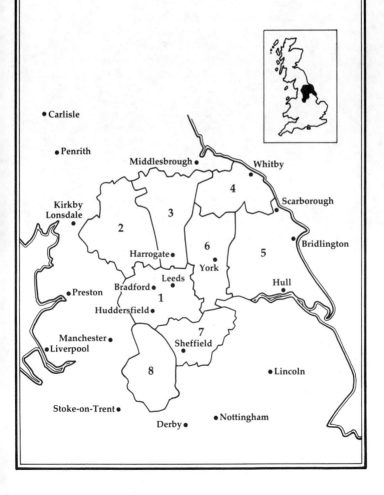

WEST YORKSHIRE

- The best of Victorian Britain, seen in the centre of the large conurbations, the mills and the excellent industrial museums
- Dramatic Pennine landscapes; the Brontë country
- Bustling markets and mill shops in the textile manufacturing heartland
- Historic stately homes in peaceful parkland close to commercial districts typify this diverse county

Five Rise Locks - Bingley

IF you start talking to locals in one of the many pubs or fish-and-chip shops between the Pennines and the Vale of York, try steering the conversation to the old days of the West Riding – one of the Viking 'thriddings', or thirds, of the ancient county of Yorkshire. Eyes will light up and memories come flooding back of the days when farmers from the Dales, businessmen from Leeds and miners from the Barnsley and Doncaster pits argued things out at County Hall in Wakefield. Yorkshire was the largest county in England but the West Riding on its own came second; it was 'God's favourite patch of His own county'.

Those days ended administratively in 1974, although many Yorkshire people refuse to accept the change. Indeed, Leeds City Council defiantly concludes its official address with 'West Riding of Yorkshire'. The contemporary boundaries of West Yorkshire are much more modest, but the county still embraces the heart of the former West Riding with its tall chimneys, Pennine moors and landscapes of the Brontë sisters and J B Priestley.

Major, conventional tourist attractions – stately homes like Harewood House and Nostell Priory, ruins such as Kirkstall Abbey and Pontefract Castle – are still within the county boundary. Haworth is one of Britain's prime tourist honey-pots, where you can buy everything from a Brontë lollipop to a Brontë sunbed (and pay inflated Brontë prices for them). But the bulk of West Yorkshire is relatively fresh to tourism, with locals still dubious about the idea that outsiders actually want to spend holidays there. Memories of visitors like Charles Dickens ('Leeds is the beastliest place, one of the nastiest I know') are not dead.

Parts of the landscape, too, leave you in no doubt that the West Yorkshire conurbation is one of the largest in Britain, with houses packed close to factories where thousands of different products are still made. The old 'Satanic' days of noise and smoke have gone, but visitors may sometimes find their surroundings overcrowded and drab. Bolling Hall in Bradford is a treasure hidden in run-of-the-mill suburbia; lovely Heath village near Wakefield looks out on to a hideous power station. Persistence is rewarded here and in areas where ribbon development can give the illusion of an endless town. Driving from Bradford to Dewsbury through the Spen Valley you may be tempted to flee to the more obviously inviting Dales; but it would be a shame to miss Oakwell Hall, the Red House and the Bagshaw Museum, and the countryside is usually just a row of terraces away.

In the busiest town centres, too, keep your eyes open for traces of an elegant past: Georgian and medieval market-towns were the industrial hives until the factories came. The ruthlessness and energy of the age of the Industrial Revolution were summarised by the Victorian statesman Brougham in a speech at Leeds Cloth Hall in 1830: 'We don't now live in the age of barons, thank God; we live in the age of Leeds, of Bradford, of Halifax and of Huddersfield.' A few years later, Leeds' industrial barons drove a railway right through the Cloth Hall where Brougham had spoken; only one section remains.

West Yorkshire has also capitalised on its gritty history; there are ingenious industrial museums, plenty of mills put to interesting new uses, such as the excellent Hockney gallery at Saltaire, and the unique clog factory at Hebden Bridge, as well as mill shops offering bargains that will gladden the thrifty. Trams and steam trains are waiting to clatter and chug you about. The by-products of a busy, hard-working part of Britain include such minor marvels as some of the best fish-and-chips in England.

The general welcome extended to visitors may sometimes be mixed with the famous Yorkshire taciturnity, deliberately deployed to try you out. Optimists who like goading pessimists will have a field day. Bradford people, in particular, delight in taking a gloomy view of things and are reputed to keep their overcoats on all summer because 'it is bound to rain eventually'. Praise of your surroundings goes down well, but keep the parameters tight. If there is anywhere a Dewsbury man scorns more than the South, it is Batley; Leeds and Bradford people virtually deny that the other exists.

West Yorkshire can be divided with manageable logic into five principal centres: Leeds, Bradford, Huddersfield, Halifax and Wakefield, each with a ring of countryside, sometimes with valleys snaking off towards the moors.

LEEDS

Leeds is the sprawling, prosperous, regional centre of Yorkshire, given in its wilder moments to claiming that it is the Capital of the North. This accolade would require the disappearance of Manchester, but Leeds has certainly established itself as the chief city on the Yorkshire side of the Pennines.

Depending on how you measure it, Leeds ranks as the third-, fourth- or fifth-largest city in Britain and its size can

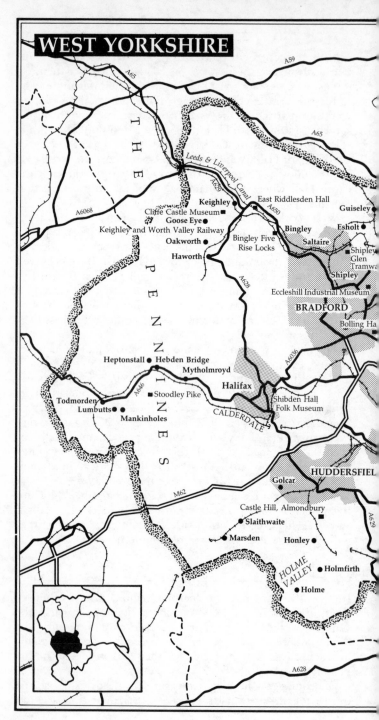

WEST YORKSHIRE

A59

A65

A65

THE

Leeds & Liverpool Canal

A6068

Keighley

East Riddlesden Hall

A650

Guiseley

Cliffe Castle Museum

Goose Eye

Keighley and Worth Valley Railway

Bingley

Esholt

Oakworth

Bingley Five
Rise Locks

Saltaire

Haworth

Shipley
Glen
Tramway

Shipley

A628

Eccleshill Industrial Museum

BRADFORD

A6036

Bolling Ha

Heptonstall **Hebden Bridge**

Mytholmroyd

Halifax

A646

Stoodley Pike

Todmorden

Shibden Hall
Folk Museum

Lumbutts

Mankinholes

CALDERDALE

P E N N I N E S

T H E

A629

M62

HUDDERSFIEL

Golcar

Castle Hill, Almondbury

Slaithwaite

A629

Marsden

Honley

HOLME
VALLEY

Holmfirth

Holme

A628

16

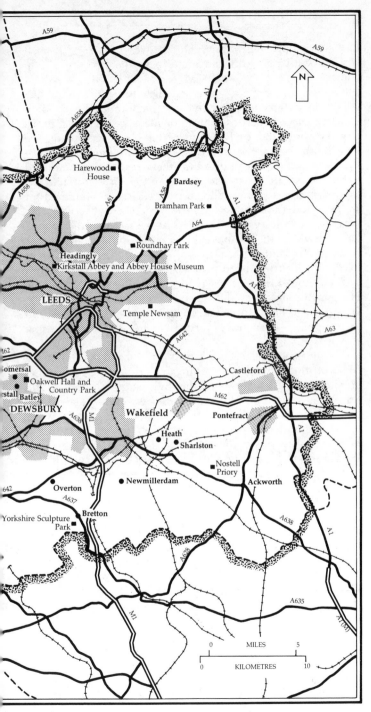

initially be overwhelming. The centre, however, is well stocked with car parks and meter bays (take plenty of 20p coins).

The centre of Leeds is a paradise for those who like Victorian architecture, and even the uncommitted may enjoy spotting carved cherubs, plump maidens and the ubiquitous city symbol, the owl. Among the best legacies of the nineteenth century are the covered shopping arcades – Queen's, Grand, Thornton's and others – a tradition continued in the 1990s with the stylish roofing of Queen Victoria Street. In wet weather, you can thread your way round hundreds of shops; modern shopping centres are linked by Victorian arcades. In County Arcade, smirk at the fact that the council has mistaken the embossed frieze of pomegranates for oranges and painted them the wrong colour. The city centre is exceptionally friendly to pedestrians. Traffic is barred from most of the square between the Headrow (nicknamed the Hedgerow since trees and shrubs were planted), Vicar Lane, Briggate and Park Row. The sheer intensity of the bustle and the shopping – a favourite Northern recreation – may take you by surprise.

The hurly-burly reaches a peak on Vicar Lane in **Leeds Market**, the largest in Yorkshire and a riot of sooty Oriental architecture. To appreciate the full range of domes and minarets, you should look upwards, which is good advice generally in these Victorian streets. Inside, a warm, crowded Babel of commerce reveals remarkable bargains, from fish to bootlaces. Just down the road, the ugly but striking **Corn Exchange** resembles London's Covent Garden; twee boutiques are set in a glorious interior, like the inside of a barrage balloon. Corn merchants still sell seed on Tuesday mornings next to the café.

The Victorians, though, would undoubtedly have preferred Whitelock's, an exceptional pub in Turk's Head Yard, a sinister-looking alley connecting Briggate and pedestrianised Trinity Street. Another vintage Victorian pub is the Victoria Family and Commercial Hotel behind the splendid **Town Hall**. Explorers venturing further afield will also be rewarded if they track down the sumptuous Victorian Garden Gate in Whitfield Place, Hunslet, and the Albion in Armley Road, Armley, which was the model for the standard Hornby model railways pub.

In your role as modern Victorian, you should also visit the grandly fitted out auditorium of the **Leeds City Varieties** (opposite Lewis's on the Headrow), Britain's oldest surviving music hall and celebrated home of the television programme, *The Good Old Days*, which ran from 1953 to 1983. Performances are an unpredictable mixture - concerts, pantomime, and one-night plays are offered, as well as music hall. **The Grand Theatre** (Upper Briggate) is the still more opulent home of Opera North – all plush, chandeliers and coin-in-the-slot opera glasses. **The West Yorkshire Playhouse**, on Quarry Hill at the foot of the Headrow, is modern, by contrast, with good repertory and a restaurant serving fare that tends towards the wholesome.

Leeds Art Gallery (open all year, Mon to Fri 10 to 6, Wed 10 to 9, Sat 10 to 4 and Bank Hol Mon), next to the Town Hall on the Headrow, is one of the best galleries outside London. It has a strong Henry Moore collection and imaginative temporary displays. The neighbouring **Leeds City Museum** is feeble; most of the city's treasures are in storage awaiting better premises but you can see an Egyptian mummy and a stuffed Bengal tiger. But **Thwaite stone-grinding mill** (open all year, daily 10 to 5; closed Mon except Bank Hol Mon), in Thwaite Lane, off the Pontefract road, and **Armley Industrial Museum** (open Apr to Sept, Tue to Sat 10 to 6, Sun 2 to 6; Oct to Mar closes at 5) have competent displays, especially interesting if you are an enthusiast of giant cogwheels and associated machines.

Leeds outskirts

The ruins of **Kirkstall Abbey** and **Abbey House Museum** (open Apr to Sept, Mon to Sat 10 to 6, Sun 2 to 6; Oct to Mar closes at 5), on opposite sides of the A65, three miles from the city centre, are worth visiting for a taste of older history. Rather a lot of the abbey itself is cordoned off, in case the Cistercian stonework should crash down on tourists, but the nave, tower and cloisters form a lovely group. The museum has an excellent recreated network of Victorian streets, including vintage slot-machines that will keep children amused (old pennies can be bought at the entrance). There is a garden for the blind, as well as a miniature railway on Sundays and Bank Holiday afternoons, but no café, alas.

Kirkstall is a stopping point on the **Leeds and Liverpool Canal Towpath Walk**, an astonishingly rural meander which begins at the **Dark Arches**, Victorian vaults which now house a reasonable arcade of small shops under Leeds City Station. The path runs reliably alongside the canal up the Kirkstall Valley to the city boundary (eight miles) and eventually into Airedale.

On the other side of Leeds, the council's **Temple Newsam** estate (signposted off the A63 Leeds-to-Selby road at Halton; open all year, Tue to Sun, Bank Hol Mon 10.30 to 6.15; Wed to 8.30; closes earlier in winter, tel (0532) 647321) is the largest urban park in Europe. Its 1,400 acres include the national collection of delphiniums and surround a magnificent Tudor and Jacobean mansion. Inside the house is a formidable collection of decorative art, a bit too formidable for children, perhaps, but they should enjoy the friendly animals at Home Farm. There are plenty of pleasant woodland walks, a café (in season) and a reasonable souvenir shop.

Just off the ring road at **Roundhay**, the park (open daily 10 to dusk) is another Victorian delight, with boating, a small funfair, and a boathouse tea-room. The Coronation hothouse in the Canal Gardens (across Prince's Avenue from the main park) offers butterflies, spiders, tropical fish and a jungle with two waterfalls – all free. This is definitely the place to go on a chilly day in Leeds.

Excursions from Leeds

The splendid gatehouses of **Harewood House** (open Apr to Oct, daily: grounds 10 to 7; house 11 to 4.30) open on to the Leeds-to-Harrogate road (A61) at Harewood, opposite the uniform estate village which was moved here *en bloc* from the park in the eighteenth century. It is a magnificent mansion with a fine formal rose garden and lovely wooded grounds that sweep down to a lake, a romantic artificial waterfall and richly planted bog garden. The separate bird garden is large and rewarding, especially for children, who will also relish the very good adventure playground. A well-run café is housed in the stables. Harewood often has outdoor events, exhibitions and rallies which add to its attractions but can lead to monumental traffic jams.

Bramham Park (summer opening times, tel (0937) 844265), just off the A1 at Bramham village is often described, with characteristic Yorkshire nerve, as West Yorkshire's answer to Versailles. This statement might raise a few eyebrows, but the park is very splendid: a formal collection of canals, fountains, cascades and woodland rides which make a change from the more usual Capability Brown school of gentle landscaping. The mansion is a graceful Queen Anne building with fine furniture, porcelain and pictures, although the interior was wholly rebuilt in 1906 after years of neglect following a devastating fire in 1826.

BRADFORD

Bradford is the second-largest, but most characterful, of West Yorkshire's cities and major towns. Although snubbed whenever possible by Leeds, it has the confident air of a place known all over the world. People in Padua or Patagonia may, just, have heard of Leeds United. But they certainly know about Bradford, the old world capital of wool. Those heady days, when the city was the greatest international textile centre, have faded, but their relics remain. **The Wool Exchange**, where the merchants fixed their prices, now houses good-cause jumble sales and local festivals. But the grandeur is still omnipresent, and the buildings are the more impressive for being built almost exclusively in Pennine stone.

The biggest mills in Britain are here and some of the finest warehouses. The central **Little Germany** area is particularly rich in solid but ornately carved commercial buildings, canyons of stone created by nineteenth-century German textile merchants (including the father of the composer Frederick Delius, who was born in Claremont, Bradford). The western suburb of Manningham is rich in carefully graded types of Victorian workers' houses: 'back-to-backs', 'throughs' (with front and back doors) and grander 'semis' for the complicated rankings of overlookers and managers. The humbler dwellings stand, literally, in the shadow of the enormous Lister's velvet mill; the grander ones down the hill towards the Bradford Beck, facing Lister (or Manningham) Park which the mill-owner donated to the city along with its purpose-built art gallery, **Cartwright Hall** (open Apr to Sept, Tue to Sun, 10 to 6; Oct to Mar closes at 5).

Another monument to the past is the extraordinary **Under-cliffe cemetery**. It is one of the finest and most florid Victorian cemeteries in Britain; one good example is the grave of the Illingworth family, on which sphinxes guard their Egyptian tomb. There is no better place in Britain than Bradford to appreciate the might, muscle and social cost of the Industrial Revolution.

But this is also an adaptable city, accustomed to change. Many of the Manningham houses, for instance, are now the homes of families from Pakistan and Bangladesh, whose arrival in the '60s and '70s added a new cultural dimension to Bradford. The city has few rivals for the scale and range of its Pakistani, Bangladeshi and Indian cuisine. Not surprisingly, 'curry weekend' holiday packages have proved a success. There are literally hundreds of small restaurants, many of

21

which may look rather offputting, but once inside provide a genuine discovery. As a general rule, be bold. Do not always expect cutlery; customers often use chapatis to scoop up the dhal, sag or succulently cooked lamb. Some reliable choices include the Silver Jubilee in Oak Lane, Karachi in Neal Street and two upmarket places: the Nawab in Manor Row and the Bombay Brasserie in Simes Street's former chapel. It is also worth trying the many sweet centres for sugary burfi, balushai and other fattening sweets – Oak Lane, Great Horton Road and Leeds Road are well stocked with them (and many outlets offer savoury food as well).

Museums

• **National Museum of Photography, Film and Television** (open all year, daily exc Mon, 10.30 to 6; café until 7.30) Towering in Prince's View above an impressive statue of a rugged J B Priestley, loyally wearing his Bradford mac, this museum is free and allows you the chance to be a TV

RHUBARB AND LIQUORICE

THE TRIANGLE of farming land between Leeds, Wakefield and Pontefract has an unusual niche in history: for centuries, it dominated British rhubarb-growing and world production of liquorice.

Rich soil (further improved by the big cities' middens and cartloads of greasy textile waste), combined with a suitable climate, encouraged the production of both rhubarb and liquorice. Forced rhubarb, grown in long, low sheds (still visible from the M1 and M62), benefited from the nip of an early winter and the presence of a large labour force. Liquorice flourished on the limestone outcrop round Pontefract and also required a lot of farmhands.

Both crops were originally grown as medicines – rhubarb had a reputation for easing wind and stomach pains and is also used today in ulcer drugs - but both became sweets. Forced rhubarb, with its delicate colours of yellow and gold, was the standard winter pudding before deep-freeze container-ships made tropical fruits available all year round. Sugar was added to liquorice in the seventeenth century, with the creation of the black medallions known as Pontefract Cakes.

Anecdotes abound about visitors to Pontefract sitting down in

newsreader, operate TV cameras, fly on a magic photographic carpet and generally explore the absorbing world of film. Don't miss a show on the giant, five-storey IMAX screen, the biggest in Britain. You have to pay for this, but you won't begrudge it. There is a good café and wine bar with a terrific view of the city.

● **The Colour Museum** (open Tue to Fri, 2 to 5, Sat 10 to 4) This museum in Grattan Road has made an unexpected success of its speciality subject – the use of colour and the history of colour chemistry. Displays are highly imaginative and the museum is a deserving past winner of the Industrial Museum of the Year award.

● **Bradford Industrial Museum** (open all year, daily exc Mon, 10 to 5) The museum is in a converted woollen mill in Moorside Road, two miles from the city centre, and signposted off the Bradford-to-Harrogate road and the Bradford ring road at Eccleshill. You can visit rebuilt local 'back-to-back' terraced houses, or see the mill-owner's house, suffocating in cumbersome High Victorian décor. The staff,

---

local cafés, ordering one of the town's famous Cakes and then being startled to receive an old penny-sized sweet in lonely splendour on a plate. Alas, they are generally as unsubstantiated as the tale of how liquorice first came to Pontefract: twigs washed ashore from an Armada galleon wrecked off the Lincolnshire coast, were found by a local schoolmaster on holiday, who made them into canes, one of which broke during a boy's punishment. The boy bit a section to stifle his pain and, hey presto, Britain's first liquorice stick was discovered.

The origin of Liquorice Allsorts is better documented: a Bassett's salesman at the turn of the century mixed up his samples and offered them to clients as 'all sorts'. Local people also recall the Rhubarb Express, a special train laid on during the winter months in the 1930s, which took 600 tons of prime crop a night to London.

Rhubarb is still grown, although on a much reduced scale, and an annual show of plants and recipes is held every spring in Garforth, near Leeds. Liquorice-making thrives in Pontefract, but the crop is entirely imported. Token trees, with their blue flowers and serpentine roots, can be examined outside Wilkinson's factory in Knottingley Road.

many of whom are retired from the wool trade, treat fleeces, explain the difference between a top and a noil and put fantastic objects like the 12-Spindle Dolly Roller and Ring Twister through their clanking paces. There are also non-wool trade curiosities like the 1919 Scott Sociable Three-Wheeler. 'I have made a car for the working man which only the rich will buy,' lamented its inventor, Alfred Scott. Bobbins cafeteria is cosy and offers that rarity in this county, a small Yorkshire pudding (larger ones are naturally available too).

Bolling Hall

(Open all year, daily exc Mon 10 to 6; closes at 5 in winter)
The Hall is reached via the Bradford ring road and is two miles south of the city centre. Although marooned in suburbia, the hall is a fascinating mishmash of different periods, full of the feel of Yorkshire grandeur. The main hall, locally known as the housebody, with its magnificent window incorporating 24 stained-glass coats of arms, was built on to a medieval peel tower in 1500 and further wings were added in Georgian times. The rooms, each with a description in braille, house an exceptional collection of Northern seventeenth- and eighteenth-century oak furniture. Fifteenth-century mod cons installed by the Bolling family were the *en-suite* privies which can be seen in the tower bedrooms. The gardens are not extensive, but they do have picnic tables.

AIREDALE

Two curiosities form a gateway to Airedale from Bradford. At Windhill in **Shipley**, **Sooty's World**, Leeds Road (open all year, Mon to Thur 10.30 to 4.30; Fri in school hols; Sat and Sun 10 to 5; café) reverently records the days of juddering, black-and-white TV, when Sooty, the scatty bear, was created by Bradford-born Harry Corbett. Just off the A6038, two miles out of Shipley is **Esholt**, a quaint hamlet once entirely inhabited by Bradford sewage workers but now famous as *Emmerdale*, the setting for ITV's eponymous soap opera. Watch out for coachloads of solemn Scandinavians, who particularly relish the series. The Commercial Inn (the Woolpack of *Emmerdale*) is a good lunch spot and there are pleasant walks in the woods above the village.

Saltaire

Just off the A650, Saltaire is perhaps the finest 'factory village' in Britain. It can be reached by train on the Airedale line and also by intermittent canal waterbuses from Shipley. It has remained virtually unaltered since it was built in the 1850s by Sir Titus Salt, who combined his own surname with that of the River Aire to name his settlement. Salt was a millionaire at forty through his success in weaving alpaca and angora wool, which other industrialists had thought impossible. Spotting pious statues, friezes and stained-glass windows of llamas and angora goats is a good game for children in Saltaire. Salt was also a fervent Liberal and built the entire town for his 2,500 millworkers to show that industrialists could be charitable. A hospital, a school, rent-free almshouses for the elderly and a chapel were all included, but no pubs. Instead, the Workers' Saltaire Club and Institute with its library, games and billiard rooms, gymnasium and lecture hall was designed, in Salt's words, 'to provide a place where you can resort to conversation, business, recreation and refreshment... all the advantages of a public house without its evils'. Notice too, as you stroll the streets named after members of Salt's family, the subtle gradations in architecture, from workers' cottages to overlookers' larger homes.

The main, vast mill, completed in 1853, now houses the national collection of paintings by the Bradford-born artist David Hockney, in the **1853 Gallery** (open daily, 10 to 5); entry is free. A stroll up Victoria Road (one of only three streets not named after Salt's relations) takes you to an excellent second-hand bookshop and the Village Bakery, with a reasonably priced café whose menu is a treasure-store of Yorkshire chauvinism: Yorkshire Dales water, tea, pudding, teacake, curd tart and three types of Yorkshire cheese. Down the hill, past the station, rowing boats may be hired on summer weekends from the Saltaire Boathouse, a lovely spot; good lunches and teas are served.

Cross the bridge, turn left through the park and about a half-mile walk will bring you to the **Shipley Glen tramway**. This Victorian funicular operates on summer weekends and bank holidays, hauling you up through woodland to a rocky moor, with a pub, ice-cream kiosk and seasonal funfair; the emphasis on sturdy fun is another part of the Victorian tradition. For travellers in a hurry, Saltaire is a matchless epitome of Industrial Revolution Yorkshire.

Bingley

Neighbouring Bingley introduces itself with the ugliest building society headquarters in Britain, inadequately screened by trailing plastic plants. These Hanging Gardens of the Bradford & Bingley Building Society are not, however, the local Wonder of the World. For that, you must make your way to the pretty green by the church, flanked by cottages and some worthwhile antique shops. Cross the A650 and sidle up Treacle Cock Alley (lined with green railings) to the superb **Bingley Five Rise locks**, part of the Leeds and Liverpool Canal. The longest continuous flight in Britain, the locks lift barges 59 feet uphill and downhill, a triumph for John Longbotham of Halifax and his team of local stonemasons who designed and built the flight in 1774. Bingley can also claim literary fame; the novelist John Braine wrote *Room at the Top* while on the staff of the Victorian Gothic town library. The model for the fictional room itself is at 13 Priesthorpe Road, still a private house and not open to the public. Bingley has two potential picnic sites: neat Myrtle Park just over the canal, and the rambling St Ives Park, a little neglected but with woods and moorland on the scenic walk up to Lady Blantyre's Rock.

Keighley

From Bingley the often congested A650 improves and the moors on either side of the valley beckon. But Keighley (pronounced Keethly) gives you several reasons for stopping off; the highlight is the main station of the **Keighley and Worth Valley Railway**, star of many period films, and much the best way of getting to Haworth. Keighley itself is solidly Victorian, with pleasantly arcaded shops in Cavendish Street. But to eat, venture to the hidden hamlet of **Goose Eye**, in a moorland clough off the road to **Oakworth**, where a paper mill once manufactured banknotes. A memorable old pub, The Turkey, is extremely hard to leave for the wide range of healthy moorland walks which start from Goose Eye. Before puffing up to Haworth with the Brontë pilgrims, you will be rewarded by visits to Keighley's two contrasting historic homes.

East Riddlesden Hall (NT, open Easter to Oct, usually 2 to 5.30 but changes; tel (0535) 607075) is a lovely gabled and mullioned manor house approached through unpromising suburbia. It is a classic West Yorkshire 'low hall', largely built in 1648 for the Murgatroyd clothmaking family of Halifax. The low stone-tiled roof sweeps protectively down over panelled rooms, ornate plaster ceilings, and original Jacobean furniture; there is a garden too, and a display of ancient farming machinery in an even more ancient barn. The café and gift shop are good, and the delightful setting, including a romantically ruined wing, is reflected in a large duck-pond.

Cliffe Castle Museum (open Apr to Sept, Tue to Sun, Bank Hol Mon 10 to 6; Oct to Mar 10 to 5) in Spring Gardens Lane, high above the A629 Skipton road, is a less obvious attraction, but worth the detour for an insight into one aspect of the Yorkshire character – the lavish spending of self-made money. The clumsily imposing building, aptly described in 1883 as 'a modernised Tudor castle in the Victorian era', is only a part of textile magnate Henry Butterfield's original fantastic mansion; the rest has been demolished. But the opulence of what remains gives a good impression of the original. The small but excellent local history museum is complemented by well-kept grounds, with a decent café connected to thriving greenhouses and an aviary.

Haworth

Devotees of the Brontë sisters may at first be upset when they see the extent of Haworth's tourism, but even the hordes of visitors trekking up the steep hill to the Parsonage and the plethora of 'gifte shoppes' with the Brontë name attached to everything have not overwhelmed the authentic atmosphere. If you find Main Street unbearably quaint, explore the quieter side-alleys. Best of all, if the weather is reasonable, follow the signs past the Parsonage Museum to one of the family's favourite walks via the Brontë Waterfalls, Bridge and Stone Chair (two miles, walking boots or strong footwear recommended) to the airy moorland surrounding the ruined farm Top Withens (a further mile); it is reputed to be the inspiration for Emily Brontë's *Wuthering Heights*.

The Brontë Parsonage Museum (open Apr to Sept, daily 10 to 5, Oct to Mar 11 to 4.30; closed 4 weeks mid-Jan to mid-Feb; tel (0535) 642323) is the other must: a painstaking preservation of the Brontë home. Much of their original furniture, auctioned off after Revd Patrick Brontë's death in 1861, has made its way back, but not everything is quite what the sisters' admirers would like to believe. The pencil doodlings on plaster, carefully screened under glass, are as likely to be the work of Victorian decorators as precocious efforts by the Brontë children. Fascinating and genuine relics include the miniature books produced by Branwell and his sisters as children.

The museum is excellent but inevitably cramped; it attracts some 250,000 visitors a year and can become very crowded in summer.

Haworth also offers a **Museum of Childhood** (open Apr to Oct, daily 10.30 to 5.30; Nov to Mar weekends and school hols) with ancient toys, and the curious grave (in Haworth cemetery) of Miss Lily Cove, Britain's first woman balloonist and parachutist who took one jump too many over the village in 1906. The tourist office overflows with information, souvenirs and ideas for excursions. Weavers restaurant (see 'Where to eat' section) beats considerable competition to end the full day best allowed for this flagship of Yorkshire, indeed national, tourism.

HUDDERSFIELD

Friedrich Engels described Huddersfield as 'the fairest of all the English industrial towns' and, although the pioneering Communist is not usually thought of as an authority on tourism, he had a good point. The town centre was carefully planned under the eye of the local Ramsden family, who owned almost all the land. The central **St George's Square**, in front of the Grade-I-listed railway station, is a classic example of Northern architecture. The main streets running from it are noble in their modest way and large parts of the shopping centre are pedestrianised: Byram Arcade and the Brook Street market are both recommended.

The George Hotel on St George's Square is a place where you can still rub shoulders with the town's remaining wool barons. If you get talking to any, don't be surprised if they pinch a piece of any woollen clothing you are wearing, rub it and give either a murmur of approval or an almost inaudible sigh of discontent; they take cloth seriously around here. Rugby League, the Northern offshoot of Rugby Union, was founded in the hotel. The food is lavish, the beer good and the atmosphere typically Yorkshire.

The **Tolson Museum** (open Mon to Sat 10 to 5, Sun 1 to 5), housed in a large textile mansion in Ravensknowle Park, runs efficiently through the history of Huddersfield and has an unusually good section on transport. There is a children's play area in the park. The winding drive up to **Castle Hill, Almondbury**, with its Iron Age ramparts, small museum, good pub and Victorian folly, gives you a wide panorama of the city and the valleys leading off into the Pennines. These are the main goal for most visitors, but enjoy the urban landscape too. Here and there, the grey roofs are broken by splashes of honey-coloured stone – house-owners have taken to turning over their solid gritstone roof tiles to use the less weathered undersides, which are still the original colour. Stone-cleaning, too, leads to vivid contrasts in these Pennine terraces: a creamy, sandblasted house stands next to a sooty neighbour. Opinions differ fiercely on which suits the landscape best.

In Huddersfield and its surroundings, study noticeboards and posters in shops for details of concerts. From the celebrated Huddersfield Choral Society to the smallest village junior band, this area is drenched in home-made, high quality music.

The Pennine Valleys

The Colne and Holme Valleys lead straight out of Huddersfield into the wild and open scenery of the Pennines. A straggle of textile towns lines each valley bottom but enhances rather than spoils the countryside. Weavers' cottages with their long rows of windows on the upper floor, to catch all available daylight, cling to the slopes above Slaithwaite and Marsden, Honley and Holmfirth. Stone walls are everywhere, stone setts and cobbles have frequently escaped the Tarmac machine.

Holmfirth has capitalised on the fame brought by the television series *Last of the Summer Wine*, the heroes of which, gormless and shrewd by turn, have brought 'a touch of Haworth' to the little town's streets. You may be trampled by a coach-tour crocodile searching for Nora Batty's terraced house. Craft shops open and close erratically and a Saturday craft market attracts a fluctuating range of stalls. The **Holmfirth Postcard Museum** (open Feb to Nov, Mon to Sat 10 to 5, Sun 1 to 5; Nov to Feb, Mon to Sat 12 to 5, Sun 1 to 5) is a more genuine attraction, based at the local printers, Bamforth's, which effectively invented the celebrated naughty seaside postcard.

Quieter rivals for Holmfirth in the Colne Valley are **Marsden**, the last town before Lancashire, and **Golcar**, a steep tumble of stone terraces and cottages on the hill above **Slaithwaite**. **The Colne Valley Museum** (open all year, Sat, Sun, Bank Hols 2 to 5) at Golcar gives a comprehensive tribute to local history – rag rugs, looms and bobbins – housed in three weavers' cottages. The village also has a stock of excellent walking guides to the neighbourhood and the Kirklees region. Golcar is best explored on foot, with its alleys and ginnels rewarding the extra effort.

A gentler arena for walkers is Merrydale (off the Holme Valley) while the eagle's nest village of **Holme** gives access to the wild, high moors leading up to the BBC's Holme Moss transmitter. Another place to savour this huge wilderness is the A635 between Meltham and Greenfield, which crosses the mournful peat wastes of Saddleworth and Meltham Moors. Decoy towns were built here by camouflage units in the Second World War to mislead enemy bombers. You may squelch across their remains.

The Spen Valley

Masked by ribbon development and a confusing web of roads, the Spen Valley between **Gomersal**, **Birstall** and **Batley** is the absorbing landscape of Charlotte Brontë's *Shirley*. The descriptions of the book's mansions, *Fieldhead* and *Briarmains*, were closely modelled on Oakwell Hall and the Red House. **Oakwell Hall and Country Park** (open all year, Mon to Sat 10 to 5, Sun 1 to 5) is well signposted off the Bradford-to-Dewsbury road. Leave your car at the first car park if you want to enjoy the 87-acre park, or drive half a mile further to the lovely stone manor house, set in well-kept gardens and hardly altered since it was built in 1583. The imaginative use in some rooms of reproduction oak furniture, which looks as new as it would have done in the sixteenth century, gives a homely feel; and skilful removal of layers of paint from the walls have revealed 'scumbled' panels – a decorative technique giving the oak-lined walls a *trompe l'oeil* effect. Enjoy the good café, souvenir shop and craft workshop.

The Red House (open Mar to Nov, Mon to Fri 10 to 5, Sat and Sun 12 to 5; Nov to Mar, daily 12 to 5) is a few minutes' drive from Oakwell Hall at Gomersal, and is a red-brick surprise in this stone-built part of Yorkshire. Recently restored, it almost looks newly built from the outside, like the modern *Dallas*-style home of a prosperous wool merchant. This is a fitting description of its owner in the 1830s, Joshua Taylor (the arch-Yorkshireman Hiram Yorke in Charlotte Brontë's *Shirley*). Taylor specialised in a heavy scarlet cloth known as 'common thick 'uns', used for the army's Redcoats. His daughter, Mary, was Charlotte Brontë's close friend and the light, airy interiors of the house are faithfully furnished and decorated in a style that would have been familiar to the young girls. Admission is free and there is a good souvenir shop in the entrance hall.

Signposted left off the Bradford-to-Dewsbury road on the edge of **Batley**, the **Bagshaw Museum** (open all year, Mon to Sat 10 to 5, Sun 1 to 5) is a treasure among Britain's idiosyncratic local history collections. A glory of 'Hollywood Gothic', especially inside, the mansion houses the curios of Walter Bagshaw, local JP and alderman. Exhibits at this free museum include a section of Flamborough Head covered in stuffed seabirds, a bizarre Oriental hoard collected by a fake Manchester mandarin and, in the gardens, a butterfly house with an enthusiastic janitor. A textile magnate built the house for £25,000 in 1875. His ghost must have walked in 1909, when, after standing derelict for a decade, it was sold to Batley Corporation for £5.

There are good walks in the Spen Valley (guidebooks are sold at all three of the above museums) and it is worth taking a detour to the Black Bull Inn on Kirkgate, behind Birstall parish church, just off the Bradford-to-Dewsbury road. The pub is a lovely survival, dating back 800 years; ask to see the old, panelled court room upstairs complete with dock and witness box. Good food is served.

HALIFAX

Halifax is the best-preserved of all West Yorkshire towns and cities, thanks to a dozy council during the demolition-mad '50s and '60s. Its greatest architectural glory, the Piece Hall, was saved from the bulldozers by one vote. The town is strikingly set in a narrow cleft of Calderdale and although a few tower-blocks have clumsily appeared on the scene, it looks the very picture of a Northern industrial town. Prince Charles is a great fan and regular visitor. It is rumoured that he might even convert a redundant mill into a Northern Sandringham.

Until the Industrial Revolution, Halifax had a different, fearsome reputation, recalled in the saying 'From Hull, Hell and Halifax, good Lord deliver us'. Draconian local measures against theft, especially of completed cloth left out in the fields on tenterhooks (the origin of the phrase) to dry and stretch, culminated in the use of the town's guillotine. Invented well before its French counterpart, the machine is commemorated by a full-scale (but not working) replica in Gibbet Street.

Main sights

• **Piece Hall** From the station, or any of several spacious car parks on the outskirts, a brief wander through the compact centre, savouring the solid Victorian stone buildings, brings you to the Piece Hall, an astonishing monument worthy of Verona or Florence. Three storeys of gracefully arcaded shops, where eighteenth-century Halifax merchants displayed their sample 'pieces' of cloth up to 60 yards long, surround a noble paved and grassed courtyard with an open-air flea market on Thursdays, general market on Fridays and Saturdays, and various fiestas at weekends. On other days, the atmosphere can be lifeless; many shops are shut, few visitors are about and the café can be soulless. But this is a cathedral of industrial Britain, a glory of the North. Appropriately, it also houses the entrance to Halifax's Industrial Museum.

• **Calderdale Industrial Museum** (open all year, Tue to Sat, 10 to 5, Sun 2 to 5) Clock in with a small admission charge on an ancient machine at this museum; it offers a slightly patchy guide to the town's remarkably diversified trades. Splendidly unconvincing model workers will keep the children amused. Much more could be made of cat's-eyes, the road reflectors invented in Halifax by the eccentric Percy Shaw, and of Mackintosh's toffee which began when the arch-Methodist Granny Mackintosh stirred her delicious recipes in a cauldron outside her terraced cottage. But the history of the domestic washing-machine and the fabulous web of moquette strands on a powerloom leave no doubt about the graft and ingenuity of West Yorkshire's Pennine manufacturers. The heat from working machinery, including a beam engine and water-wheel, also makes the ground floor an ideal refuge in winter.

• **Shibden Hall Folk Museum** (open Apr to Oct, Mon to Sat 10 to 6; Nov to Mar 10 to 5, Sun 12 to 5; Feb, Sun only) The domestic side of a wealthy manufacturer's life is well displayed at this museum on the A58 from Leeds, a mile-and-a-half from the centre of Halifax. The half-timbered fifteenth-century house is somewhat dark and gloomy but well-stocked with complementary furniture and includes an interesting nineteenth-century 'village' in its stableyard, with mock-ups of assorted ancient trades. The park offers steep walks, a miniature railway and a boating lake.

• **Eureka** Britain's biggest hands-on museum for children opened in 1992 at a cost of £10 million – money well spent on this larger and much more colourful Northern complement to the Science Museum's successful Launch Pad and Bristol's Exploratory museum, tel (0422) 330069.

• **Wainhouse Tower** If you are lucky, your visit may coincide with Whit or August Bank Holidays when the 400 steps of this needle-like folly, the town's tallest building, are open to the public; the belvedere is impressive.

CALDERDALE

The A646 from Halifax to **Todmorden** snakes beside the River Calder through a landscape which vies with the Holme and Colne Valleys for Pennine perfection. Savour its mixture of romantic countryside, gentle copses steeply banking up to the wild moors, and small, picturesque mill towns. Becks foam down the hillside cloughs to the River Calder while the canal descends in stately pounds between its recently restored locks. At **Mytholmroyd**, turn left over the canal to one of the prettiest corners, where the village of **Cragg Vale** clusters round the church of St John-in-the-Wilderness. The Hinchcliffe Arms Hotel has a small display about the infamous Cragg Coiners, an eighteenth-century coin-clipping and minting gang of extreme, though now somewhat romanticised, thuggery. Newer settlers have brought a gentler spectacle, an Indonesian gamelan band which frequently plays at concerts in Calderdale and is worth hearing.

In the main valley, farms and the occasional Jacobean yeoman's hall perch on the few shelves which interrupt the steep slopes. The local council, doing its best to bring in new industry, often bewails the lack of flat land suitable for factories. The few existing sites were seized by the Victorians for mills like **Maude Walkley's clog factory** (open all year, daily 10 to 5), the last in Britain, recently rebuilt after a disastrous fire, and separated by bluebell woods from the outskirts of Hebden Bridge.

Hebden Bridge

This tight little mill town, clinging to some of the steepest slopes in the valley, is nicknamed Yorkshire's Hampstead because of the media, legal and other professionals who have colonised its picturesque streets. Commuting to Leeds and Manchester, or working from fax and computer-stuffed 'telecottages', they follow an earlier invasion of '60s 'Good Lifers' and the odd hippy, many of whom also remain. Finishing off this exotic human cocktail are the original gritty Hebdeners, personified by the town's most famous contemporary son, Sir Bernard Ingham.

They live side-by-side in streets with biblical names like Machpelah (an Old Testament graveyard) or the distinctive 'flying freehold' houses. These are 'back-to-backs' built, as it were, on top of one another because of the steep hillside. The top two floors, entered from the street above, are one house;

the bottom two, entered from the street below, another one. The problem of giving the top house its own freehold, legally separate from that of its neighbour below, was only solved by a special Act of Parliament unique to Hebden Bridge which legalised the concept of a 'flying freehold'.

Hebden Bridge is full of good cafés, pubs and offbeat shops and the tourist office will overwhelm you with local literature and souvenirs. Horse-drawn and ordinary canal trips are available. **Automobilia** (open Apr to Sept, Tue to Fri 10 to 5, Sun 12 to 5; Mar to Nov, Sat 12 to 5 and Bank Hol Mon) Billy Lane, Old Town (a mile-and-a-half from the town centre) is an interesting transport museum where the brave may hire out ancient cars.

An outstanding walk from Hebden Bridge is along the splendid cobbled street that crosses the packhorse bridge and rakes sharply up to **Heptonstall**, an exceptionally fine huddle of Pennine cottages grouped round an octagonal Wesleyan chapel and two Anglican churches, one a picturesque ruin. The graveyard is the resting place of the poet Sylvia Plath, whose husband Ted Hughes, the Poet Laureate, was born at Mytholmroyd. The **Old Grammar School museum** has had a rocky time recently but is now operational, tel (0422) 354823.

Todmorden, further up the Calder Valley, is a quieter version of Hebden Bridge. The traditional boundary with Lancashire plays funny tricks here, dividing the town hall and, more crucially, the cricket club pitch. It is a good base for wild and windy walks to Pennine outposts like **Lambutts**, **Mankinholes** and the monument at **Stoodley Pike**. An unusual treat at Clough Bank above the town is the **Todmorden Amateur Astronomy Centre**, tel (0706) 816964. Planetarium shows can be booked and special events are advertised throughout the year.

WAKEFIELD

Pit workings on the outskirts of town, a grim prison and a clumsy power station may initially provoke an urgent desire to leave, rather than linger in Wakefield; tourism is still in its infancy here. But that has a bonus: people are not visitor-sated, as you sometimes (and understandably) find in Haworth, Holmfirth or Hebden Bridge. In pubs, cafés and museums, the people want to help, to make your stay enjoyable.

Wakefield actually has a long history to be proud of; 'clean, handsome and rich,' said Daniel Defoe. The **Cathedral** is fine and the public buildings in **Wood Street**, along with graceful Georgian houses in **St John's Square** (off the Leeds road) bear witness to the city's long reign as the county town of West Riding. The medieval **Chantry Chapel** on Chantry Bridge across the Calder is one of only four in Britain (though its dismal state reflects the mountain Wakefield's tourist promoters have to climb). The **Elizabethan Gallery** or **Old Grammar School**, tel (0924) 295796, holds various exhibitions throughout the year and has been well-converted into a small gallery next to Wakefield market.

The city centre is small and easily walkable from the bus station and both railway stations. Drivers may like to leave their cars in the multi-storey car park attached to the Ridings shopping centre, partly to see if they can find them again. Imaginative use of the hillside makes the centre original (and coachloads come from all over Yorkshire to shop here) but extremely confusing. The **Art Gallery**, Wentworth Terrace, has an excellent twentieth-century art collection and the **Museum**, Wood Street, is well organised with a particularly good room on the naturalist and eccentric Charles Waterton of nearby Walton Hall.

Excursions from Wakefield

You need your wits about you to find routes out of Wakefield and to thread your way along minor roads, often bereft of signs as though a wartime invasion were imminent. But the countryside is refreshingly gentle and very different from that of the Pennines and Dales. Large estates flourished here and many mansions and parks have survived the now declining era of intensive coal-mining.

Newmillerdam, four miles south on the A61, is a typically quiet spot with two pubs and a restaurant serving a good choice of food. Drive or walk across the dam to the lakeside woodland park where you can fish or work off your lunch over 25 miles of designated walks. **Nostell Priory** (open Apr to Oct, weekends only, Sat 12 to 5, Sun 11 to 5; July and Aug, daily exc Fri 12 to 5, Sun and Bank Hols 11 to 5) is National Trust-owned, and is the ancestral home of the St Oswald family. Designed by Robert Adam, it is one of West Yorkshire's finest stately homes, approached across a lake, and set in a beautiful country park. The house also has outstanding, specially commissioned Chippendale furniture. It is reached from the A638 Doncaster road.

Within Wakefield's city boundaries, the remains of **Sandal Castle**, signposted left off the A61 Barnsley road, crown a high, grassy and moated mound with a sweeping view. Perfect for picnics and for children to let off steam, this is the very hill that the Grand Old Duke of York marched his men up and down. Just as close to the city centre, but left off the Doncaster road, is **Heath**, known appropriately as the 'village of mansions'. Practically all of its handful of houses are eighteenth-century piles built by Wakefield merchants and prettily set around a grassy common criss-crossed by neat lanes. The King's Arms, Heath, is a glorious old pub, gas-lit and full of panelled nooks; it offers good food including double Yorkshire puddings for the hungry.

A few miles towards Doncaster, **Sharlston**'s dour mining façade hides the sixteenth-century Grade-I-listed Sharlston Hall. It is private property, but worth a discreet peep from the common for a picture of how this coal-blighted area used to look. Another three miles along the road, the village of **Ackworth** clusters attractively round its Quaker boarding school. The Plague monument commemorates the time when food was left at that spot by neighbouring villagers, when the disease cut the inhabitants off from the rest of the world. **Badsworth**, a little further on, is another unexpectedly pretty village and the base of the Badsworth hunt whose member-ship includes local miners; an unusual pastime in a traditional colliery area.

The **Yorkshire Mining Museum** (open all year, daily 10 to 5) in the old Caphouse Colliery at **Overton** on the Wakefield-to-Huddersfield road is relatively new and much praised. The highlight here is an underground tour. You will be equipped with a miner's headlamp and given the chance to crouch in some of the strikingly narrow seams. The claustrophobic will find plenty to do above ground: there is a good museum, and rides, a café, a shop and some lovely surrounding countryside for picnics.

The district's other outstanding museum is the **Yorkshire Sculpture Park** at Bretton Hall, Bretton (open all year, daily 10.30 to dusk). This free park is one mile along the Hud-dersfield road from junction 38 of the M1. Works by Henry Moore, Barbara Hepworth and a great parade of sculptures and statues by other artists are placed in the lovely eighteenth-century gardens and park. Visiting exhibitions are frequent and the café in the walled garden is a delightful surprise after the initial impression of municipal dreariness at the informa-tion centre.

Pontefract

The three nearby towns of Normanton, Castleford and Knottingley are best left to the really determined explorer, but Pontefract is another matter. The town is one of the most historic in Britain, now reviving after traces of its glorious past had worn perilously thin. Coal-mining came, the gentry fled and the lovely centre was sadly mauled. The 'improving' council of the '50s and '60s even blew up the remains of the glorious Elizabethan New Hall and had grotesque plans (now penitentially on display in the charming library museum) to devastate the main shopping streets.

But today the attitude is completely different. Heroic efforts have been made to tidy up the centre. The ancient **Buttercross** looks across at smartened Georgian and medieval buildings. A wander round the small, well-pedestrianised core is rewarding. The **Museum** in Salter Row (open all year, daily 10.30 to 5), an outstanding example of extravagant art nouveau architecture, has helpful staff and a small but satisfying amount of material on the history of Pontefract, including its long connection with liquorice (see box, p.22). Most astonishing, though, and indicative of the town's former glory, is the painting of the castle before Cromwell deliberately ruined it in 1649.

Even in its present state the **Castle** is striking. Although approached through rather tatty surroundings, the fragments of stonework soar up the steep central mound and circle the wide, green bailey where kings and queens regularly came and went. One of them, Richard II, went abruptly, murdered in a dungeon in a manner which may enthral the bloodthirsty. The castle's dungeon-like underground chambers may be visited at 11am.

Pontefract's other outstanding excursion is also under-ground, even more limited in access times, but a treasure if you can arrange your visit to include it: the extraordinary **Brother Adam's Hermitage** (open four Saturdays each summer 2 to 4; (0977) 797289). Admission is free, but tickets are required and must be booked in advance from the library museum, which will also give you the dates. Brother Adam retreated there in 1368, scooping out a bedroom and a small chapel. The Hermitage is reached down subterranean stairs below the hospital on Southgate and was rediscovered after the Second World War when a workman fell through a hole above it. Its fragility limits the opening times.

WHERE TO STAY

BRADFORD

Restaurant Nineteen

North Park Road, Heaton,
Bradford BD9 4NT
TEL (0274) 492559
Rather an exotic restaurant with
rooms opposite Lister Park.
Rooms are very comfortable but
the décor may be a bit flamboyant
for some; the restaurant has an
excellent reputation.

££ *All year exc one week at Chr and
2 weeks in Aug; 4 rooms; Access,
Amex, Visa*

HALIFAX

Holdsworth House

Holdsworth, Halifax HX2 2TG
TEL (0422) 240024
This seventeenth-century house
with mullioned windows and
beamed ceilings is popular with
business people while retaining a
private house atmosphere. The
warmly lit public rooms are full
of antiques and the bedrooms are
pretty and individually furnished.

££ *All year exc 24–28 Dec; 40
rooms; Access, Amex, Diners, Visa*

HAWORTH

Weavers

15 West Lane, Haworth BD22
8DU
TEL (0535) 643822
Lots of interesting pieces and
antique furniture clutter the
public rooms and give the hotel,
created out of converted weavers'
cottages, warmth and
atmosphere. The four bedrooms
are decorated with flair and are
pretty. A good place to relax after
a delicious dinner.

£ *All year; restaurant Tue to Sat
evenings, also Sun lunch in winter; 4
rooms; Access, Amex, Diners, Visa*

HUDDERSFIELD

Wellfield House

33 New Hey Road, Marsh,
Huddersfield HD3 4AL
TEL (0484) 425776
A small hotel on a busy main road
but inside all is peaceful. The
decoration throughout is
Victorian in style, to match the
age of the house. Bedrooms are
full of homely touches.

£ *All year exc Chr and New Year; 5
rooms; Access, Visa*

LEEDS

42 The Calls

42 The Calls, Leeds LS2 7EW
TEL (0532) 440099
An extremely chic, civilised hotel
in the town centre. Public areas
are not huge but every comfort
and convenience has been thought
of in the smart, spacious
bedrooms.

£££ *All year exc one week at Chr;
39 rooms; Access, Amex, Diners,
Visa*

LINTON

Wood Hall

Linton, Nr Wetherby LS22 4JA
TEL (0937) 587271
Lovely eighteenth-century
country house hotel in beautiful
grounds overlooking the Wharfe
Valley. Professionally run, yet
informal and relaxed. Bedrooms,
all different, are large and well
equipped.

£ *All year; 44 rooms; Access, Amex, Diners, Visa*

LIVERSEDGE

Lillibet's Restaurant-with-Rooms
64 Leeds Road, Liversedge WF15 6HX
TEL (0924) 404911

The addition of more bedrooms and refurbishment of existing ones really makes this more of a hotel. It is a bright, comfortable place to stay with the added delight of good food.
£ *All year exc one week at Chr and 2 weeks Aug; 13 rooms; Access, Amex, Visa*

WHERE TO EAT

HUDDERSFIELD

Paris II
84 Fitzwilliam Street
TEL (0484) 516773
An offshoot of the Paris in Leeds (see entry) with fair prices, few frills and fresh food. Good starters include black pudding and liver parfait, with plenty of fish for the main course. Excellent value 'early bird' menu from 6–7.30.
Mon to Fri 12–2, 6–10.30, Sat 6–10.30; Access, Amex, Visa

Ramsden's Landing ★
Aspley Wharf, Wakefield Road
TEL (0484) 544250
A large, crowded brasserie with above-average French-inspired food. Well-executed imaginative cooking includes poached Finnan haddock with an aïoli sauce, duck breasts with blackberry sauce or rack of lamb. A reasonable vegetarian selection and good desserts.
Mon to Fri 12–2, 6–10, Sat 7–10.30; Access, Visa

LEEDS

Brasserie Forty Four
44 The Calls
TEL (0532) 343232

a new split-level restaurant, seating about 100, in a smartly renovated former grain warehouse. Long modern and eclectic menu features dishes with arresting and fresh flavours from pasta to Yorkshire pudding, lime-marinated fish to chargrilled chicken. Moderately priced for the city centre. Good-value two-course set lunch. A good place to stay.
Mon to Fri 12–2.30, 6.30–10.30, Sat 6.30–10.30; Access, Amex, Visa

Bryans ★
9 Westwood Lane, Headingley
TEL (0532) 785679
A genuinely British fish-and-chip shop, seating 140 people. Generous portions of consistently good fish with crisp batter and chips fried in lard. Reasonable prices.
All week, Mon to Sat 11.30–11.30, Sun 12–8.30

Hansa's ★
72–74 North Street
TEL (0532) 444408
A Gujarati vegetarian restaurant in a row of converted shops outside the city centre. Good, honest home-cooking includes bhajias, dhals, masala and thalis. Excellent choice of desserts. Service may be slow when full.

Tue to Sat 6–10.30; closed 25 and 26 Dec

Paris
36A Town Street, Horsforth
TEL (0532) 581885
An upstairs restaurant with somewhat basic décor, but fair cooking and generous portions at reasonable prices. The French-inspired menu includes cassoulet and beef bourguignonne, plus English steak pies or beef and horseradish. A good-value 'early bird' menu includes half a bottle of house wine. Friendly service. (See also Huddersfield)
All week 6–10.30; Access, Amex, Visa

POOL IN WHARFEDALE

Pool Court
Pool Bank
TEL (0532) 842288
Very professional hospitality is offered in this sturdy yet luxurious house. The menu features a mix of high fashion and English dishes including perfectly hung grouse, breast of Aylesbury duck in a calvados sauce, or the freshest of fish. A good-value no-choice set menu. Also a good place to stay, with six excellent bedrooms.
Tue to Sat 7–10; Access, Amex, Diners, Visa

SHELLEY

Three Acres Inn ★
Roydhouse, Nr Huddersfield
TEL (0484) 602606
A very well-run and pleasant pub with views stretching for miles. A wide choice of bar food (lunch only) with a good-value set-lunch and more expensive evening meals in the restaurant. A good range of real ales.
All week 12–1.45, 7–9.45; Access, Amex, Visa

YORKSHIRE DALES

- Beautiful Pennine landscapes of high, gritstone moors and classic limestone gorges, caves and underground rivers
- Scattered farmsteads and stone villages clustered around becks and informal village greens
- Superb territory for outdoor activities and walking, with the Three Peaks challenge and 60 miles of the Pennine Way

Settle to Carlisle Railway

THE YORKSHIRE Dales National Park is the third largest of the 11 National Parks of England and Wales. It is a semi-wild, semi-manmade scene with subtle nuances of dimension, contour, colour, and texture. The primeval forests have long been cleared; open pasture and heather moorland constitute the rule, woodland the exception. Even conifer plantations, now common in so much of upland Britain, are a rarity. By the end of the Dark Ages, the settlement pattern was largely determined, with Anglian, Danish and Norse settlers established in farmsteads and hamlets in woodland clearings. Hawes, Sedbergh and Grassington comprise the only towns within the National Park's 680 square miles, and none are of great size; even today, sheep and cattle easily outnumber the human population.

Uniformity is the key to the charm of the Dales: stone villages scattered over long, lonely dales beneath windswept moors. The area really cries out to be walked, if only to see aspects unseen by flitting motorists. The many paths are well-maintained and magnificently varied. But there are plenty of scenic drives, too.

Domestic buildings are typically built of large limestone blocks, with gritstone used for the lintels, mullions, corner-stones and doorheads (frequently adorned with the date of building and the initials of the original owner). The load-bearing walls are strong enough to support flagstone roofs. Since the designation of the Dales as a National Park in 1954, permission for new building has become difficult to obtain, and strict guidelines exist to ensure that new development is in keeping; in recent years this control has spread to include farm buildings too.

Some of the most visited places are Malham, Aysgarth Falls, Grassington, Hawes and Bolton Abbey. Virtually all of the villages and hamlets make good bases and there are plenty of B&Bs and hotels. Wharfedale and Wensleydale are centrally located, Swaledale and Dentdale are more remote but full of delights. Essentially it is an area to be outdoors enjoying the countryside as there's not much in the way of indoor sightseeing.

LOWER WHARFEDALE

From its source above Langstrothdale, the trout-laden River Wharfe runs through some of the loveliest and subtly varied of Pennine landscapes. While the upper dale is narrow and overshadowed by wall-like hills, the middle dale displays the bare bones of the Great Scar limestone in the bright-green turf. Downstream, the transition into more mellow countryside is abrupt; the walls are dark gritstone, the woodlands extensive, and the contours mild. Except for a few miles either side of Conistone, an easily managed and much trodden path follows the river for the length of the dale.

Bolton Abbey and surroundings

The Bolton Abbey estate (open access), owned by the Dukes of Devonshire, forms a gateway into the Dales from the south. Gently lowland in character, the estate is quite unlike the rest of the Dales. The medieval abbey ruin and its adjacent church grace the green banks of the Wharfe, a scene faithfully captured by J M W Turner in 1809. Level paths lead upriver into mature woodlands and around the oddly named Valley of Desolation where landslips occur with some regularity. A group of Augustinian canons founded the abbey in 1154. They practised a communal life, with a strict daily routine of prayer, worship, teaching and running hospitals. The abbey buildings developed, but the west tower was started in 1520, just before the Dissolution, and was never completed. Today it is of dual interest for its medieval features and for an imaginative nineteenth-century restoration by George Street. During the latter period Pugin added a rich show of stained-glass depicting the stories of the Gospel, and paintings on the rebuilt east wall of 11 plants atop biblical symbols. You can still see the arcading and tracery in the choir ruins, but the cloister, dormitory and chapter-house are only stone foundations on the lawn. Bolton Hall (not open) close by is an early nineteenth-century extravaganza, bristling with turrets and mock-medieval castellations. Bolton Abbey gives its name to a small, immaculate village adjacent to a vast car park.

A couple of miles upriver, the **Strid** is a narrow millstone-grit channel through which the Wharfe accelerates on its southwards journey. The car park gives quickest access to the majestic Strid Woods, where sessile oaks shelter a diverse butterfly and bird population and carpets of bluebells in spring. A free leaflet detailing nature trails is given out at the kiosk, with details of what you can expect to see on five colour-coded walks. To the west, above Barden Bridge, stands the strange semi-ruin of Barden Tower (free access). Now uninhabited, it was an administrative centre when the

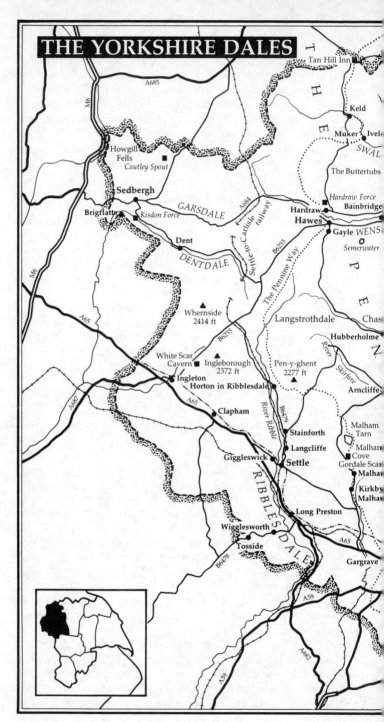

THE YORKSHIRE DALES

Tan Hill Inn

Keld

Muker · Ivel

SWAL

The Buttertubs

Howgill Fells
Cautley Spout

Hardraw Force
Hardraw Bainbridge
Hawes

Sedbergh

GARSDALE

Brigflatts
Kisdon Force

Gayle WENS
Semerwater

Dent

DENTDALE

P

E

Whernside
2414 ft

Langstrothdale Chas

Hubberholme

White Scar
Cavern Ingleborough
2372 ft

Pen-y-ghent
2277 ft

Arncliffe

Ingleton
Horton in Ribblesdale

Clapham

Malham
Tarn

Stainforth

Langcliffe

Malham
Cove
Gordale Scar
Malha

Giggleswick Settle

Kirkby
Malha

Long Preston

Wigglesworth

RIBBLESDALE

Tosside

Gargrave

Settle-to-Carlisle railway

The Pennine Way

River Ribble

River Skirfare

A685

M6

M6

A65

A684

B6255

B6255

B6479

A687

A65

A65

A59

A59

B478

A682

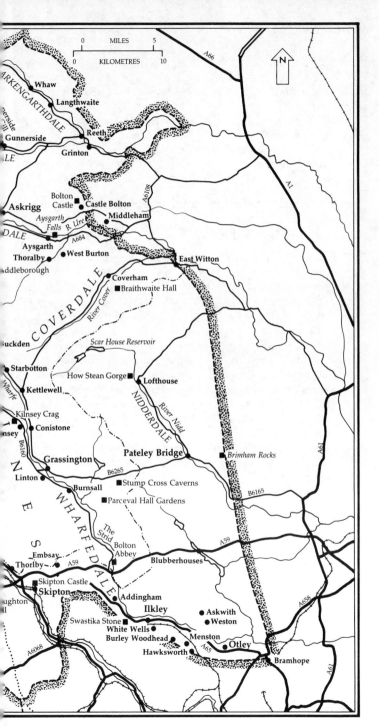

MILES 0 — 5

KILOMETRES 0 — 10

N

ARKENGARTHDALE

Whaw
Langthwaite
Reeth
Gunnerside
Grinton

Askrigg
Bolton Castle
Castle Bolton
Middleham
Aysgarth Falls
R. Ure
DALE
A684
Aysgarth
Thoralby
West Burton
East Witton
ddleborough

Coverham
Braithwaite Hall

COVERDALE

River Cover

Scar House Reservoir

uckden

Starbotton
How Stean Gorge
Lofthouse
Kettlewell

NIDDERDALE

River Nidd

Kilnsey Crag
nsey
Conistone

Grassington
Pateley Bridge
Brimham Rocks
Linton
B6265
Burnsall
Stump Cross Caverns
Parceval Hall Gardens

B6165

The Strid
Bolton Abbey

WHARFEDALE

Embsay
Thorlby
A59
Blubberhouses
Skipton Castle
Skipton
ughton
Addingham
Ilkley
Askwith
Weston
Swastika Stone
White Wells
Burley Woodhead
Menston
Otley
Hawksworth
A65
Bramhope
A6068

B6160
Wharfe

A66
A1
A6108
A61
A658
A59

45

dale was part of the royal hunting forest. The Clifford family built the adjacent Priest's House in 1485. It was later converted into a farmhouse and is now run as a guesthouse and restaurant.

The charming village of **Burnsall** on the banks of the River Wharfe owes much to Sir William Craven. Though born in Appletreewick about a mile to the south, he turned his favours to Burnsall: he financed the building of the fine four-arched bridge, the village school and the rebuilding of the church of

---

A FARMING TRADITION

FARMING is an essential part of the Dales scene, providing both the texture of the landscape and a rural life-style. Milk-tankers squeeze along narrow lanes and four-wheel drives carry stock to market, but deeply traditional elements exist side-by-side with the late-twentieth century agricultural methods. Unfertilised herb-rich hay meadows present spectacular shows of wild flowers before the single cut of the year, stone barns are all around (although many are disused) and village shows are major events. Wensleydale Cheese is still produced in Wensleydale, and the calendar of sheep-farming follows the age-old rhythm of lambing in April, shearing in early summer, followed by dipping a month later, and tups (rams) put to ewes in November. Aptly, the Yorkshire Dales National Park emblem shows the head of a Swaledale tup, the black-and-white faced breed found throughout the northern Dales; further south, the Dalesbred, identified by a facial marking of black and two white patches, predominate, while the irregularly marked Rough-Fell breed wander the Howgill Fells. Each breed is known for its hardiness rather than the quality of its wool, the coarseness of which makes it suitable for carpets. The sheep spend most of the year outdoors (and can survive for days beneath snowdrifts) on the exposed rough grazing lands and moorland that make up most of the area of the National Park. The fertile valley floors constitute cattle pastures. Lucrative grouse-shooting rights ensure the preservation of large areas of heather moorland, especially on Barden and Conistone moors, and on the hillsides above Swaledale.

The Dales farming tradition dates from the period of Stone Age hunters and the first farmers of the Neolithic period. In the twelfth century the land was made up of hunting forests and monastic estates. Most of the Dales farmhouses date from 1630 to 1730, when a new class of yeomen farmers emerged. This occurred following

---

St Wilfred. He was twice Lord Mayor of London, where he had made his fortune. About a mile east of Appletreewick you can visit **Parceval Hall Gardens** (open Easter to end Oct, daily 10 to 6) with 16 acres of woodlands, rockeries and shrubberies.

Grassington and around

Grassington is the main centre in Wharfedale. The cobbled back-alleys, known as folds, are prettified and the centre looks

---

the sell-offs of the great abbey estates and granges after the Dissolution of the Monasteries; the freeholds were acquired first by gentry and London merchants, and then by the sitting tenants. As farms were rebuilt, the dimensions of the old cruck constructions were inherited: typically bays of sixteen feet by twelve, with the front door opening directly into the living room. Stone barns, built as byres to winter four cows, proliferate throughout the Dales, especially in Swaledale where there is virtually one in every field.

Up to 1780 much of the lands were common grazing grounds. In the following 40 years most of the dry-stone walls were built, transforming the area and spelling doom for many small farms. The regular geometry of these walls is now a major component of the landscape. Low intensity farming goes hand-in-hand with the Dales' diverse wildlife. But changing trends in farming practices, particularly toward mechanisation, and the low profitability of hill-sheep farming, have threatened the Dales' landscape as well as its rural economy. Without sheep nibbling newly grown shoots and keeping the undergrowth at bay, much of the area would quickly revert to scrub, while in the low-lying meadows the incursions of new farming techniques, particularly the introduction of chemical fertilisers and pesticides, reduce the incidence of wild flowers. Subsidies to hill-farmers have helped redress the balance, particularly with the designation in 1986 of the Pennine Dales as an Environmentally Sensitive Area (one of six areas in Britain), covering parts of Swaledale, Waldendale, Dentdale, Wharfedale and Arkengarthdale. Farmers in these areas are offered grants for maintaining traditional farming practices. Farm buildings for many years fell outside the strict development control applied to other developments within National Parks, and some ugly factory-style barns have appeared, but this control has recently been extended to cover new farm buildings.

carefully groomed. If you don't mind crowds in high season it makes a good base, with plenty of interesting shops and no shortage of tea-shops. The main shops and some fine Georgian buildings line the main square. Old Hall, thirteenth-century in origin, glimpsed from an alley to the left of the Devonshire Hotel, is the dale's oldest manor house. Across the square from the hotel, the volunteer-run Upper Wharfedale Museum houses local bygones and exhibits relating to past life in the area. The National Park Information Centre adjoins the main car park. North-east of the village, you can see remnants of the lead-mining days on Grassington Moor and, by contrast, a mile north-west is the Grass Wood nature reserve.

Linton, across the Wharfe, has an attractive green crossed by a clear beck. The village almshouses were built by Richard Fountaine in 1721 for six poor men or women and are the earliest example of classical architecture in the Dales. Linton church (of Norman origin) also serves Grassington and Threshfield and has a square tower with a bell-cote. The building was much altered in the fifteenth century and has been restored since; sadly, its greatest treasure, a crucifix of c.1000, was stolen in 1980. Furnishings in the Lady Chapel are the work of Robert Thompson of Kilburn (see page 105), and bear his ubiquitous mouse carvings.

On the B6265 between Grassington and Pateley Bridge, **Stump Cross Caverns** (open Apr to Oct, daily 10 to 5.30, Nov to Mar 11 to 4) are the only 'show caves' in the Dales that you can walk around without a guide; Wolverine Cave is one of the best features.

Kilnsey Crag, trimmed by glacial action in the last major Ice Age, looms menacingly over the village of **Kilnsey**. The 170-foot high rock has the largest overhang in the country and is a considerable challenge for rock-climbers; the race to the summit is the highlight of the village show in August. Immediately south of Kilnsey, **Kilnsey Park** (open daily 9 to 5.30; closes at dusk in winter) offers trout-fishing, a fresh-water aquarium and a 'Dales life' display, with exotic pigs and a sample chunk of dry-stone wall. You can visit the shop, where trout and game are on sale, without paying the admission fee for the rest of the site. Pony-trekking is available at the riding centre in Conistone, just across the river; for details tel. (0756) 572861.

UPPER WHARFEDALE

In the Ice Ages, glaciers straightened and broadened the dales, seen here to classic effect as the modest Wharfe flows along the grand, corridor-like valley. The villages are small and simple: **Starbotton** is tiny, **Buckden**, established as a village in the Norman hunting forest, is not much larger. Both offer rewarding walks, high up on to Buckden Pike or along the limestone terrace above Cray and Hubberholme, from where there are panoramic views down the dale.

Kettlewell is the major settlement of the upper dale just off the main road and a very popular centre for walkers. Former lead-miners' cottages and barns and the old smelting-mill up Dowber Gill are reminders of the prosperous days of the late-eighteenth and early-nineteenth century. A steep road leads north-east from the village over the high moor to drop into Coverdale. **Arncliffe**, just off the main dale, was built on an area of drained gravel on the otherwise wet floor of Littondale, the valley of the River Skirfare. Cottages and porched barns surround a large oblong green. The sides of the dale are grooved by field terraces known as lynchets, dating from 1200–1350, when oxen ploughed the land for corn and other arable crops. Western exits from Littondale are spectacular, leading above the gorge of Cowside Beck to Malham Tarn or heading north-west to Litton and then carrying over open moor between Pen-y-ghent and Fountains Fell.

As the dale narrows and deepens, Upper Wharfedale merges imperceptibly into **Langstrothdale**; maps still name the hillsides Langstrothdale Chase, a legacy of the hunting days. At the western end, commercial forestry impinges on the scene. Tiny **Hubberholme** has the dale's only church; it is a beauty, with a rare rood-loft of 1558 (which somehow escaped Elizabeth I's decree that such adornments should be removed) and pews embellished with carved 'Kilburn mice' (p. 105).

MALHAMDALE

Malham

Malham is a starting-point for explorations into a quite remarkable limestone landscape – natural pavements, scars, gorges, sink-holes and waterfalls; the geological significance and history can be studied in detail in the National Park visitor centre in the village. The crowds have been coming here for well over a century and by day it is extremely touristy, although not over-commercialised. Plenty of cafés and pubs cater for the influx, but it reverts to a more natural pace in the evenings.

The four-mile **Malham Trail** published by the National Park takes in the major features of the area: Malham Cove, Malham Tarn, Gordale Scar and Janet's Foss. On the road to Settle the huge quarry-like cliff of **Malham Cove** suddenly looms into view. Towering 250 feet over a natural amphi-theatre, the crescent-shaped Cove was created by the erosive powers of glacial ice and meltwater. Charles Kingsley joked that the black lichen and moss clinging to the Cove could have been made by a chimney sweep falling over the edge; the idea stayed in the writer's mind and finally emerged in his book *The Water Babies* (published in 1863) when Tom the sweep comes across the Water Babies in the River Aire.

The **Pennine Way** climbs the left-hand side of the Cove to emerge on to a fine example of a limestone pavement, where the acid contained in rainwater has attacked the joints to form deep, regular fissures known as grikes. From here you can continue north along Watlowes, a classic 'dry valley', to the sink-hole near Malham Tarn where Malham Beck plunges underground. **Malham Tarn** is Yorkshire's second largest lake. It is noted for its natural rather than visual interest; the swampy fen that surrounds the shores supports sedges, brown mosses and purple moor-grasses and has been designated a nature reserve for its botanical and bird-life. **Gordale Scar** to the south-west is an extraordinary gorge and best approached on foot. The original cave system collapsed leaving a narrow gorge forbiddingly overhung by towering limestone crags. There is limited roadside parking by a double bridge (one bridge for cars, one for walkers) near the gate at the entrance of the dale. At busy times, you should walk the $1\frac{1}{2}$ miles along Malham Beck from the village, turning left along Gordale Beck as signposted. Before the road is joined you will see **Janet's Foss**, a modest but pretty waterfall, in a verdant setting where the beck trickles over a cone of tufa (a calcium carbonate encrustation); Janet, the queen of the fairies, is supposed to live behind.

A mile south of Malham, **Kirkby Malham** is a quiet village yet the church serving the dale is one of the area's grandest: plain in style, not conspicuously over-restored, with box pews throughout, a sundial above the porch and late-sixteenth-century roof timbers. The finest of the pews, dated from 1631 to 1723, are in the north aisle.

RIBBLESDALE

Settle

Settle is a compact town focused on a large market-square, which bursts into life on Tuesdays when it is filled with food- and clothes-stalls. The Town Hall and the Shambles – a two-layered building, arcaded in its lower storey – stand in the middle. Behind, in a maze of tight lanes and yards sloping steeply uphill, you will find The Folly, Settle's most outstanding house, built in 1675 for a wealthy tanner; its two-winged façade shows off elaborate lintels and windows. Further up, steep paths zigzag to a lone flagpole, from where there is a dizzy view over the town's slate roofs. The revival in fortunes of the Settle-to-Carlisle railway line has brought many visitors to both towns. Good shops in Settle cater for most needs: second-hand books, and equipment for walkers and cavers in particular. The centre suffers a bit from traffic congestion, being a main road junction, and trucks from the nearby limestone quarries rattle along its narrow main street.

• **North Craven Heritage Centre**, Chapel Street (open all year, weekends and Bank Hols daily 2 to 5, also July to Sept, Tue to Fri) Displays arranged on two floors are devoted to the local history of the area. Exhibits include cases of cobblers' and chemists' equipment and panels on the conservation of Settle's buildings and aspects of rural life.

• **Yorkshire Dales Falconry and Conservation Centre** (open all year, daily 10 to 5.30, or 10 to dusk in winter; closed Christmas Day) The aviaries at the Centre are constructed to recreate semi-natural habitats, allowing close-up views of birds of prey, which include barn and tawny owls, eagles, griffons, vultures and hawks in addition to falcons. Regular flying demonstrations take place throughout the day, weather permitting; around 4 to 4.30 in the afternoon you can watch the birds being fed. The Centre is just outside the town on the A65 bypass.

The village of **Giggleswick** is joined on to Settle but has a totally different character; seventeenth- and eighteenth-century cottages line the quiet village street which leads past an old market-cross to the boundary wall of its public school.

Settle-to-Carlisle Railway

This is one of the main attractions in the Dales. After years of uncertainty, during which British Rail seriously considered its

51

closure, the future of this majestically scenic 71-mile line, completed by the Midland Railway in 1876, at last looks rosy. Its spectacular 24-arch viaduct at Ribblehead had developed structural problems of rotting mortar and fracturing stone. BR reduced its services until the line's tourist potential was realised. Spurred on by a spirited campaign by the Friends of the Settle-to-Carlisle Line Association, BR set up a trust which is funding the renovation of the structures on the line; these include 9 intermediate stations, 13 tunnels and 17 viaducts. It is the only railway line in the country to have conservation area status.

The best of the scenery occurs between Settle and Appleby, but Carlisle itself is an easy place to spend a few hours with the medieval cathedral, castle and Tullie House Museum as the main highlights. From Settle the line snakes along Upper Ribblesdale, where the upland scenery becomes increasingly remote; Pen-y-ghent, Ingleborough and Whernside are the peaks in view; the route continues past Dentdale and Garsdale to enter the Eden Valley at its head. As you travel further north you can see the Pennines and the eastern parts of the Lake District.

Around Settle

The most appealing of the three villages in upper Ribblesdale, **Langcliffe** has a spacious and idyllic green overlooked by a large oak tree. One house bears the stone figurine which was once the sign for the Naked Woman Inn, which was forced to close after a murder following a brawl in 1876 that involved navvies working on the construction of the Settle-to-Carlisle line.

Stainforth, to the north, is known mostly for two nearby waterfalls. **Stainforth Force** lies by a narrow packhorse bridge constructed in the 1670s; here the Ribble tumbles over shallow limestone steps making a popular and well-shaded place for bathing and picnics. **Catrigg Force**, a broken fall of over 50 feet, involves a steep half-mile walk up Goat Scar Lane to the south-east of the village.

Hikers attempting the Three Peaks Challenge (see p.257) and Pennine Way walkers converge on **Horton in Rib-blesdale**, a long, somewhat bleak village. But all around is the grandest of the Dales scenery: the Three Peaks – **Whernside** (2,414 feet; 736m), **Ingleborough** (2,372 feet; 724m) and **Pen-y-ghent** (2,277 feet; 694m) make a distinguished trio and a tough full-day's walk. Pen-y-ghent is closest to Horton, and like Ingleborough (see below) is riddled with potholes. The entrances to **Hull Pot** and **Hunt Pot** are close together and easily seen from a walk along the Pennine Way (see walk on p.260); the way turns north at Horton and passes **Sell Gill Holes**, another fine aperture. Most impressive of all is **Alum Pot**, a vast 200-foot opening; access is by way of a private footpath from North Cote Farm (fee payable) at the village of Selside to the north of Horton. The B6479 joins the Ingleton-Hawes road at **Ribblehead**, where the great **Ribblehead Viaduct** dominates the austerity of the open wastes. The small (50 to 150-foot-high) rounded hills in this area are good examples of drumlins, made of debris deposited by glaciers.

Clapham

A stream fringed by a grassy bank divides the lovely main street, with tea-shops and craft-shops in abundance. Clapham village and its hall (the latter not open to the public) were largely rebuilt by the Farrer family in the 1820s. *The Dalesman*, a most widely read regional magazine, is published here. The hall is now an outdoor education centre, but the visitor can enjoy its planted woodlands. **The Reginald Farrer Trail** (small toll payable), leading off from the top end of the main village street takes you through the woods and past the sombre artificial lake. Reginald Farrer (1880–1920) travelled all over Asia collecting wild flowers, shrubs and trees; the plant species he introduced to Europe numbered over a hundred and included Farrer's Gentian and some twenty varieties of rhododendron. Also on the Trail, guided tours of **Ingleborough Cave** (open daily 10.30 to 5.30; tours at half-past the hour; access along Reginald Farrer Trail, one mile each way) take in the first 600 yards of a 7$\frac{1}{2}$-mile system that extends well beneath neighbouring Ingleborough. The most famous entrance into the cave system is at **Gaping Gill** on the moor below the summit of Ingleborough.

Fell Beck cascades 340 feet down into the unseen depths of an immense chamber that could comfortably swallow up York Minster. In 1983, 88 years after the first descent, cavers abseiled into it and successfully reached the Ingleborough Cave resurgence for the first time. For the general visitor, access to the bottom is possible on spring and summer bank holidays, when local caving clubs set up a winching-chair to get you to the bottom.

Stout footwear and a stiffish climb will get you to the summit of **Ingleborough** (2,372 feet) and one of the great views of the Pennines. South are the Forest of Bowland and Pendle Hill, both in Lancashire, east and north lie the Dales, while to the west you may see the Lake District fells and Morecambe Bay. Ramparts of the Dales' only Iron-Age camp are discernible on the summit. East of Clapham above Arstwick village, Norber Boulders are dark blocks of Silurian slate transported by glacier from the head of the valley half a mile away.

Ingleton

Once a textile-mill village and quarrying centre, the town expanded in 1885 when a company was formed by local people with the aim of turning the previously inaccessible gorges of the Rivers Twiss and Doe into a trail; paths were created and footbridges constructed, and excursion trains brought day-trippers in ever-increasing numbers, drawn by the romantic beauty of the place. Geological faulting and the co-existence of limestone, slate and shale have created the spectacular changes of level that are a feature of the **Ingleton Waterfalls**. Pecka Fall is a series of cascades descending a natural staircase of limestone steps. Further up, water gushes over Thornton Force, where the layering of vertically bedded slate beneath horizontally bedded limestone presents itself as clearly as a cross-section from a geology book. The path leads on across open pasture and drops into the Doe gorge where the Beezley and Snow Falls twist and foam among crooked rocks beneath a canopy of oak trees, finally dropping into a gloomy chasm. The whole trails takes about two hours and stout shoes are recommended as the paths are quite rocky and uneven.

On the B6255 between Ingleton and Chapel-le-Dale, **White Scar Cavern** (open daily 10 to 5.30; 10 to 4.30 in winter; closed at Christmas) is another spectacular cave. Billed as Britain's largest 'tourist' cavern, the one-mile visit is also one of the more expensive, but there are some fine formations. For most of the way the tour follows an underground river, and as the cave is susceptible to flooding, it may be closed without notice.

Kirkby Lonsdale is just outside the National Park boundary in the Lune valley and has an unmistakeably Cumbrian character: narrow cobbled streets, eighteenth-century yellow-grey stone and colour-washed houses, a dignified central square and shops geared to its market-town function rather than to tourism.

The nineteenth-century writer John Ruskin was so moved by the outlook from the churchyard over a loop in the River

Lune, with the Pennines for a backdrop, that he rated it one of the finest views in Europe. Ruskin's View, as it has become known, remains much the same, although trees have grown up in front of a gazebo and you need to look out from the railings nearby.

DENTDALE AND THE NORTH-WEST

The River Dee and the Clough River flow west-to-east along Dentdale and Garsdale respectively. Valley roads are the main thoroughfares; the dales are steep-sided, scattered with farm-steads, and characterised by a higher proportion of hedgerows than the rest of the Dales. Modern county boundaries place this corner of the National Park in Cumbria.

Sedbergh and the Howgill Fells

The little market-town situated at the mouths of Dentdale and Garsdale is set right against the foot of the **Howgill Fells**, themselves a great mass of Silurian-slate-folded rocks that strongly resemble the eastern fells of the Lake District. The fells are glorious, but tough, walking country and it is a relief to arrive in the main street, narrow and cobbled and lined with well-preserved shop-fronts – Mitchell's pharmacy is a minor gem, double-fronted and with curved glass. Behind the main streets, several old yards and back-alleys survive. Davis Yard has the upturned barrel of a cannon at its entrance, reputedly left by Bonnie Prince Charlie who made his getaway on a packhorse cart laden with knitwear. On the other side of the street, King's Yard is flagged and contains a tiny square of carefully restored cottages. A couple of miles south-west of Sedbergh, **Brigflatts** is the second oldest Quaker Meeting House in the country, and the earliest one in the north. A simple stone building of few pretensions, it was erected in 1674–5 and has a plain interior of oak benches and a gallery, with whitewashed walls. A Quaker burial ground is nearby.

To find **Cautley Spout waterfall**, take the A683 north-east of Sedbergh and park by the Cross Keys hotel and head towards Kirkby Stephen until a signpost points left over a footbridge, where a path joins a track and bends round to the right. The fall tumbles down 600 feet from the Howgill Fells into a large U-shaped valley.

Dent

South-east of Sedbergh the delectable village of Dent is well worth seeking out. Both northern and southern approaches to this isolated village are exciting and part of its appeal.

The village itself is huddled against the outside world, a 'stage-set' arrangement of tightly built cottages and tiny streets. The tawny-coloured, uneven cobblestones that make it memorable sweep right up to each front doorstep and a memorial of Shap granite stands at the centre, commemorating Professor Adam Sedgwick (1785–1873), a founder of modern geology who contributed much to our understanding of the landscape and who made a study of the geography and history of Dentdale. Dent was once famous for its worsted stockings but factory competition killed-off the cottage industry. The village still attracts plenty of visitors but today a knitwear outlet is the only echo of that heyday. St Andrew's Church, at the edge of the village, has a fine chancel floor of polished, dark limestone known as Dent marble, a seventeenth-century pulpit and box pews and brass memorials to the Sedgwick family.

WENSLEYDALE

Broad and mellow, **Wensleydale** lacks the striking confines of Upper Wharfedale and the melancholy grandeur of Swaledale. There are a number of attractive villages – some grouped around greens, others ranged linear fashion along streets – and some fine waterfalls. **Addleborough**, just south of Bainbridge, is one of the distinctive flat-topped summits. Otters are occasionally seen on the dale's main river, the Ure, and on the River Bain.

Wensleydale and Swaledale together form the essence of 'Herriot Country'. This is the region made known to many by the autobiographical novels (*All Creatures Great and Small*, and others) of the country vet, James Herriot; the popular television series adapted from the books has brought the Yorkshire Dales into thousands of homes. Richmond Museum displays the TV set of the vet's surgery.

Cheese production has made Wensleydale a household name. The cheese recipe originated with the monks of Jervaulx Abbey, and has been handed down and adapted, with local farmhouse variations (Coverdale, Swaledale and Teesdale) developing in the seventeenth century as Shorthorn cattle were introduced into the area and ewes' milk was replaced by cows' milk. In the late nineteenth century creameries opened at Masham, Coverham and Thoralby. Kit Calvert, a local man, bought the factory in Hawes and ran it until his retirement in 1966. The Hawes creamery in Gayle Lane has experienced difficult times and has closed.

Hawes

Wensleydale's market-town on the route of the Pennine Way has become a busy tourist resort. The centre is somewhat dominated by the main road, but when the weekly cattle-market is in full swing between August and September the town is full of local colour; 140,000 sheep and lambs and 12,000 cattle are auctioned here each year, making it one of the main cattle centres in the Pennines. Hawes has a smattering of 'plastic-looking' cafés and souvenir shops but there are plenty of places to browse: second-hand bookshops, Elijah Allen's grocery shop where you can buy smoked or own-label Wensleydale cheese, and if you're looking for a skipping-rope or a dog lead there is a shop that makes its own rope on the premises. Hawes' prettiest corner is where the beck cascades under the main street. For an insight into the area, visit the **Dales Countryside Museum** (open daily Apr to Oct; winter openings, tel. (09697) 494), in Station Road. This is a well-presented folk museum that displays objects gathered from all over the Dales, particularly Wensleydale. Cheese- and butter-making exhibits feature strongly, and there are displays of implements and bygones from the days when lead-mining, hand-knitting and sheep-farming were all thriving local industries.

From Hawes church, a flagged path known as Bealer Bank, heads across a field to **Gayle**, a hamlet predating Hawes and dominated by its saw-mill. Look out for the two waterfalls, Aisgill just above the village, and Gayle Force below the bridge.

North of Hawes at the tiny village of **Hardraw**, you can reach **Hardraw Force** through the Green Dragon Inn (a small fee is payable). It is worth it to see England's tallest single-drop waterfall plummet 96 feet over a lip of limestone. Hardraw Force has been famous since Victorian times, when Blondin, the renowned tightrope-walker, made a crossing, and audiences queued for brass band concerts. The concert tradition has been recently revived, with a brass band competition held in May.

Askrigg

Before Hawes gained its market-charter and turnpike traffic in the eighteenth century, Askrigg was a major trading centre.

Today its winding, climbing street still promises something of a small town, with three-storey buildings, a market-cross and late Perpendicular church with an unusually fine timber roof. But the shops are 'villagey', and most people come mainly to look at 'Skeldale House', the house adopted as the home of James Herriot for the purposes of the TV series *All Creatures Great and Small*.

Bainbridge

South of Askrigg, Bainbridge is somewhat dominated at busy times by the main dale road that bisects it, but it has a charming and trim village green as a centrepiece. The village stocks are displayed intact and the whole place is well-preserved, with neat chain-link fencing and picnic benches. Behind the cottages a low hillock – a drumlin – peeps above the roof-tops; this was the site of the Roman fort of *Virosidum*, occupied from from AD 80 until the main withdrawal in AD 395. Look out for the Roman road, metalled in parts, close to Bainbridge from where you can enjoy exhilarating views over Wensleydale and Raydale (the valley of the River Bain). Below, to the south, **Semerwater** is Yorkshire's largest glacial lake, created when debris left by a retreating glacier piled up, damming the Bain. The legend goes that a beggar who was refused food and shelter by all the village except a kind shepherd and his wife, put a curse on it and the whole village was drowned, submerged beneath the lake. This story was given further credence when in 1937 the ancient remains of a village were found after part of the lake was drained; road access is from just below Countersett.

Aysgarth

The most popular beauty spot in the Dales teems with tourists in season. Reached from a National Park visitor centre just north of the main-road village **Aysgarth Falls** stretch about half a mile along the Ure, tumbling down a series of wide ledges. Like many such features, they can be a disappointment in dry weather, and the crowds may be a further deterrent, but in winter, and after heavy rain, the peaty torrent is worth seeing. The Upper Falls are near the road-bridge but the drop is negligible (the bridge provides the best viewing platform); the Middle Falls drop over a single terrace; the Lower Falls tend to be less crowded as they entail a ten-minute walk, and mainly consist of water racing over flat rocks. Aysgarth church occupies a lovely site on the opposite bank; the building dates from 1866 but contains a lovely sixteenth-century screen rescued from Jervaulx Abbey at the time of the Dissolution. **The Yorkshire Museum of Carriages and Horse-drawn Vehicles** (open daily 11 to 5, Easter to Oct) close to the Upper Falls, was the former Yore Mill, producing cotton and then flour up to 1959. A display of historic carriages includes a brougham, a hansom cab, a horse-drawn charabanc and an antique milk-float.

Bolton Castle

(Open Mar to mid-Nov, daily 10 to 5; for winter opening times tel. (0969) 23981) A couple of miles north of Aysgarth, the Castle is a mighty symbol of feudalism; the towering quadrangular bulk of the castle states its presence over **Castle Bolton**, the first estate village built in the Dales, and over the former hunting forest of Wensleydale. Three of the Castle's four towers, which fortify the corners, stand to their original 100-foot height; the fourth partly collapsed in a storm in 1761. Constructed in 1379 by Sir Richard Scrope, the first Baron Scrope of Bolton, the castle survives remarkably close to its original state, and although it is partly ruined there is an impressively deep and gloomy courtyard at its centre and a grand view of Wensleydale from its roof. Despite its appearance, the castle was meant for comfortable living rather than as a defence. A visit takes you over the living-quarters, including the rooms where Mary Queen of Scots was kept between 1568 and 1569.

Bishopdale

West Burton is one of the villages in this lesser known dale that should not be missed. The huge village green lined with former quarrymen's and miners' cottages suggests a larger population than there is now. It is a charming place and if you arrive or leave at the north end of the village, look out for the beck cascading over a small waterfall. **Thoralby**, nearby, also has a pretty waterfall.

Coverdale

In this the easternmost of Wensleydale's tributary valleys, the River Cover rises between Great Whernside and Buckden Pike and runs through Coverdale, often alongside the lonely road from Kettlewell. **East Witton** village is near the confluence of the Cover and the Ure and was rebuilt in the 1800s by the Earl of Ailesbury. He kept to the plan shown on the estate map of 1627 but excluded five cottages in the centre, leaving a spacious, sloping green as an attractive feature. A couple of miles to the west, **Braithwaite Hall** stands just above the road to Coverham, a seventeenth-century house owned by the National Trust but let to a tenant and run as a working farm. The flagged hallway, staircase and eighteenth-century panelling can be seen by arrangement with the tenant for a small fee (open May to Oct, tel. (0969) 40287 for an appointment).

SWALEDALE

Swaledale may be less visited than Wharfedale and Malhamdale, but its beauties are no less considerable or varied. The landscape here is traditional, with Swaledale sheep, now widespread in northern England for their hardy qualities, stone barns in profusion and a great number of uncultivated meadows; these present a blaze of yellow in June when buttercups, globe flowers, meadow vetchling and birdsfoot-trefoil are out, with thistles providing splashes of purple.

Yet the dale also bears the scars of its time before 1840 as the major lead-mining area in the Dales. The process was first carried out by surface digging, then levels (or 'adits') were driven horizontally into the hillsides and shafts were sunk. The ore went to the smelting-mills. An unusual feature of mining in the dale was the use of 'hushes', where streams were dammed to make ponds, from which torrents of water would be released to wash down and break up any lead-rich veins ('orebodies') in the rock. Today the hushes of **Gunnerside Gill** and heaps of orange-grey spoil make spectacular gashes on the scene, and stone-arched entrances to adits and eerie ruins of smelting- and crushing-mills haunt the landscape. After 1840 the industry began to decline with cheaper ore available from overseas and the population, 8,000 in 1801, dwindled to the 2,000 or so inhabitants here today.

Buttertubs Pass and Muker

Three roads connect Wensleydale to Swaledale, each climbing high on to the moor. Beside the Hawes-to-Thwaite road you will see the **Buttertubs**, a series of potholes into which streams tumble. Passing farmers on the way to market used to lower their butter into the holes to allow it to cool. Further up in the Swaledale direction the road reaches its highest point at 1,726 feet.

A tight-knit village, with a pub and tea-rooms and a tiny network of backstreets around its Elizabethan church, **Muker** stands in the loveliest part of Swaledale. Kisdon Hill forms one of its steep sides and there are beautiful walks along the Swale. The mile-and-a-half to Keld is one of the best walks in the Dales, and you can change sides of the river on your return. **Keld** at the far end is a grey village of chapels, cottages and a youth hostel. It is a lovely walk from here to **Kisdon Force**, not a gigantic water leap, but beautifully set amid deciduous trees and spectacular crags.

Gunnerside

The village stands on the fringe of Swaledale's most vivid reminders of the lead industry. The path upstream along the gill takes you into the hub of it: the most spectacular sections occur after two miles, where the remains of the Old Gang Mines – in operation up to 1900 – are seen. A longer walk taking in this valley and leading over into the finest part of Swaledale is described on p.263. The humpback seventeenth-century bridge at **Ivelet**, a mile west of Gunnerside, still its original width, is a minor classic of its kind.

Reeth

A lovely, spacious green fronted by cottages, inns and the comfortable Burgoyne Hotel forms the centre. The village was formerly busy as a commercial centre for the dale when knitting and lead-mining flourished, but its market and old industries have gone and Reeth has now reverted to rural calm, enlivened by its role as an excellent base for visiting the dale.

A sign on one side of the green leads you to the **Swaledale Folk Museum** (open Easter to Oct, daily 10.30 to 6), an enthusiastically compiled assortment of bits and pieces related to the dale – cheese-making tubs, brass band ephemera, bibles, and wool-making memorabilia. It is similar in content to the Wensleydale museum at Hawes and observant visitors will have fun spotting the subtle differences in bygone life-styles in the two dales.

Arkengarthdale

The road from Reeth to the Tan Hill Inn (p.62) heads along Arkengarthdale, the northernmost dale in the National Park, initially fringed by the high wall of Fremington Edge. Again, old lead-workings – shafts, miners' tracks, hushes, spoil, ruins of smelting-mills and crushing-mills – are scattered throughout. The dale seems to specialise in odd place-names: Whaw, Eskeleth, Arkle Town and Booze. **Langthwaite** is minute, but the major village, its square entered via a narrow bridge.

Until the church was built at Muker in the late-sixteenth century, the only consecrated burial ground in Swaledale was at **Grinton**. Coffins had to be carried for miles over rough tracks which became known as the Corpse Way. **Grinton church** which has been dubbed the 'cathedral of the Dales' dates from Norman times but a thorough rebuilding in the fifteenth century gave it its long, low and wide appearance.

Further west along the same road, at a point south of Healaugh, the 15-foot-high, grassy ramparts of an Iron-Age fort known as **Maiden Castle**, lie above and can be reached by footpath. The site is some 200 feet across and a major legacy of the dale's earliest settlers.

THE NORTHERN FRINGES

The northern part of the National Park merges into the uplands known as the Northern Pennines; these contain some of the bleakest and most solitary hill-tops in England, presenting a very different picture to the intimate, complicated limestone landscapes of the southern Yorkshire Dales. In particular the drive up to the **Tan Hill Inn** crosses a desolate moors landscape – comparable to the vast wastes of western Dartmoor. The inn, the highest in England (1,732 feet above sea level) and close to the boundary point of North Yorkshire, County Durham and Cumbria, was built at a meeting of packhorse routes which have since become little-frequented roads.

NOT QUITE THE NATIONAL PARK

Like most artificial boundaries, the borders of the Yorkshire Dales National Park have an arbitrary air. Valleys or even fields are divided at the stroke of an office-bound pen. Parts of Wharfedale, cast out from the officially holy ground, are every bit as beautiful as neighbouring stretches which come within the park. The wild moors of upper Nidderdale, beyond Pateley Bridge, are a particularly surprising exclusion, and indeed, as a belated consolation prize, they have just been made an Area of Outstanding Natural Beauty.

They were left out partly because the water authorities, which have used upper Nidderdale as a reservoir for nearly 100 years, did not want to encourage people on to their moorland catchments, but equally, the park's domain could not run on indefinitely. The dogleg of Nidderdale, lower Wharfedale (south from Addingham) and the shallow valley of the Rivers Aire and Ribble between Skipton and Giggleswick, have many compensations, too, for being denied park status. The pressure of tourism is not so intense; locals are less harassed by fierce planning restrictions; and the sense of discovering secret places by yourself can be more satisfying.

That said, this area just outside the National Park is far from untrodden. It has two of the Dales' most important touring centres in Skipton and Pateley Bridge. Both are good bases for exploring the complicated landscape of valleys and ridges leading up to the Pennine summits and the Lancashire border. Ilkley is a third, well-placed town with a strong local history. A few miles further down the Wharfe, Otley is an archetypal little market-town, snugly placed below the the rocky hillside of The Chevin.

Walkers can choose from the Brontësque moors around Cowling to the charming defile of the How Stean waterfalls, near Middlesmoor, whose marketing tag of 'Yorkshire's Little Switzerland' is not entirely fanciful. Monuments include one of Britain's most charming castles at Skipton and the mighty dams at Angram, Scar House and Gowthwaite which quench Bradford's thirst.

Skipton

To the west, Skipton has set out its stall to be the 'Gateway to the Dales' and it serves this function efficiently. A bypass for the A65 Leeds-to-the-Lakes route has relieved the town centre of traffic; strollers can enjoy the fine townscape of Market Street and the bustling market-stalls lining its pavements in relative safety.

Flanked by handsome, largely eighteenth-century houses and shops, the street leads up to Skipton's twelfth-century parish church and the deceptively modest front gate of the town's main attraction, **Skipton Castle** (open all year, daily 10 (Sun 2) to 6 (4pm Oct to Feb); closed Christmas Day). Beyond the Norman arch with its motto *Desormais* (the Clifford family motto, 'Henceforth!') picked out in stone, a lawned courtyard leads to a flight of steps and the castle's entrance. One whole wing of the fortress is private flats; but the public section, guarded by four immense millstone grit-towers, is an ample delight. The frowning bastions open on to delicate Conduit Court. It is like discovering a quiet Elizabethan manor house inside an enormous stone box. The castle has a splendid dungeon (where the guide enjoys teasing children by turning out the lights) and a memorable garderobe, or medieval lavatory, cantilevered out over the Eller Beck which forms a partial moat. One captive in the dungeon told his subsequent trial at York that he had never been so well fed as when in the custody of Lord Clifford.

The Craven Museum (closed Tue), tel. (0756) 4079, is on the top floor of the Town Hall in High Street, with modest but informative displays on Dales geology, archaeology, farming and lead-mining. The Craven Heifer, a vast beast bred by the vicar of Bolton Abbey and sold for a nineteenth-century record of £200, is duly honoured. Her name has been given to many West Riding pubs. A ten-minute walk down High Street and Swadford Street brings you to the picturesque canal basin, where narrowboats tie up in front of cafés, shops and pubs. A waterbus is available for trips down to Cononley and, the prettiest route, up to Gargrave.

On the north-eastern rim of the town, **Embsay** village has its own **steam railway** (talking timetable on (0756) 795189) which puffs up and down a two-mile track. The bookshop at the station has an outstanding collection of local history, archaeological and railway books. Embsay village has an attractive centre and a pleasant by-road leads to the glories of Bolton Abbey only four miles away.

Around Skipton

The favourite tourist route to the Dales leads north to Grassington and the spectacular landscape beyond. Almost equally busy, the A65 heads off towards Settle, Ingleton and ultimately the Lake District, skirting the National Park boundary as far as Giggleswick and passing through lovely countryside. Two road hazards to look out for in this area: quarrying is still a thriving industry in the Yorkshire Dales and huge lorries pound along the roads. Less alarming, a sudden hiss may alert you to a party of sturdy Yorkshire cyclists, heads down, pounding away in their skintight cycling gear and riding several abreast like a multi-coloured swarm.

Taking the A65 north, you may be stopped at **Thorlby**, shortly after leaving the Skipton ring road, by a rare set of cattle traffic-lights, activated by a local farmer to get his herd safely across. Two miles further on, you arrive in **Gargrave**, a large, handsome village with several antique, craft and sheepskin shops and a pretty green on either side of the River Aire, with road and pedestrian bridges criss-crossing the river. A pleasant side-road leads off left to **Broughton** and Broughton Hall (see below), while a right-turn just before the village takes you into the splendours of Malhamdale in the National Park.

Long Preston, the last village before the A65 enters the National Park, has a lovely green with a maypole surrounded by mellow Dales houses; from here you can walk or drive into the final empty quarter of this Yorkshire *ultima Thule*. A gated road loops round the lonely farmhouses of **Wham**, while at **Wigglesworth** a comfortable country pub, The Plough, offers good food. A little further west, the hamlet of Tosside has had a split personality since local government changes in 1974: the village institute, former vicarage and caravan site are in Yorkshire, the pub, shop and church are in Lancashire.

As an alternative to the A65 you can thread your way back from here on by-roads to the A59, running west from Skipton to Clitheroe, to visit **Broughton Hall** (open Summer Bank Hols and weekends in June; otherwise by appointment (0756) 792267). This handsome mixture of eighteenth- and early-nineteenth-century architectural styles reflects the fortunes and building enthusiasm of the Tempest family, who still live here.

From Broughton, a quiet road leads south and up on to the Pennine moors (crossing the Pennine Way beyond Elslack), a little-frequented corner with much of the atmosphere, but few of the visitors, of the Brontë heartland a few miles south. Several gritstone hill villages huddle against the wind and weather.

LOWER WHARFEDALE: ILKLEY AND AROUND

The A65 climbs south-east of Skipton over the watershed from Airedale to Wharfedale. **Chelker reservoir**, at the summit, is a famous stopping-off point for migratory birds; 'twitchers' fill the car-parking bays and stand sentinel with binoculars and telescopes. Beyond, a left-turn leads to a brief detour from the main road to **Addingham**, known to many simply as the last stop before Bolton Abbey, but an attractive village in its own right and a notable walking centre with the start of the **Dales Way** close by; footpath maps are available at Ilkley tourist information centre. Street names such as Druggist Lane and Sugar Hill bear witness to its long history as a farming and weaving centre.

Ilkley

Ilkley has a rather grand air – very grand in King's Road (up to the left off the A65 coming into the town from Addingham). A splendid Lutyens villa, **Heathcote**, stands here, now under corporate ownership. Leeds and Bradford businessmen colonised the sleepy market village in the nineteenth century and some of them turned their hand to marketing the icy moorland springs as a spa – the 'Malvern of the North'. The modest but painstaking **Manor House Museum**, housed in a mullion-windowed, sixteenth-century building just behind the parish church, tells the town's story entertainingly, with a wealth of Victorian hype for the magic of the chalybeate (iron-rich) springs – 'mellifluent, diaphanous, luminous, transparent, pellucid, immaculate and unequalled in purity', according to one of the more modest brochures. People came in large numbers to take the waters. The museum, tel. (0943) 600066, also has a lively art gallery with touring exhibitions.

As the museum's archaeological collection also shows, Ilkley's origins, and their surviving traces, go back far beyond the spa. The mystifying **Swastika Stone**, the oldest known rock-carving in Yorkshire, is thought to be part of a related culture. It stands by Woodhouse Crag, a short step beyond **Heber's Ghyll**, a natural wooded ravine on the edge of the moor, landscaped by the Victorians into a manageable wilderness with small waterfalls and a series of rustic bridges.

The moor proper lies up behind the town, a favourite place for ramblers and picnickers. The sturdy may be tempted by the paved trod from **White Wells** (the original, humble spa developed in 1760 by a local squire) right across the moor to Bingley, calling halfway at Dick Hudson's, a welcoming pub celebrated by J B Priestley, Howard Spring and generations of walkers. A more modest target is the famous **Cow and Calf** group of rocks, a characterful scrambling ground with time-worn steps allowing the reasonably fit to conquer the immense, isolated boulder of the Calf.

Ilkley's compact town centre is a pleasant place to wander around. Some of the shops are particularly interesting: Humphrey's confectioners, on the right of the Leeds Road just beyond the town centre (going south), makes its own chocolate – milk, plain and white – while you watch. The swirling churns are tipped into moulds and you can sally out with an edible tennis racket, golf clubs, chess set or other curiosities.

Otley's Neighbourhood

The most picturesque route down the dale to Otley starts from the Cow and Calf, a scenic run through **Burley Woodhead** to Menston. You can follow the road to either **Hawksworth** or Menston, both huddles of old, dark cottages and terraces. **Menston** has a station on the Leeds-to-Ilkley line and is just down the road from the world-renowned **Harry Ramsden's** fish-and-chip shop at White Cross roundabout, Guiseley, where the A6038 joins the A65. Don't be put off by the almost permanent queue; it moves rapidly. Inside, plump, contented diners lay into items like 'Baby Haddock' (twice as big as a normal fish). Harry's is a self-conscious tourist attraction but has a genuinely interesting place in social history. Its owner was determined to make a 'common' meal respectable by gracing it with 'posh' surroundings. He succeeded triumphantly.

Another alternative route to the busy A65 between Ilkley and Otley lies across a graceful suspension bridge, on the left shortly after Ilkley. This side road winds gently to Denton and its fine hall (not open to the public) and St Helen's church, both by John Carr of York. The quiet lane continues to Otley through the peaceful villages of **Askwith** and **Weston**, the last with lovely Elizabethan Weston Hall. Visits are by written appointment, but the house is viewable from the equally delightful part-Norman church.

Otley

Otley people are understandably proud of their thriving market-town. It is smaller than Ilkley, but far more of a community. The annual Victorian Fayre at the end of November has the streets packed with costumed revellers; fund-raising goes on incessantly for the much-loved Wharfedale district hospital; Leeds, which theoretically controls the town, is regarded with suspicion and contempt. The visitor, stopping at one of the pubs, cafés or restaurants, may absorb a little of this characterful ambience, which more than compensates for the lack of more specific attractions.

The town's part-cobbled streets make an attractive place for a stroll: a statue honours the cabinet-maker Thomas Chippendale, Otley's most famous son, next to some dignified Georgian town houses and a cobbled market-square. The market has an exceptionally colourful tradition – founded in the twelfth century, it was notable up to the First World War for its 'eye lickers', who would offer to lick away incipient cataracts. Several ginnels (alleys) and passages house a good range of shops.

Otley has a lot of modest but satisfying vernacular architecture, plus one or two surprises. The brightly tiled houses in Guycroft, off Westgate Street, were built with material intended for a swimming-pool which was never constructed. The miniature tunnel in the parish churchyard commemorates more than 30 navvies killed during the building of the nearby Arthington railway tunnel in the 1840s.

Beside the medieval bridge spanning the Wharfe, there is a small, well-kept park where rowing-boats can be hired in summer. Above the town, The Chevin is a long, striking hillside serrated with glacial outcrops and boulders, thick strands of trees and coverts of bracken and long grass. **The White House visitor centre** (open 1 Apr to 31 Oct, Sat and Sun, 1 to 4.30) has an historical exhibition, maps, leaflets; teas are served, too.

The A660 up The Chevin leads to **Bramhope** which has an exceptionally rare Puritan chapel, one of very few religious buildings dating from the Cromwellian interregnum, with a fine triple-decker pulpit, box pews and font. Staircase Lane, behind the chapel, is an old packhorse route connected by a footpath to the Arthington Tunnel entrance. The route is reproduced in miniature in the Otley churchyard memorial.

NIDDERDALE

Leaving Otley by the less-frequented road to **Blubberhouses** (straight on north after the bridge over the Wharfe) is more rewarding than the official B6451 road to Pateley Bridge. Heather-covered moorland lies on your left and lovely views of the Washburn Valley to your right. You can just see, too, the eerie-looking giant golf balls of Menwith Hill, a government 'listening post' on the edge of Blubberhouses Moor. When you reach a skew junction at Blubberhouses church, turn right and immediately left up Hardisty Hill. This bleak moorland, where the trees are permanently bent from being buffeted by the wind, is grouse-shooting country.

Pateley Bridge

Very much the centre of Nidderdale, Pateley Bridge serves an essentially agricultural area. You will be aware that you are in walking country as soon as you find the car park: 'Washing of boots within these premises is strictly forbidden' proclaims a sign outside the ladies' lavatories.

The compact town, winner of three Britain in Bloom awards, is ideal for shopping and browsing. A good selection of cafés and shops in the high street is gradually being added to by development of the delightful courtyards which lie just behind it.

Nidderdale Museum (open Easter to end Sept, daily 2 to 5; winter Sun only 2 to 5; groups at any time by prior arrangement), in King Street, was extensively renovated in 1992. It is a fine example of what can be achieved by enthusiasts. Begun in 1975 in only four rooms, it now occupies the whole of Pateley's former Union Workhouse, with its recreated Victorian shops and displays illustrating every aspect of life in the Dales, from religion to transport, and costume to agriculture. It was voted National Heritage Small Museum of the Year in 1990.

Don't leave Pateley Bridge without a visit to the ruined church of St Mary, set in an outstandingly pretty churchyard at the top of Old Church Lane (a continuation of the high street). There is only one caveat: your peace is likely to be disturbed only by the heart-stopping noise of jet fighters on exercise.

To make your way up Nidderdale, cross the river from Pateley Bridge and turn right. A few miles further on is the **Water Mill Inn**. This was a working flax-mill until as recently as 1967; its huge 11-metre (36-foot) diameter water-wheel has been restored to working order and if you are lucky, you will see it in operation. Roaring fires, good food and a few rooms. Children welcome.

The head of Nidderdale gives every appearance of a dead end, but a steep moorland road leads out of the valley at **Lofthouse** to Masham, offering superb views on the way. For a small fee, you can also take the waterworks road to **Scar House reservoir**, a pretty route to a bleak destination where the wind always seems to blow and immensely healthy walks can be taken round the reservoir to Angram dam, still higher up. The infant River Nidd has an interesting habit of vanishing for prolonged periods into the potholes which seam this harsh but invigorating landscape.

How Stean Gorge, well-signposted at Lofthouse village,

is the dalehead's most popular attraction, a precipitous ravine carved by the furious How Stean Beck on its descent from the encircling moors. Potholes were gouged out by the water and a leaflet reminds visitors that all caves can be dangerous (and dirty; Cat Hole is pungent with rabbit droppings). Go armed with a torch.

Leaving Pateley Bridge on the Harrogate road B6165, turn left at the sign for **Brimham Rocks** (National Trust), a wonderful collection of tors, balancing rocks and pinnacles, strangely weathered and a challenge as a series of scrambly climbs. Most of the rock formations don't allow the inexperienced climber to get very far. The sculptor Henry Moore, who bicycled here as a boy, acknowledged a debt to the rounded and sometimes eerily human-looking shapes.

WHERE TO STAY

ARNCLIFFE

Amerdale House
Littondale, Nr Skipton BD23 5QE
TEL (0756) 770250
A very beautiful and peaceful spot with views down Littondale to the River Skirfare. Bedrooms and public rooms are comfortable, with relaxing atmosphere.
££ *Mid-Mar to mid-Nov; 11 rooms; Access, Visa*

BOLTON ABBEY

Devonshire Arms Country House Hotel
Bolton Abbey, Nr Skipton BD23 6AJ
TEL (0756) 710441
A smart and expensive former coaching inn just outside Bolton Abbey. Owned and decorated by the Duchess of Devonshire, it is an elegant and luxurious base for exploring the Dales.
£££ *All year; 40 rooms; Access, Amex, Diners, Visa*

GRASSINGTON

Ashfield House
Grassington, Nr Skipton BD23 5AE
TEL (0756) 752584
A pretty, seventeenth-century house close to the centre of this busy village. It has simple, appealing furnishings in the bedrooms and offers a friendly welcome and good English food.
£ *Feb to Nov; 7 rooms*

MASHAM

King's Head
Market Place, Masham HG4 4EF
TEL (0756) 689295
This straightforward, popular inn dominates the main village square. It is traditionally furnished and homely; an excellent base for visiting the Dales.
£ *All year; 10 rooms; Access, Amex, Diners, Visa*

REETH

Arkleside Hotel
Reeth, Richmond DL11 6SG
TEL (0748) 84200
Just east of the village green this
small, stone house provides a
friendly welcome. Well-prepared
food makes this an inviting base
for the area.
£ *Mar to Dec; 8 rooms; Access, Visa*

Burgoyne Hotel
Reeth
TEL (0748) 84292
This mainly Victorian, long,
stone house dominates the village
green. The hotel has been
decorated with flair and taste, and
you will be well looked after.
Bedrooms are as spacious as the
rest of the house and extremely
comfortable; most have lovely
views over the moors.
£ *All year; 8 rooms; Access, Visa*

SEDBUSK

Stone House
Sedbusk, Nr Hawes, Wensleydale
DL8 3PT
TEL (0969) 667720
This turn-of-the-century stone
house is in a lovely garden and has
a welcoming atmosphere.
Panelling and log fires are the style
here and the bedrooms, though
simple, are comfortable.
£ *Mar to Nov, weekends only in
Dec and Jan; 15 rooms; Access, Visa*

WEST WITTON

The Wensleydale Heifer
West Witton, Wensleydale DL8
4LS
TEL (0969) 22322 Fax (0969)
667720
Right in the middle of the village
this pretty, whitewashed inn
makes a good base. Sometimes
the pub gets very busy and guests
can escape to the bedrooms which
are varied but generally
comfortable.
£ *All year; 19 rooms; Access,
Amex, Visa*

WHERE TO EAT

DENT

Stone Close ★
Main Street
TEL (058 75) 231
An old stone farmhouse, now an
all-day café-cum-B&B. Daytime
offerings include salads, oak-
smoked trout and Yorkshire curd
tart. For the short, set-price menu
prior notice is essential.
Inexpensive wines. *All week,
10.30–3.15, 7.30 (prior notice for
D); closed Jan and first 2 weeks Feb;
tea-shop closed mid-week Nov to mid-
Mar*

HETTON

Angel Inn
Hetton
TEL (075 673) 263
First-class restaurant and
brasserie-style bar food; in the
main dining-room the set-price
menu offers seasonal choices such
as provençal fish soup with aïoli,
seafood 'moneybags' fish features
strongly and sticky toffee
pudding. Exemplary wine list.
*Mon to Sat, D only, and Sun L,
12.15–2, 7–9.30; Access, Visa*

ILKLEY

Bettys
32–34 The Grove
TEL (0943) 608029
One of the famous tea-shops,
open til evening for omelettes,
filled rolls, light meals and
peerless cakes.
All week 9–9

THRESHFIELD

Old Hall
Threshfield
TEL (0756) 752441
Comfortable country pub that's
very popular. A blackboard menu
lists bar food inspired by global
cuisines: Italian seafood salad,
chicken wings with Chinese
sauce, cassoulet and Landlord's
steak pie. Generous helpings.
Well-kept Timothy Taylor's beer.
*All week, 12–2, 6.30–9.30; closed
Mon, Jan to May*

WATH-IN-NIDDERDALE

Sportsman's Arms
Wath-in-Nidderdale
TEL (0423) 711306
Old stone Dales pub now
operating as a restaurant-with-
rooms, though still retaining the
bar for beer and lunchtime
snacks. *All week, exc Sun D, 12–
1.45, 7–10; Access, Amex, Diners,
Visa*

EAST WITTON

Blue Lion
East Witton
TEL (0969) 24273
Country pub with interesting,
seasonal and fairly priced food.
Plenty of game and fresh fish.
Good desserts and coffee.
Friendly atmosphere. *All week,
12–2.15, 7–9.30, exc Sun and Mon
D main restaurant closed; Access,
Visa*

HARROGATE, RIPON AND THE NORTH

- Harrogate, one of Britain's great spa towns, well-practised in entertaining visitors
- Ripon's ancient cathedral, with dozens of historic daughter churches
- An exceptional concentration of attractive market-towns, all with thriving markets
- Castles, stately homes and famous gardens, set in gentle countryside

Middleham Castle

Between the Dales and the North York Moors, the wide plain of York funnels up towards Darlington and County Durham; it is flattish farming country, but full of history as the Great Northern Route to Scotland (and 'Easy Way South' for kilted invaders in the past). The A1 drives with Roman certainty and straightness up the spine of this part of Yorkshire, a road for going places rather than gentle touring. Its bad reputation for accidents is slowly being changed by improvements and repairs.

Harrogate has little difficulty tempting the traveller off the A1 to the west. It marks the entry to a fascinating landscape of great estates and mansions with parkland, which fringes the foothills of the Northern Dales all the way to Richmond and the Durham border. Some of these, like the Studley Royal estate incorporating Fountains Abbey, are in the front rank of British tourist attractions, hugely popular (with good reason), highly organised and the subject of libraries of books. But others, like Markenfield Hall or the decaying Eden of Hackfall Woods, are wonderfully tranquil. Although you are in prime tourist territory in this part of Yorkshire, parts remain the preserve of the determined, explorer-minded few.

The same applies on the east of the plain, between the A1 and the Hambleton and Cleveland hills, where farming again dominates a somewhat amorphous area, currently trying to establish itself under the name of Herriot Country. The tag brings the coaches, meeting up with Captain Cook Country tours operating around Great Ayton, once the home of the great navigator. But there is more than enough room for them. You are not going to feel crowded pottering around villages like Ainderby Steeple, with its cottages and four-teenth-century church, or Leake's tiny settlement by the A19.

If you explore this wedge of North Yorkshire, you will notice many gradual changes. The accent alters gently from the slowish, rounded vowels of the 'traditional' Yorkshire accent in the south to the Geordie-like twang which begins to dominate from Northallerton northwards. Isolated farms offer a tremendous range of home-grown or bred products, from milk to goslings; craft businesses abound. The magnifi-cent architectural range of the churches in the area has the added attraction, especially for children, of looking for the wooden mice carved by Mousey Thompson of Kilburn on his furnishings.

Above all, this is a pretty area, in the best sense of a debased word. The countryside is gentle and characteristically English, the villages all that a foreigner with notions of Merrie England could wish for. The market-towns complete the landscape, nearly matchless in Britain as a set of scarcely spoiled, old mellow housing grouped around lively, cobbled squares. The light-coloured stone buildings are not blackened, either, like some of their sooty neighbours in West and South Yorkshire, although you may spot one intriguing exception. Chimney flues are often clearly marked on the outside of buildings by a blackish stain, caused by the sulphurous acid in smoke from the hearth which seeps through the limestone. In some cases, poor-quality stone has been so weakened that it has had to be replaced by brick.

HARROGATE

Harrogate is one of the best and most comfortable holiday bases in the whole of Yorkshire, a largely Victorian town, the entire history of which has been based on pampering visitors. The spa's heyday reached a climax one August day in 1911 when no fewer than three Queens spent the night in local hotels, to paroxysms of social delight from Yorkshire worthies. The same season saw more than 75,000 humbler visitors take the healthy but nauseating sulphurous water. 'It makes a good sort of purge if you can hold your breath long enough as to drink it down,' wrote the seventeenth-century traveller Celia Fiennes, whose horse refused to go anywhere near the spring's stench.

Harrogate has a reputation as a genteel retirement town these days, and well-to-do pensioners potter about or may be seen playing bridge in their mansion flats (some of Yorkshire's most expensive properties) overlooking the open, grassy Stray. But it was not always so. In 1629 Dr Michael Stanhope complained that posh patients were put off the waters by 'the meaner sort, who would wash their soares and cleanse their besmeared clouts (clothing) where others would afterwards dippe their cups to drinke'.

Even without such tainting, Harrogate water is pretty unpleasant to most tastes but is none the less permanently available, free under a fierce local covenant, at the Royal Pump Room which is now an excellent small museum. Sip some water, then reward yourself with the much more enjoyable form of hydrotherapy of a Turkish bath, available in vaguely oriental surroundings at the Royal Baths Assembly Rooms. You can also get a sense of the town's nineteenth-century past

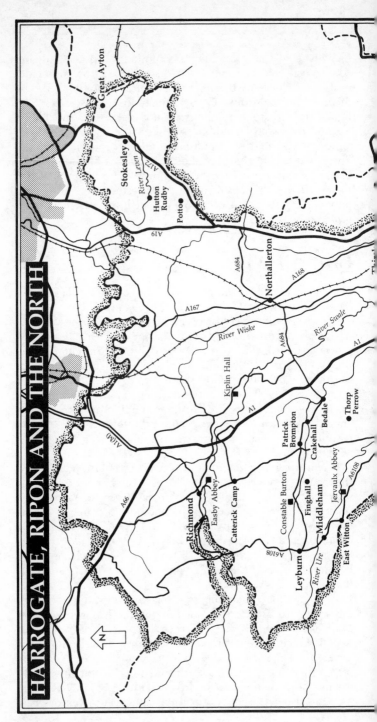

HARROGATE, RIPON AND THE NORTH

Great Ayton

Stokesley

Hutton Rudby

Potto

River Leven

A172

A19

Northallerton

A684

A168

A167

River Wiske

River Swale

A684

A1

Thirs[k]

Kiplin Hall

A1

A1(M)

Thorp Perrow

Patrick Brompton

Crakehall

Bedale

A6108

A66

Richmond

Easby Abbey

Catterick Camp

Constable Burton

Finghall

Middleham

Jervaulx Abbey

A6108

Leyburn

River Ure

East Witton

N

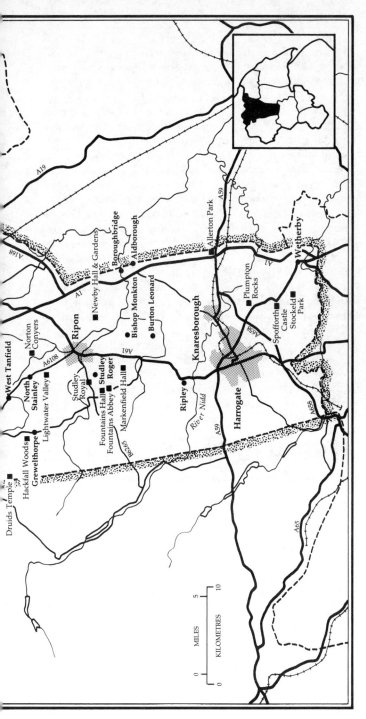

at some of the many hotels, notably the enormous Majestic and the Old Swan, where Agatha Christie was discovered after her breakdown and mysterious disappearance in 1926.

Taking the waters is no longer the medical rage, but Harrogate's hotels still thrive, serving the modern conference centre (the subject of great controversy locally after its building costs ran out of control). Delegates from the National Union of This or the British Association of That are almost always to be found sauntering Harrogate's streets or the Stray, wearing their name badges and looking for a free table in one of the many tea-rooms. Conference organisers also appreciate the compact and classy nature of Harrogate's shops, which serve one of the most prosperous areas of Yorkshire. Antiques, though seldom cheap, are a speciality.

Heavy Victorian architecture and blackened gritstone can make the town centre dour on a dull day – compared, say, with honey-coloured Bath – but the buildings are generally low-storeyed and often relieved by graceful cast-iron canopies. Harrogate has also been an almost permanent winner of Britain in Bloom competitions and its parks, floral displays and trees festooned with lights encourage a holiday atmosphere, albeit sedate. The town was built on relatively high moorland, however, and can be unexpectedly nippy in late spring or early autumn. There are good train and bus services, plentiful car parks and a two hour disc-parking system (discs are free at all local shops) which tries to relieve the frequent congestion.

AROUND THE TOWN

The sulphurous spa water was first discovered at Tewit Well when in 1571 Captain Sir William Slingsby disturbed a flock of plovers (nicknamed peewits or tewits after their sharp call), reined in his horse to watch them and discovered a stinking spring. Another 88 sources of the water, forced up through a geological fault, have since come to light. Exploitation for medicinal treatments began in earnest in the nineteenth century, helped by Harrogate's strategically central position in Yorkshire. The present domed and Tuscan-columned **Tewit Well** is essentially eighteenth-century, aggrandised by the Victorians, and splendidly sited on one of Harrogate's most valued possessions, the green and open Stray. This wide, 200-acre arc of grass, which stretches right into the town centre, was cleared from the Forest of Knaresborough under the Enclosure Act in 1770 and is theoretically preserved for all time.

One wedge of it leads almost to the **Valley Gardens**, a classic Victorian pleasureground in a steep clough. Ornamental gardens cover 18 acres, with a boating-pond for the rolled-up trouser and model yacht brigade. A tea-room is housed in an elegant structure of cast-iron and glass and you can dally on the 600 foot-long Sun Colonnade, designed in 1933 for convalescents and invalids to take tentative steps towards the outdoors.

The central spa complex, the **Royal Baths Assembly Rooms** at the foot of Parliament Street, is a pleasant place to potter under cover, have a coffee to the sound of string trios and plunder the well-stocked leaflet racks of the tourist information centre. Combine enjoyment of the building's architecture with a visit to the nearby, octagonal **Pump Room Museum**, and you will understand and appreciate the heyday of taking the waters.

Harrogate's **Theatre Royal** is another building worth examining, a good example of art nouveau, also with a café and bar. Its theatrical reputation is extremely high and its repertory productions and traditional family pantomimes are regularly praised by national critics. **The Mercer Gallery**, Swan Road, has a good collection of nineteenth- and twentieth-century paintings. Of the many tea-rooms, **Betty's** at the top of Parliament Street is a Yorkshire institution whose almost perpetual queue moves rapidly. Try one of their Warm Fat Rascal cakes and choose from an impressive range of exotic teas and coffees in the associated shop.

Shopping is a prime occupation in Harrogate and is much-advertised for spouses of delegates to conferences. The quality of the shops is probably the highest in Yorkshire and there is the enormous attraction of a very compact town centre: essentially James, Oxford and Cambridge Streets, with antiques shops concentrated on the little hill down (and behind) Montpellier Parade and Parliament Street. Exotica here is plentiful and almost always the genuine article; prices are accordingly at the top of Yorkshire's price range. Farrah's Harrogate Toffee is an obvious, cheaper souvenir, and there is plenty of more modest shopping, including a new and lively market hall, opposite the station.

On the edge of the town, **Harlow Carr Gardens** in Crag Lane are the Kew of the North, run by the Northern Horticultural Society, with an interesting range of plants which flourish in Yorkshire's marginally colder climate. Spelling perfectionists may like to know that Harlow Car is the correct, original name, but the gardens were so regularly assumed to be a car showroom, that a second 'R' was added in 1989. The 68 acres include a Museum of Gardening and restaurant (although it is worth seeking out the nearby eighteenth-century Squinting Cat pub in Whinney Lane, Pannal Ash, signposted off the B6162). On the other side of Harrogate, off the Wetherby road, the 250-acre Great York-shire Showground has frequent fairs and festivals. The show itself, usually in the second week in July, is a spectacular jamboree which causes traffic chaos for miles around.

AROUND HARROGATE

South-east on the A661, **Spofforth Castle** is a picturesque but sparse ruin where Harry Hotspur was supposedly born. His ancestor, Henry Percy, received a Licence to Crenellate what was really a fortified house rather than a major fortress in 1308; neighbouring rockfaces are cleverly incorporated into the defences. Spofforth's small village was the birthplace of Laurence Eusden (1688–1730) who became Poet Laureate after writing flattering verses about the influential Earl of Newcas-tle. He is widely considered the worst-ever holder of the post.

Stockeld Park (open 1 to 31 July, Tue to Sun 2.30 to 5.30), a mile nearer Wetherby, is an imposing eighteenth-century pile by James Paine with a wide 'crinoline' staircase (the balusters bowing outwards to cope with ladies' dresses) curving grace-fully upwards from an oval hall to a glass dome. Cream teas are available at weekends, more modest refreshments on weekdays.

Allerton Park (by the A1/A59 junction) is an entirely different sort of mansion, built in 1848-51 by the Mowbray and Stourton family to celebrate the return of Catholics like themselves to political and social acceptability. The vast, Dracula-like pile finally proved too much for them in the 1970s and the present earl lives in the converted stables, with the gaunt, spiky-roofed house now owned by an American multi-millionaire. He is pouring money into a painstaking restoration, which you can admire on Sundays from 10 to 4.

Plumpton Rocks are a less Transylvanian form of Romantic landscape, close to the junction of the A661 Harrogate-to-Wetherby road with the B6163 to Knares-borough. Huge boulders of millstone-grit, weathered into fantastic shapes, ornament a valley with a six-acre lake and plenty of woodland paths and picnic spots. The grounds were planned in the eighteenth century to complement a mansion being built by Daniel Lascelles (whose relations had bought the Harewood estate), but he never completed the building and moved instead to neighbouring Goldsborough Hall (now a nursing home). At the end of the A661, **Wetherby** is an ancient coaching stop on the Great North Road, now bypassed. The Thursday market is smallish but lively and there are some reasonable traditional shops, including an all-providing ironmongers. The **Ebor Way**, a 70-mile walk from Helmsley to Ilkley, leads along the Wharfe, with many pleasant riverside picnic spots, especially towards Wood Hall and Harewood (see page 20).

Knaresborough

Knaresborough, scarcely three miles from Harrogate, is a remarkable little town perched on precipitous limestone cliffs above the River Nidd. Beside the railway viaduct that straddles the river on slender arches, the huddle of varied houses, cobbled alleys and flourishing gardens seems astonishingly exotic, especially on a hot summer's day.

The town's main attraction is the extraordinary **Mother Shipton's Cave** and **Petrifying Well**, strictly enclosed in a highly organised, highly priced and over-touristy complex, but still a remarkable sight. Limey water drips down a smooth cliff-face and petrifies objects hung in its path (hats, shoes and especially teddy bears). Within a few weeks, they are solidly enclosed in a limestone coating and sold in the souvenir shop. In 1488 the alleged prophetess Mother Shipton was born (inevitably during a thunderstorm) in the neighbouring, satisfyingly damp and mossy cave. Endless fun can be had trying to relate her somewhat generalised predictions to specific modern events.

Less dramatic, but unexploited and therefore quieter, is the half-forgotten hermitage of **St Robert**; the third oldest shrine in England, it is reached down beetling steps on the opposite side of the Nidd, 20 minutes' walk along Abbey Road from the Blands Hill bridge. **The House in the Rock**, carved out in 1720, is another minuscule troglodytic curiosity.

Knaresborough's small town centre is excellent for a stroll, with plentiful cafés, pretty streets and an attractive market-place. Here England's oldest chemist's shop dispenses its own secret recipe for lavender water. Markets are on Wednesday, when you will meet the town crier (often about at other times, too) in his fine red coat. Upmarket shopping is limited, compared to Harrogate, but the Gordon Reece Gallery has a good range of Oriental arts, crafts and carpets.

Make sure that your walk takes in the fragmentary remains of the **castle** on its fine site dominating the river below. The friendly guides may not be historically reliable about the dungeon, but their gruesome tales delight most children. The unusual sallyport tunnel, only rediscovered in the late 1980s, takes you from the grassy castle yard through the rock into the moat. Defenders used the tunnel for lightning raids on besiegers. **The Old Court House** in the castle's pleasant gardens is scarcely altered from the fourteenth century and houses a small museum featuring Blind Jack of Knaresborough, who laid out local roads in spite of his handicap. Take one of several paths down to the river where cafés, ice-creams and rowing-boats for hire abound on Waterside. For the energetic, the **Nidd Gorge trail** leads back towards Harrogate through miniature, craggy defiles.

Like Harrogate, Knaresborough is well-served by public transport, especially the railway which links the town to Leeds, Harrogate and York from an excellent Victorian station whose buildings include a number of small shops.

EN ROUTE TO RIPON

A short detour off the main Harrogate-to-Ripon road, well signposted at its nearby roundabout, brings you to the stone-built estate village of **Ripley**, decorously laid out near Ripley Castle. The houses' uniform Gothic windows pretend to an older pedigree than the 1820s, when the village was rebuilt by the forceful Sir William Amcotts Ingilby of Ripley Castle. Whilst visiting Alsace-Lorraine, he was so struck by a Gothicky village there that, on his return, he effectively recreated it to replace the original, much scruffier Ripley. There is even an 'Hotel de Ville' towards the end of Main Street. Most of the houses are still occupied by current or retired employees of the Ripley Castle estate; a post office, half-a-dozen shops, an art gallery, church and the Boar's Head Hotel overlooking a cobbled market-square (with stocks) complete the village. Look for the weeping-cross in the churchyard; around its base are niches in which penitents could kneel to pray.

Entrance to the **Castle** (open Sun and Bank Hols, May to Sept) and grounds is from the square. The present occupants, Sir Thomas and Lady Ingilby, are the twenty-eighth generation of the family to have lived here since the 1320s. They run the estate as a tight, modern business, providing conducted tours of the Castle. The rooms date from the 1500s to Georgian times, and include a secret room which lay undetected behind panelling until it was rediscovered in 1963. The gardens are open to the public and rooms can be hired for private functions. Most recently, a major renovation of the hothouses has been undertaken to accommodate the tropical plant collection which Hull University could no longer maintain. The landscaped view from the Castle terrace is lovely, especially photogenic if the cows in the field opposite co-operate by trooping down to the lake. A pleasant tea-room has been made in converted outbuildings and a museum of old farming equipment and machinery is to be found on the other side of Main Street at Birchwood Farm.

A quiet, pleasant and well-signposted route leads to Fountains Abbey (see page 86) from Ripley – a good way of avoiding the A61 to Ripon which is often bedevilled by lorries and impatient commuters. Just before the Abbey, the somewhat spooky-looking derelict chapel on the hill is Howe Hill Tower, converted into a folly when Fountain's Abbey was landscaped in the eighteenth century. You can also thread your way to Ripon itself via the pretty villages of **Burton Leonard** and **Bishop Monkton** – both have welcoming pubs. The main road must be braved, however, to see one of the outstanding houses of Yorkshire, all the more enticing for only being open on Mondays between April and October (and even then closed for lunch). This is **Markenfield Hall**, unsigned and unadvertised, a moated and fortified, partly thirteenth-century manor house reached down a farm track marked only with a bridleway sign (Hell Wath Lane). You come on this fairly abruptly, a left turn off the A61 shortly after the Markington/ Bishop Monkton crossroads, three miles south of Ripon. The seventeenth-century gatehouse opens on to a lovely courtyard surrounded by the old buildings. Climb the ancient stairs which lead out on to the roof and contemplate the swans sculling in the moat. The path across the fields to Ripon makes a good circuit if combined with a bus back.

Ripon

Wonderful signs of considerable antiquity welcome visitors to Ripon on every major approach road with the quaint slogan: 'Stay Awhile Amid Its Ancient Charms'. This is an easy invitation to accept; the town is attractive and its **cathedral** of St Peter and St Wilfrid is magnificent. The west front was considered by Pevsner to be one of the noblest Early English examples in the country. Inside, take time to look at the locally carved misericords in the choir-stalls. The Saxon crypt, built around AD670, is one of the earliest Christian survivals in England and has the peaceful air of a place where prayer and worship have been conducted for generations. The cathedral is beautifully set, just behind the market-square. On the first Saturday in August, a colourful procession through the town, complete with a bearded and mitred 'St Wilfrid' on horseback, culminates with a cathedral service to celebrate this extremely worldly saint's return from foreign exile in AD686.

The **market place** (with markets on Thursday and Saturday) is all you might hope for with its mixture of Georgian and medieval buildings surrounding wide stretches of paving. For most of the week it becomes a car park, but on Thursdays market-traders set up their stalls around the central obelisk, erected in 1781 to commemorate the 60 years as an MP for Ripon of William Aislabie of Studley Royal. Stand near the obelisk at 9pm to watch (and be deafened by) Ripon's paid hornblower 'setting the watch' with a blast at each of the obelisk's four corners, a 1000-year-old tradition which once assured the inhabitants that they were safe in the hands of the nocturnal watch (who also became liable to pay compensation for any thefts committed before dawn).

The town's narrow, winding streets are ideal for a stroll, as are the **Spa Gardens** with a choice of not-too-strenuous activities, including bowls and pitch-and-putt, and a Victorian bandstand which is the scene of Sunday afternoon concerts in summer. The nearby racecourse offers thirteen racing days a year. Children are more likely to enjoy the **Prison and Police Museum** (open Apr to June and Sept, daily 1 to 5; July and Aug, Mon to Sat 11 to 5) housed in a former cell-block in St Marygate. Satisfyingly gruesome exhibits depicting early forms of punishment and hard labour can be enjoyed from the security of the twentieth century, together with a history of law and order.

Boroughbridge and Aldborough

Leaving Ripon for Boroughbridge on the B6265 you can visit **Newby Hall** and **Gardens** (open 1 Apr to 30 Sept daily, exc Mon (open Bank Hol Mon), 11 to 5.30) on the way. Pass Ripon Racecourse, cross the river and turn first right for Skelton. The long approach to the lovely Adam house of Newby is through a fine example of English parkland. There are all sorts of different gardens to explore within the 25 acres of grounds, including formal paved areas and traditional herbaceous borders leading down to the River Ure. Kingfishers are not uncommon, but the tranquillity can be deceptive; track down the garden's hidden monument recording a nineteenth-century drowning catastrophe involving the local hunt. There is also a miniature railway and an exceptionally well-designed children's adventure garden as well as an excellent self-service restaurant. The Compton family and their ancestors have lived here since the seventeenth century, and have managed to keep a lived-in atmosphere despite grand rooms, tapestries, much sculpture and Chippendale furniture, and the bedroom where the Queen Mother stayed. (For details of special weekend events, tel. (0423) 322583.)

A few miles south-east of Ripon, Boroughbridge and Aldborough are such close neighbours that it makes sense to visit them together. **Boroughbridge** earned its living as a coaching post, as the bridge built here over the Ure formed an important link on the Edinburgh–London route which became the A1. Now that the town is bypassed, it is a quieter place for visitors but fortunately seems to have survived the blow to business that bypassing can inflict. There is an attractive mix of architectural periods in the small town centre and a remarkably large market-cross built in the Victorian age when big generally meant beautiful.

Boroughbridge was a Norman creation, and the original street pattern survives. Neighbouring **Aldborough**, as its name – 'The Old Town' - implies, was the original Roman settlement. It is an outstandingly pretty Georgian village, worth visiting for its own sake, even if it was not concealing some of the most extensive Roman remains in the country. Villagers digging their gardens frequently unearth pieces of pottery, spoons and coins, but the impracticability of excavating the entire remains of Isurium Brigantum – once the capital of the Brigantes, the largest tribe in Roman Britain – is self-evident. However, you can view a lengthy though low-coursed portion of Roman wall by English Heritage's small but good museum, in a peaceful, tree-shaded setting of great charm. A footpath meanders delightfully between pasture and local back-gardens to two intricate mosaic pavements, preserved under cover in their original positions. An even better one is now in Leeds City Museum; others, alas, were destroyed in past centuries but still more, almost certainly, are buried under present-day Aldborough.

Boroughbridge and Aldborough have always been a natural settlement, occupying a spectacularly strategic position on

Britain's north-south artery, and they offer another, even older monument. In fields off Roecliffe Lane stand the **Devil's Arrows**, three gritstone menhirs (18, 21 and 22^1/$_2$ ft high) dating back to Neolithic or Early Bronze Age. Gaunt and lonely, they have that special atmosphere of the inexplicable and very old.

Fountains Abbey and around

Taking the B6265 Pateley Bridge road out of Ripon leads you to one of Yorkshire's foremost beauty spots (indeed now a World Heritage Site consecrated by UNESCO), **Fountains Abbey and Studley Royal** (National Trust, Abbey and Garden daily, exc 24 and 25 Dec and Fri in Nov, Dec and Jan; Jan to Mar and Nov and Dec, 10 to 5 or dusk if earlier; Apr to June and Sept, 10 to 7; July and Aug, 10 to 8; Oct, 10 to 6 or dusk if earlier; deer park all year during daylight hours). Cistercian monks found this idyllic pasture by the River Skell to build their abbey in 1132. By the eighteenth century the graceful, ruined buildings provided a dramatic ornament for the superb landscaped gardens started by John Aislabie and finished by his son William.

The Aislabies' mansion of Studley Royal was burnt down in 1945 but the estate is glorious and has been tidied-up and restored by the National Trust, which took over from North Yorkshire County Council in 1983. Follies and temples are dotted about the 793 acres of grounds and you can picnic beside one of the several lakes, while fending off assorted water-fowl. The Abbey's extensive ruins are in a magnificent setting. Guided walks are available on half-a-dozen days in the year; open-air concerts and firework displays are held on summer evenings. **St Mary's church** (open end Mar to Sept, daily 1 to 5), incongruously Victorian to some, is none the less the masterpiece of William Burges; on Boxing Day you can join the traditional four-mile pilgrimage from Ripon Cathedral to the Abbey. Fountains Abbey is the National Trust's most visited property and in 1992, after much controversy, a new entrance and visitor centre opened to enhance facilities which had grown piecemeal. The stone and slate-roofed building was allowed on condition that it was screened with landscaping of almost Aislabian proportions, involving no fewer than 30,000 trees and shrubs. An older and usually quieter approach is through the village of **Studley Roger** via a grand uphill drive towards St Mary's church. You can then walk to the Abbey through the heart of the Aislabies' park.

The other traditional entrance at Fountains Hall is now intended for the disabled.

Fountains Hall (open Apr to end Sept, daily 11 to 6; Oct to Mar, 11 to 4) was historically a separate estate from Studley Royal. The hall is an unusually tall and slender-looking Jacobean mansion, so beautiful inside and out that all but the most flinty-hearted must forgive the unpleasant Sir Stephen Proctor, fines collector for James I, for raiding the ruined abbey's stone to build the hall in 1611.

After all this culture, you are unlikely to escape a visit to **Lightwater Valley Theme Park** if you have children with you (open Easter to Oct, daily 10 to 5; June, July and Aug tel. for details (0765) 635368). This theme park (of indeterminate theme) is second in size only to Flamingoland in Yorkshire, but is very well screened from the surrounding area, four miles north of Ripon on the A6108. Your entrance fee covers most of the fun-fair attractions, including white-knuckle rides of which the worst (or best, depending on your point of view) are the Soopa Loopa, Rat and seemingly endless Ultimate. Food is available but basic, and weekend crowds can be huge.

A quieter afternoon near Ripon can be guaranteed at lovely **Norton Conyers** (open Easter, May to mid-Sept, Sun and Bank Hol Mon, 2 to 5.30), a late-medieval house owned and occupied by the Graham family since 1624. In the 'they slept here' league, Norton Conyers must come near the top, claiming James I, Charles I and James II as past guests. Charlotte Brontë stayed too and the house is one of the putative models for Thornfield Hall in *Jane Eyre*. Modern film directors would find Norton far too gentle and mellow for their Gothick ideas of Brontë mansions, especially the peaceful eighteenth-century walled garden which helps supply the small garden centre with unusual hardy plants.

FRINGES OF THE NORTH YORK MOORS

Leaving Ripon on the Thirsk road, over the Ure, with the bishop's comfortable mansion screened by trees on the hill to the left, you cross the A1 and then the River Swale (placidly different from its rugged, picturesque reaches in the Pennines), with the flat and intensively farmed landscape relieved only by the bluish-green escarpment and its prominent, carved white horse beyond Thirsk. Welcome to Herriot Country! Like it or not, the sobriquet borrowed from the immensely successful stories of a Thirsk vet, Alf White, has been given to an enormous swathe of Yorkshire between the Northern Dales and the North Sea. In places which were already well-visited, like upper Wensleydale or Helmsley, this has been a mixed blessing; but it has given a boost to less spectacular destinations such as Thirsk itself, Northallerton, Bedale, Leyburn and the many villages of the surrounding plain.

Thirsk

Thirsk has other claims to fame. It is the headquarters of Austin Reed and the conventionally minded may be reassured to know that they share the small market-town with one of the greatest concentrations of warehoused suits in Britain. More obviously appealing, the market-square (home to about 70 stalls on Mondays and slightly fewer on Saturdays) is a delightful set piece of largely Georgian buildings, cobbles, pubs and rural shops (waxed jackets? birdscarers? seeds? You are spoilt for choice). James Herriot's fictional home in Darrowby, as he calls Thirsk, is at the vet's working surgery in Kirkgate, just opposite the birthplace of a famous local lad. Thomas Lord, the founder of Lord's cricket ground, started life at No. 16, now the tourist information office and a modest folk museum.

Watered by the Swale, the Wiske and the Cod Beck, the gentle countryside north of Thirsk is only modestly interesting, with the Hambleton escarpment and the more distant hills of the Dales tempting visitors away like opposing magnets. Tractors chug, crops grow and signs point to villages with suitably agricultural names like Thornton-le-Beans. The A168, regularly enlivened by low-flying jets from the big RAF base at Leeming alongside the A1, leads to Northallerton, the county town of North Yorkshire and a place of legendary prosperity.

Northallerton

No one has actually proved the frequent claim that more tax is paid here per head than anywhere else in Britain; and North Yorkshiremen are perhaps less inclined to put their wealth on show than their counterparts in the West Riding. The long main street, however, has a contented air, a wide range of shops for a small town and that ultimate mark of Yorkshire respectability (shared only with Ilkley, Harrogate and York), a Betty's Café and Restaurant. On Wednesdays and Saturdays,

North Yorkshire's biggest market brings 100 stalls and much extra colour and life.

A wander round the centre is enjoyable but specific attractions are few and the information kiosk in the large, free car park (behind the shops that line the western side of the high street) has virtually no information on the town itself, amid stacks of material on other North Yorkshire attractions. The Fleece Inn is the oldest of several characterful pubs, used as a base by Charles Dickens during his hunt for the evil 'Yorkshire schoolmasters' flayed in Nicholas Nickleby. The **Hambleton leisure centre** (tel. (0609) 777070 for opening times) and pool at Stone Cross has a reasonable array of flumes, waves and sprays in a vaguely sub-tropical setting, useful if your visit coincides with gloomy weather. Rail links are good as the station is on the East Coast main line.

Two miles north on the A167, a memorial stone marks the site of the colourful Battle of the Standard. A large but undisciplined Scottish army was routed in 1138 by Northern troops led by an unpromising combination of elderly churchmen and rural knights who were also well past pensionable age. Their secret weapon was the standard, an extraordinary mixture of flags and holy relics on a sort of cart, which inspired the home side and allegedly struck terror into the Scots.

Turn right shortly after this to explore across country, and over the A19, via little-frequented lanes which lead eventually to **Hutton Rudby**, an old sail-making centre once surrounded by fields of blue-flowered flax which was spun into linen. New housing encroaches on the outskirts, but the long village green is lovely, with ancient trees, pretty terraces of cottages and two welcoming pubs. Down by the River Leven, the part-Norman church stands grandly, flanked by trees and, rising behind, the Cleveland escarpment is a marvellous mixture of woodland, hidden hanging valleys and glimpses of distant moor. **Potto**, just south, is where the 40-mile Lyke Wake Walk from Osmotherly to Ravenscar was first planned by a local, and very engaging, farmer and writer, Bill Cowley.

Stokesley

Along the Leven to the north-east, Stokesley is the market-town for this far corner of Yorkshire; market day is Friday. Two fine squares, West Green and College Square, are linked by a wide High Street with the little Town Hall in the middle. Cobbled stretches separate the shops from the road and the

Leven winds behind the houses, crossed by a generous series of footbridges. A particularly pretty walk is between the White Swan pub at the junction of West End and Levenside and Stokesley bridge. The many small curiosities *en route* include a wall plaque with a kangaroo by the path on the east bank of the Leven, just south of White (or Church) Bridge, which commemorates Stokesley lass Jane Pace, the first white woman to settle in Victoria, Australia. The Stokesley & District Local History Study Group's three guided walk leaflets make this an ideal town to look at in some depth, to follow the ups and downs of textiles, brewing and local agriculture. The large Stokesley Show is held on the permanent showground every September.

Great Ayton

Three miles along the A173 and at the present Yorkshire border with Cleveland, Great Ayton is another town extremely well-served by local historians. With more obvious reason. In spite of the marvellous surroundings, crowned by the 'Yorkshire Matterhorn' of Roseberry Topping, Great Ayton's most famous son, Captain James Cook, made his name by escaping the village and discovering distant lands. His former schoolroom is a friendly little **museum** with erudite maps displayed alongside an amateur colour snap of a turtle, supposedly left in New Guinea by Cook, which died only in the late 1970s. The village is splendidly set along the Leven, with a handsome Quaker school, good pubs and traditional shops doing friendly battle (Suggitt's Ices vie with Worthy Pearson's). Gentlemen should be sure to visit the very rare figure-of-eight-shaped Victorian urinal at the junction of Little Ayton Lane and Station Road – loyally defended against acquisitive folk museums by the parish council. Cook relatives are buried in the south-east corner of the graveyard surrounding All Saints' Church.

GATEWAYS TO THE DALES

For the explorer of the western side of the A1, embarking from Ripon, quiet country lanes lead north-east through pretty villages like Wath, past Norton Conyers and through Thornborough and Well, to the shady splendours of **Thorp Perrow arboretum** (access all year). Mature conifers and oaks, some of which have been here since Henry VIII's reign, grow alongside rare species in more than 60 acres of well-planned grounds. Three miles north, **Bedale** stands on either side of a typically handsome wide main street, yet another of the type in which the North Yorkshire plain is so rich. The **church of St Gregory** looks down across the cobbles, with a small museum and information centre on the other side of the road in Bedale Hall, an interesting complex of buildings but currently somewhat the worse for wear.

For museums, it is better to continue north-west along the A684 to **Crakehall**, a delicious English village whose manor house generously, and very untypically, opens its fine front door straight on to the village green, rather than hiding away behind rhododendrons and wellingtonias. On the other side of the main road in an old Methodist chapel the **Museum of Badges and Battledress** (open Apr to Sept, Tue to Fri 11 to 5; Sun 2 to 6; closed Mon) houses exhibits that range from the spiked helmets of 1900 to the hi-tech camouflage of the modern soldier. Veterans can prove to their offspring how much webbing they had to blanco, and what enormous boots they were forced to polish. On the Leyburn road out of the village, the verges of which are bright with poppies and marguerites in early summer, **Crakehall Water Mill** (open Easter to Sept, Tue, Wed, Thur, Sat, Sun 10 to 5 and Bank Hol Mons) offers stoneground flour and a chance to see a well-preserved, working seventeenth-century mill. As the road undulates gently through Patrick Brompton and Finghall, the lower slopes of the Wensleydale fells are clearly visible ahead, distracting from the plainer, immediate surroundings. But, before Leyburn, there is one delightful, unexploited detour, through a lodged gateway and down a parkland drive (dotted with 'Beware Children' notices) to the £1 honesty box for the gardens of **Constable Burton Hall**. The house, by John Carr of York, was built in 1768; it is a fine example of an eighteenth-century English mansion, surrounded by well-tended flowerbeds, borders and lawns with interesting and unusual plants. A homely, revolving summerhouse faces the informal car park. The house, home of the Wyvill family since 1762, is only open occasionally when the Wyvills are away (usually a couple of weeks in summer) but can also be visited by appointment, preferably in groups (tel. (0677) 50361). The gardens are open daily. Don't confuse Constable Burton with better-known Burton Constable near Hull.

Leyburn

Leyburn has more of a frontier feel than any of the market-towns further into the plain. The hills of the Dales are very close now; peewits may screech overhead as you approach the town and the battered Land Rovers of Dales sheep-farmers clatter over the cobbles in the market-square. On the wall of the Black Swan pub in the square a full-size, metal-toothed mantrap, once used to deter poachers, reminds you that the hills abut the great estates of the York plain. Leyburn is very much an agricultural town. The dignified post office building in the main square is largely occupied, wholly appropriately, by an emporium offering peat, compost, mowers, seeds, nuts and bolts and a vague but intriguing line called 'fancy goods'.

For £35 a head, three holidaymakers can tour from here in James Herriot's 'actual' Austin A40 Devon used in the TV series (tel. (060982) 478). However you travel, the road to Aysgarth and Hawes is almost irresistible and the route between Leyburn and Ripon is altogether memorable.

Middleham

Just the other side of the River Ure is one of North Yorkshire's finest surprises. Crossing an imposingly fortified bridge, whose stout, stone towers (part of a vanished suspension system) are let down by a notice warning 'One vehicle at a time', the A6108 climbs a hill into Middleham, a village with the particular fascination of a place which history has sidestepped.

Middleham's imposing castle was the headquarters of the future Richard III when he ruled as Protector of the North before seizing the throne. He also came here regularly as king and the Middleham Jewel and Middleham Ring, found by amateur archaeologists in the 'Treasure Field' below the castle walls and now displayed in the Yorkshire Museum at York, suggest that the court ceremonial here was as lavish as at Whitehall.

But Richard lost at the Battle of Bosworth and so Middleham slumbers – picturesquely and appropriately, given the king's reputation, around a family butcher's shop called Richard's. The **castle** (English Heritage, open Apr to Sept, daily 10 to 1, 2 to 6; Oct to Mar, Tue to Sun 10 to 4) is splendid and the **Old School Arts Workshop**, with its spiralled modern sculpture outside, offers unusually original displays, books and souvenirs. There is a good choice of pubs and cafés and a pleasant old Central Stores with a delicate, nineteenth-century ironwork verandah. Envy the Stablelads' Welfare Trust which has its office in this delectable place – where racehorse-breeding and training is a lynchpin of the local economy.

Middleham is special; but exceptional charm persists along the road south-east to **Jervaulx Abbey**, through the lovely village of **East Witton**, with its twin, mellow-stone terraces separated by a sloping green planted with fine, mature trees. The Abbey is another distinctive place: the only one of the great Yorkshire abbeys in private (and thoroughly enlightened) ownership, which has made the ruins subtly different from the neat, well-tended monuments in government or National Trust care. Wild flowers are encouraged and a sense of wilderness recalls the Romantic illustrations of the eighteenth century when every 'horride ruine' was festooned with creepers. High Jervaulx farm uses its surplus milk quota to make an unusually good and wide range of ice-creams, marketed throughout Yorkshire, which you can sample comfortably on the premises.

The slopes of the fells guarding Nidderdale rise above the road on to Ripon, well-screened with conifers and mixed woodland and guarding two splendid fancies that belonged to eighteenth- and nineteenth-century land-owners. In the woods above Leighton reservoir, half-a-mile off the narrow, invigorating road from Masham over to Lofthouse in Nidderdale, stands the **Druids' Temple**, a scaled-down Stonehenge replica built in the 1820s by William Danby, squire of the castellated mansion Swinton Park (private) nearly three miles nearer Masham. This quaint, atmospheric structure, part folly, part a project to relieve unemployment, is equalled by the decaying grottoes and pavilions of **Hackfall Woods** (free access) at **Grewelthorpe**, just north of Kirkby Malzeard, where you can explore a romantic, folly-filled landscape which is gradually being rescued by conservationists from decline into an over-riotous wilderness.

Masham

The A6108 meanwhile continues through flatter country, with mature and carefully sited trees bearing witness to the long, local tradition of wealthy estates, to the town of Masham, famous for its Theakston's Old Peculier brewery. Daily tours around the brewery are offered (booking essential, tel. (0765) 689544). Novices can discover the origin of Old Peculier's name in the informative visitors' centre; the drink itself can be sampled at a wide range of characterful pubs, especially round the huge square. Market day is Wednesday; it is sometimes a small affair, but often has good bric-a-brac. The **market square** is also a good place to park, both for a town walk and for the brewery, whose enormous drays may come uncomfortably close to your car if you try to park nearer the brewery. The surrounding houses form a handsome group and **St Mary's church**, in the south-east corner, has some enjoyable monuments to the likes of Sir Marmaduke Wyvill and Sir Abstrupus Danby (ancestor of the Swinton Stonehenge builder). The acrostic brass inscription on the west wall, to Christopher Kay and his grandmother Jane Nichollson, is also highly satisfying. On the same side of the square you will find the King's Head Hotel, and a hundred yards behind it, an opportunity to watch molten glass being miraculously transformed into vases, bowls and paperweights at **Uredale Glass** (open Easter to Oct, daily 10 to 5; closed Sun and Mon rest of year; closed Jan).

The road to Ripon from Masham passes the riverside panorama of **West Tanfield**, delightful and locally famous (you are unlikely to leave Yorkshire without finding a picture of it on a table-mat or hotel wall). The houses nestle between the Ure and the grey, protective walls of the **Marmion Tower**, imposing but merely the gatehouse to the vanished castle of the Norman family of Marmion. A delicate oriel-window spies down on the cottages, several of which are ancient chantry-houses built for priests by the Marmions. You cannot go inside either the houses or the Tower, but West Tanfield is a pleasant place to pause and the effigies of Marmions in St Nicholas' part-thirteenth-century church are notable for their over-sized sculpted dogs, one with an exceptionally long tail.

Just before the entrance to Lightwater Valley theme park (p 87) on the final stretch to Ripon, **North Stainley** has a slightly foreign-looking, immaculately kept hall in redbrick (private) and a pointed-roofed village lock-up. Notice the farmer's signs on the left-hand verge announcing proudly that his crops are organic – a quaint exception in a county of intensive and modern agriculture.

RICHMOND

Gathered a little nervously around its immense and reassuring castle, Richmond guards the entrance to Swaledale and the far, north-western reaches of Yorkshire (which stretched much farther into the Pennines before local government changes in 1974). The Swale rampages under a steep cliff and is always a stretch of water to treat with caution, especially in winter. The town is a place of hilly streets, lovely old buildings and plentiful greenery. Perpetually dominating the landscape is the keep of the Norman **fortress** started in 1071 by Alan the Red.

North Yorkshire is so rich in well-preserved market-towns that choosing the best is fraught with difficulty and argument; but Richmond's superb setting, castle and townscape have brought it more fame than rivals like Leyburn or Stokesley. There are consequently more visitors and more tourism. You may get slightly fed up, especially if you come from Surrey, with constant reminders that Richmond, Yorks, rather than any of the 70 Richmonds named after it worldwide, was the home of the famous Lass of Richmond Hill.

She was Frances L'Anson who married the song's writer Leonard McNally in 1787, after a childhood at Hill House, the delicate Venetian windows of which look out on Pottergate (now flats). Following her dainty footsteps, and summoning up some puff for all the slopes, explore pretty streets like Newbiggin, with its trees, Cornforth Hill and The Green by the bridge across the Swale with its glimpse of the **Culloden Tower** folly, a lovely viewpoint with riotously Gothick details (now a private holiday let). The cobbled **market-place** is England's biggest, sloping (like everything else in Richmond) past the **Georgian Theatre**, the second oldest theatre in Britain. Exceptionally well-preserved, with its box benches and side galleries, this is a thriving theatre and watching one of its productions is a Yorkshire treat. There are short guided tours, a little museum and the coffee bar/gallery (with exhibitions of local art) operates 11–5, Mondays to Saturdays.

Early-bird visitors will hear both the start and finish of the 8pm to 8am curfew, still marked by the bells of Trinity Church in the market-place, where the town crier once lived on the ground-floor with the bell-rope handy by his bedside so that he did not have to get up to ring the morning peal. The twelfth-century church has been well-converted into the **Green Howards' Museum** (open Feb to Nov, tel. (0748) 822133), adding an extra appeal to a tour of the military relics of Yorkshire's most famous regiment, war photography, 80 uniforms, 3,000 medals and the blood-stained pistols once owned by a Duke of York.

The army has always been part of Richmond's world because of the town's strategic position on the highway

North, and today its streets are often busy with off-duty troops from nearby Catterick Garrison, the biggest military centre in the North. Many ex-servicemen cannot resist a brief tour of the accessible fringes of the busy camp, but security is naturally high and the buildings mostly date from the 1920s and are undistinguished. Better for military enthusiasts to travel a little further south down the A1 and hope to catch a Tornado roaring aloft from RAF Leeming.

Better still, **Richmond Castle** (open Apr to Sept, daily 10 to 6; Oct to 31 Mar, Tue to Sun 10 to 4) is a wonderful military collection of towers, curtain-walls, an enormous keep and so many minor ways in and out that you wonder how the Constables managed to keep it effectively defended. Fortunately they were not often required to do so; the castle saw little active service, which accounts for the notable amount of Norman stonework that remains intact.

Literary pilgrims can meanwhile contemplate the house where Lewis Carroll stayed while a boarder at Richmond Grammar School from 1844 until 1846. The twelve-year-old Charles Dodgson had moved with his family to Croft, on the Durham border, where his clergyman father had accepted a living. The ten miles was too far to travel every day, so the young pupil stayed in Richmond at what is now **Swale House** in Frenchgate. Charles's talents were recognised by his headmaster who wrote to his parents at Croft Rectory: 'I do not hesitate to express my opinion that he possesses...a very uncommon share of genius'. But in proper Victorian manner added,'You must not entrust your son with full knowledge of his superiority over other boys'.

Easby Abbey (English Heritage, open Apr to Sept, daily 10 to 6; Oct to Mar, Tue to Sun 10 to 4), a mile east of the town centre via a very pleasant riverside walk, is a beautifully set complex of twelfth-century ruins, on the banks of the River Swale and below Easby's Georgian hall. The fourteenth-century chapter-house stands next to the surviving parish church of St Agatha, with trim lawns leading to the cloister and other remains beyond. The Abbey was founded by Premonstratensian monks; some of their delicately carved, canopied stalls were saved at the Dissolution and can be seen in St Mary's parish church, Richmond, (along with good misericords, some adorned with bagpipe-playing pigs).

Six miles south-east of Richmond, on the B6271 near **Scorton** (not to be confused with Scotton, to the south) lies the seventeenth-century mansion of **Kiplin Hall** (house and grounds open mid-May to end Aug; 2 to 5 Sun, Wed, Bank

Hol Mon; afternoon teas Sun only), built by Lord Baltimore, founder of the State of Maryland. Oak-panelled rooms contain portraits of the Calvert family and collections made by succeeding owners.

Richmond is also a favourite and well-placed base for the glories of Upper Teesdale, from High Force waterfall to the splendid Bowes Museum, just outside Barnard Castle. They lie outside this book's scope, but *en route* to them, take in the **Stanwick Iron Age Fortifications**: six miles of first century earthworks with an interesting restored section 400 yards north of the road from Stanwick to Forcett.

WHERE TO STAY

HARROGATE

White House
10 Park Parade, Harrogate
HG1 5AH
TEL (0423) 501388
Just off the A6040 but only a few minutes' walk to the town centre, this is a very convenient place to stay. Original furnishings and bright fabrics mix easily with lots of antiques to create a relaxing, comfortable atmosphere.
££ *All year; 10 rooms; Access, Amex, Diners, Visa*

MARKINGTON

Hob Green
Markington, Harrogate HG3 3PT
TEL (0423) 770031 Fax (0423) 771589
A pretty, grey-stone building covered in creeper about a mile from the village set a little above the roadside. Some of the bedrooms could do with redecoration but the majority are good, furnished with a mixture of antiques and fitted furniture. Public rooms are sometimes taken over by conference groups.

££ *All year; 12 rooms; Access, Amex, Diners, Visa*

MASHAM

King's Head
Market Place, Masham
HG4 4EF
TEL (0765) 689295
On the main market-square and owned by Scottish and Newcastle, this jolly inn is very much at the centre of things. The cosy and welcoming atmosphere attracts locals as well as visitors, although the dining-room is slightly more formal in atmosphere.
£ *All year; 10 rooms; Access, Amex, Diners, Visa*

MIDDLEHAM

Greystones
Market Place, Middleham DL8 4NR
TEL (0969) 22016
Overlooking the market-square, this small Georgian guesthouse offers simple, brightly decorated rooms and a good, home-cooked evening meal.

£ *Feb to Nov, Christmas and New Year; 4 rooms*

Miller's House

Market Place, Middleham DL8 4NR
TEL (0969) 22630
Your hosts at this charming small hotel provide lots of information about local sights. Bedrooms and public rooms are very comfortable with good-quality decoration and furnishings.
£ *Feb to Dec; 7 rooms; Access, Visa*

THIRSK

Sheppards Hotel & Restaurant

Front Street, Sowerby, Thirsk YO7 1JF
TEL (0845) 523655 Fax (0845) 524720
A converted seventeenth-century farmhouse set around a cobbled courtyard on the edge of the village. Family-run, it is decorated in country-style with dried flowers, flagstoned floor in the brasserie and chunky pine furniture. Homely, individually decorated bedrooms.
£ *All year exc first week of Jan; 11 rooms; Access, Visa*

RICHMOND

Howe Villa

Richmond DL10 4TJ
TEL (0748) 850055
A friendly small hotel in a peaceful setting near the River Swale, with lovely views from the first-floor dining-room and sitting-room. The comfortable bedrooms are either on the ground-floor or in the annexe.
££ *Feb to Nov; 5 rooms*

RIPLEY

The Boar's Head Hotel

Ripley, Harrogate HG3 3AY
TEL (0423) 771888 Fax (0423) 771509
A Georgian pub/hotel right in the heart of the estate village on the cobbled main square. It has been comfortably refurbished into quite an up-market hotel, with public rooms and bedrooms furnished with antiques and good-quality fabrics. Large breakfasts set you up for the day and there's a good choice at dinner.
££ *All year; 25 rooms; Access, Amex, Visa*

WHERE TO EAT

HARROGATE

Betty's *

1 Parliament Street
TEL (0423) 502746
The original Betty's, a small chain of tea-rooms catering for traditional tastes. Light savouries, good baking, full cream teas, speciality teas and coffees.
All week 9–9

Drum & Monkey

5 Montpellier Gardens
TEL (0423) 530708
Once a pub, now a busy bar and restaurant on two levels. Fresh fish is on the menu, not meat. Shellfish starters through salmon trout to brandy chocolate fudge cake. The wine list is short, sharp and keenly priced.
Mon to Sat 12–2.30, 7–10.15; closed Chr to New Year; Access, Visa

Millers

1 Montpellier Mews
TEL (0423) 530708
Short, precise menus offer fresh
fish, fungi, game and classical
sweets. Dinner is fixed-price,
lunch a more affordable *carte*.
Can be expensive.
*Mon to Sat, exc Mon D, 12–2, 7–
10; Access, Diners, Visa*

MASHAM

Floodlite

7 Silver Street
TEL (0765) 689000
An unassuming restaurant in a
substantial house. Serious and
accurate cooking, but without
over-elaboration, includes much
game and fish with excellent
desserts.
*Fri to Sun 12–2 (other days by
arrangement), Tue to Sun 7–9.30;
Access, Visa*

MOULTON

Black Bull

Moulton
TEL Tel (0325) 377289
Good bar-snacks at lunch-time
including excellent seafood
pancakes. In the evening there is
up-market dining in either the
conservatory or the renovated
Brighton Belle coach: huge
portions of sole, turbot or ox
tongue with vast platters of
perfectly cooked vegetables.
*Mon to Sat 12–2, 6.45–10.15;
Access, Amex, Visa*

NORTHALLERTON

Betty's *

188 High Street
TEL (0609) 775154
A smaller branch of this
illustrious chain, resulting in
queues for their light lunches,
tempting tea-breads and cakes.
*All week 9–5 (10–5.30 Sun);
Access, Visa*

NORTH YORK MOORS

- Heather moors, deep, green dales and memorable views
- Villages of quiet rural charm
- The finest section of Yorkshire's coast, with high cliffs and charming fishing villages
- Interesting monastic remains
- One of Britain's longest and most scenic nostalgia railways
- Stone crosses on the moors, wild daffodils, the Cleveland Way

Young Ralph Cross

THE NORTH York Moors were officially designated as a National Park in 1952. The coast defines the eastern side; the southern fringes dip gently to the Vale of Pickering, and to the west and north escarpments slope off to the Vale of York and industrial Teesside.

Driving across the centre of the region reveals the strong contrasts between high, gently undulating moors, and a series of fertile, green dales dotted with farms and remote hamlets. Forestry Commission plantations make up 15 per cent of this landscape, notably the fringes of the Cleveland Hills in the north-west and in the area north-east of Pickering. Agriculture is mixed but livestock farming is the major activity with Herdwick sheep, with their unmistakable speckled black faces, and cattle in most areas. In the lower-lying parts, and near the coast, fields of barley and bright yellow rectangles of oilseed rape are visible in summer.

The moors cover 40 per cent of the National Park's 553 square miles and constitute the largest continuous tract of heather moorland in England. The wiry carpets of bell-heather are a blaze of purple in August and September. Controlled burning of the moors between November and March encourages the growth of new heather and provides vital nourishment for the sheep and red grouse.

Drive, walk or ride up on to the moor and you're aware of an eerie stillness – a vast uncluttered landscape, huge skies and sometimes not a soul around. Yet for much of its human history the upland was busy with activity. Several thousand ancient mounds (known as tumuli) are the only traces of past habitation. Some of these are grouped together: John Cross Rigg, south-west of Whitby, comprises 1,200 such features. Stone circles from the same period are thought to have been constructed for ritualistic purposes. A number survive: among the most notable are the Bridestones in Bilsdale (40 stones, 40 feet diameter) and Standing Stones Rigg north-west of Scarborough (24 stones, 32 feet diameter). Evidence of the Romans' presence is scantier, but you can see a well-preserved stretch of Roman road known as Wade's Causeway, and north of Pickering, at Cawthorn Camps, traces of a Roman training camp.

In addition to many ancient tracks and a few paved trods, the North York Moors have a rich legacy of medieval stone crosses dating from the Norman conquests, thought to have been erected as waymarkers. Young Ralph Cross at the heart of the moors is the National Park emblem.

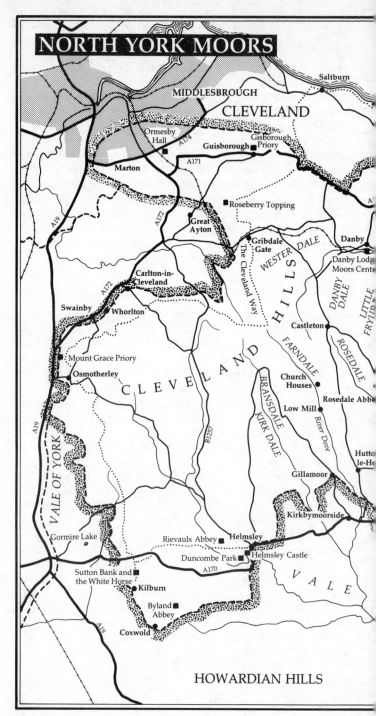

NORTH YORK MOORS

Saltburn

MIDDLESBROUGH

CLEVELAND

Ormesby Hall

Guisborough Gisborough Priory

Marton

A171

Roseberry Topping

Great Ayton

Gribdale Gate

Danby

WESTER DALE

The Cleveland Way

Danby Lodge Moors Cent

Carlton-in-Cleveland

CLEVELAND HILLS

DANBY DALE

LITTLE FRYUP

Swainby

Whorlton

Castleton

FARNDALE

ROSEDALE

Mount Grace Priory

CLEVELAND

Church Houses

Osmotherley

BRANSDALE

Low Mill

Rosedale Abb

River Dove

KIRK DALE

B1257

VALE OF YORK

Hutto le-H

Gillamoor

A19

Kirkbymoorside

Gormire Lake

Rievaulx Abbey Helmsley

Duncombe Park Helmsley Castle

A170

VALE

Sutton Bank and the White Horse

Kilburn

Byland Abbey

A19

Coxwold

HOWARDIAN HILLS

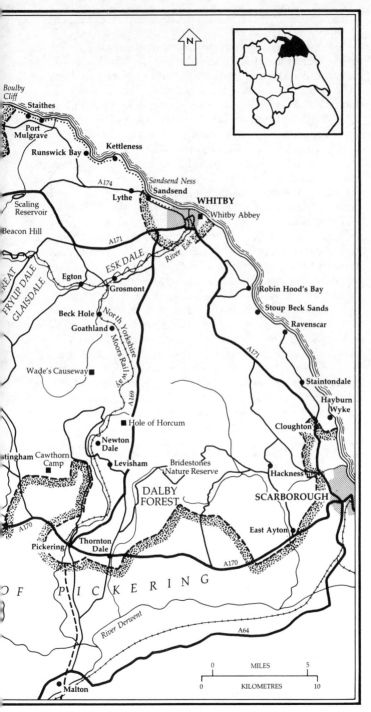

Boulby
Cliff
Staithes
Port
Mulgrave
Kettleness
Runswick Bay
Sandsend Ness
A174
Sandsend
Lythe
WHITBY
Whitby Abbey
Scaling
Reservoir
Beacon Hill
A171
River Esk
ESK DALE
Egton
Robin Hood's Bay
GREAT
Grosmont
Stoup Beck Sands
FRYUP DALE
Beck Hole
North Yorkshire
Ravenscar
GLAISDALE
Goathland
Moors Railway
A171
Wade's Causeway
A169
Staintondale
Hayburn
Wyke
Hole of Horcum
Cloughton
Newton
Dale
stingham Cawthorn
Camp
Levisham
Bridestones
Nature Reserve
Hackness
DALBY
FOREST
SCARBOROUGH
A170
East Ayton
Pickering
Thornton
Dale
A170
O F   P I C K E R I N G
River Derwent
A64
0   MILES   5
0   KILOMETRES   10
Malton

103

Superimposed on much of the moors landscape are legacies of several mineral industries, most of which have ceased operations. Alum, a double sulphate of potash and aluminium, which is used as a mordant or fixer in dyes and for tanning leather, was processed from shale at Belman Bank near Guisborough between 1607 and 1880. The manufacture involves adding ammonia, which at one time meant shipping in human urine from London pubs. Bracken collected locally was burned to make potash. In the mid-nineteenth century coal-measure shales were discovered to contain suitable material for making alum and the industry moved to the coal-fields. Iron production, established by the monks of Rievaulx in 1576, was another important industry. All surface deposits disappeared in the early-nineteenth century and mining for ironstone commenced in 1836 when a 34-inch-thick seam at Grosmont was exploited by the Tyne Iron Company; the same seam reached the cliffs at Skinningrove, where it was worked until 1958.

Jet-mining peaked in the nineteenth century, catering for Whitby's new tourist trade, and the spoil heaps can still be seen along the 900-foot contour on the Cleveland Hills. Low-grade coal, whinstone (for road surfacing) and sandstone (for building – the raw material for the Houses of Parliament was quarried here) – are some of the natural products of the area. Mineral excavation is now for limestone, as at Spaunton Quarry near Kirkbymoorside, and potash, mined at Boulby.

THE HAMBLETON HILLS AND THE WESTERN MOORS

Coxwold

The southernmost village in the National Park which merges into the Howardian Hills is also one of the most charming. Trim grassy banks beneath spreading trees line a sloping street of terraced cottages built from local stone. The fifteenth-century church with its octagonal tower has some fine Georgian features – box pews, pulpit and chancel – and monuments to the Bellasis family. In 1760, Laurence Sterne (1713–1768) was appointed curate and rented a house nearby, later nicknamed Shandy Hall (open June to Sept, Wed and Sun 2.30 to 4.30), 'shandy' being an old Yorkshire word meaning eccentric. Sterne spent his last and some of his most productive years in this rambling house, completing *Tristram Shandy* and *A Sentimental Journey*. The Sterne Trust took over the derelict house in 1963 and completely restored it. The present tenant has a fine collection of Sterne's books and original manuscripts. It is a place for literary pilgrims rather than of mainstream interest. Sterne was buried just outside the porch of Coxwold churchl; his epitaph records:

Sterne was the man who with gigantic stride
Mow'd down luxuriant follies far and wide...

Byland Abbey

(English Heritage, open Good Fri or 1 Apr, whichever is earlier, to 30 Sept, daily 10 to 6; Oct to Apr, Tue to Sun 10 to 4) Built in 1177, this was the largest Cistercian priory church in England, 330 feet long and 140 feet wide at the transept. The ruins lack the setting of Rievaulx (see p.108), but the jagged silhouette of its great west front soaring up to a broken rose window hints at past splendours. There are sections of tiled floor within the church, and scanty remains of the living quarters and cloister buildings.

Sutton Bank

This great inland cliff forms a buttress to the Hambleton Hills at the south-western corner of the National Park. Stop at the visitor centre on the A170 and take the path running above the woods, with an abrupt 600-foot drop immediately below, for huge views across the Vale of York and far over the high Pennine chain. To the south the path heads along to the **White Horse**, a hill-carving 314 feet by 228 feet. A schoolmaster and his pupils from Kilburn created this magnificent beast in 1857 and it is regularly freshened up with new chalk clippings. **The Cleveland Way** long-distance footpath north of the A170 along the cliff-top gives equally impressive views; narrow paths lead down to Gormire Lake, one of only three natural lakes in Yorkshire. Designated as a nature reserve, it is an important centre for botanists and bird lovers. The natural history of **Sutton Bank** is explained in an exhibition at the National Park information centre.

Kilburn, a village south of Sutton Bank, is best known for the workshop of Robert Thompson. Throughout this century the Thompson family have been producing high-quality woodwork: church pews, crucifixes and domestic furniture. Look out for the Kilburn mouse, their trademark, on every piece.

Osmotherley

At the western tip of the National Park, Osmotherley once had the status of a market-town. It is large but 'villagey' and virtually unspoilt, with broad verges and pretty stone cottages ranged around a 'T' of streets. John Wesley, the founder of Methodism in England, is reputed to have delivered one of his many sermons from the low stone table next to the old market-cross. The village is also the starting point for the arduous **Lyke Wake Walk** (see p.271) and there's good walking to the north, along the Cleveland Way. Just out of Osmotherley, the solitary restored chapel of Our Lady of Mount Grace is a popular place of pilgrimage for Roman Catholics.

Mount Grace Priory

(National Trust, open Good Fri or 1 Apr, whichever is earlier, to 30 Sept, daily 10 to 6; Tue to Sun, 10 to 4) Lying at the foot of the slopes below Osmotherley, this is the best-preserved of ten Carthusian houses in England, operative from 1398 until closure in 1539. The order practised a particularly austere life-style; vowed to silence, the monks lived in solitary confine-ment in two-storey cells, each within a walled garden. Food was served through an L-shaped hatch so that recipients couldn't see the person serving. One of these cells has been reconstructed so you can fully appreciate the rigours of monastic life. You can also visit the ruins of a prison where monks who slipped from the strict regime, or who had made an unsuccessful run for it, were incarcerated. The priory church, the most intact feature of the site, was built in the late-fourteenth century but remodelled and given its bell-tower in 1420.

Swainby

Once an ironstone-mining village, Swainby is now quiet and neat, with Scugdale Beck flowing beside the broad main street complete with green verges and white painted wooden railings – quite a contrast to the towering slopes of the Cleveland Hills behind. The neighbouring village of **Whorlton** was all but wiped out by the plague in 1428 and the ten survivors moved to Swainby. There is not much left to see now, except an abandoned castle and a partially ruined church.

North-east of Swainby, **Carlton-in-Cleveland** is another agreeable, long village beneath the Cleveland Hills, with the old alum-workings clearly visible on the hillside above.

RYE DALE

From its source in the high moors of the Cleveland Hills, the Rye follows a course through a landscape that wavers in characteristic North York Moors fashion between austere upland and pastoral lowland. Ryedale is also the official name of a rural district, a larger area that covers much of the National Park in addition to the countryside around Malton and Pickering.

Helmsley

Standing on the brink of Rye Dale, Helmsley is both the starting point of the Cleveland Way and the headquarters of the National Park Authority. A stream, lined with red-roofed houses, runs through the centre of this cheerful market-town, with its cobbled main square surrounded by old inns, and plenty of craft and bookshops. The market-place is filled with clothes- and food-stalls on Fridays, dwarfing Helmsley's miniature equivalent of the Albert Memorial, the canopied Gothic monument commemorating the second baron of Feversham (1798–1867). Just off the market-place stand the impressive fragments of Helmsley Castle and the entrance to Duncombe Park.

Helmsley Castle

(English Heritage, open Good Fri or 1 Apr, whichever is earlier, to 30 Sept, daily 10 to 6; rest of year Tue to Sun, 10 to 4) Walter L'Espec, a law officer of the Royal Court, began the castle in the twelfth century and it was modified and adapted for residential use throughout the medieval period. Sizeable grass earthworks are all that remain of the original phase of building. You can get a good idea of the south barbican gatehouse that dates from the thirteenth century and the massive scale of the ruined east tower; it stands defiantly as a cross-section of the original, complete on one side. The castle had an uneventful history until the Civil War in 1644 when a six-month siege culminated in capture by Thomas Fairfax's Parliamentary forces. It was lived in at the time by the Royalist Duke of Buckingham who fled, only to return thirteen years later in order to regain cunningly his property by marrying Fairfax's daughter. After the Duke's death Charles Duncombe bought Helmsley and Rievaulx, although he spent most of his time in London where he was made Lord Mayor.

On his death, his son-in-law, Thomas Brown, abandoned Helmsley and built Duncombe Park close by.

Duncombe Park

(Open Easter to Oct, Sun to Thur 11 to 6; tickets to see grounds only are also available) In 600 acres of parkland, Duncombe Park was built in 1713 to the designs of William Wakefield, who is thought to have been advised by Sir John Vanbrugh. The style is essentially baroque with Palladian touches and later modifications; fires gutted the building in 1879 and 1895. What you see today is a turn-of-the-century mansion, with a grand entrance hall of Corinthian columns and stone reliefs. Opulent ground-floor reception rooms include a library and a 115-foot-long oak-panelled saloon. After a sixty-year stretch as a girls' boarding school, the house is once again the residence of the Duncombe family, the barons of Feversham.

The landscaped gardens cover 35 acres with paths that take you through the woods and down to the Rye. One of the most remarkable features is the half-mile long grass terrace adorned with a Doric temple at one end and an Ionic rotunda at the other. There is an obvious similarity to the more celebrated terrace set out by the younger Thomas Duncombe at Rievaulx Abbey, three miles up the valley.

Rievaulx Abbey

(English Heritage, open Good Fri or 1 Apr, whichever is earlier, to 30 Sept, daily 10 to 6; Tue to Sun 10 to 4) Rievaulx (pronounced 'Reevo') is one of the great abbey ruins of England. The scene captivated Cowper and Dorothy Wordsworth, and was painted by Cotman and Turner. The highlights are the nave of 1140-45, the earliest large-scale Cistercian nave in Britain, and the thirteenth-century choir, although quite a large part of the monastic living-quarters have survived too.

The abbey was founded in 1131 by the Cistercians, an order devoted to communal life, prayer, self-sufficiency and the attainment of perfection. Within half a century Rievaulx owned 6,000 acres and 14,000 sheep – the first flocks on the North York Moors. The Abbey's greatest period of prosperity was under its third abbot, Ailred (c. 1110–1167), who was made a saint for his pains.

Rievaulx Terrace

(National Trust, open end Mar to end Oct, daily 10.30 to 6 or

dusk if earlier; last admission 5.30; Ionic Temple closed 1 to 2)
Striping a hillside less than half a mile from the Abbey, the
Terrace is one of the finest examples of the eighteenth-century
landscape garden tradition. As with the terrace at Duncombe
Park, Rievaulx Terrace consists of a serpentine lawn half-
a-mile long with a classical temple at each end. The Tuscan
Temple, a rotunda of sandstone columns, is almost certainly
modelled on the Temple of Vesta at Tivoli. It is not open, but a
mirror by the window gives you a view of the highly
decorated interior dome. The Ionic Temple is a rectangular
banqueting hall, lavishly furnished in the classical style, with
intricate wood carving and an ornately painted ceiling by
Guiseppe Borgnis.

North-west from Rievaulx a minor road takes you on an
unusual journey up the loneliest parts of Rye Dale, skirting the
eastern flanks of the Cleveland Hills before climbing on to the
moors and dropping to Osmotherley.

FARNDALE

On the moorland road from Castleton to Rosedale and
Hutton-le-Hole, the two Ralph Crosses stand at the heart of
the North York Moors. 'Young Ralph' is near the road and
'Old Ralph' is less prominently located a few hundred yards
away. A little further east you should see 'Fat Betty', the
popular name for the White Cross, a wheelhead stone where
travellers used to leave coins for the passing poor. From this
plateau you can see over Rosedale, Farndale and north into Esk
Dale.

South-west of Farndale at the southern end of Bransdale,
the Hodge Beck flows south between the forestry plantations
surrounding Kirk Dale. **St Gregory's Minster** sits in solitary
splendour here. Largely rebuilt in the nineteenth century, it
also retains an outstanding example of an Anglo-Saxon
sundial. The quarry about 200 yards from the church is where,
in 1821, a quarryman discovered the remains of a hyena and
other 70,000-year-old bones in a cave on the site; they are on
display in the Yorkshire Museum in York.

Hutton-le-Hole

One of Yorkshire's 'picture-book' villages, pantiled limestone
cottages line either side of the long village green, with Hutton
Beck flowing down the middle. The grass is kept under control

by Scottish Blackface sheep, which graze freely throughout the village. A discreetly placed car park at the top of the street helps keep cars out of the village centre.

In the centre of the village, the **Ryedale Folk Museum** (open Easter to late Oct, daily 10.30 to 5.30) has a fascinating collection of buildings re-erected and furnished to evoke the social history of the area and give some idea of old rural life-styles. Among the exhibits are workshops (of a cobbler, a tinsmith and a cooper), a 500-year-old cruck-house from Danby, a photographer's studio, a cottage parlour and kitchen, and a gypsy caravan.

Farndale stretches north of the village, and is famous for its wild daffodils. If you happen to be here in Spring the sight is spectacular, with flowers spreading through the valley and along the River Dove. The well-trodden path between **Low Mill** and **Church Houses** is the best way of seeing them. William and Dorothy Wordsworth visited Farndale and were captivated by the sight. In 1955 Farndale was designated a nature reserve and the flowers, once endangered by greedy visitors and market-traders, are now protected by law.

Lastingham

About one-and-a-half miles east of Hutton-le-Hole, Last-ingham is a peaceful, compact village in a sheltered, low-lying position. The church is quite remarkable, built above the perfectly preserved Norman apsidal crypt (unique in this country in having a nave and side aisles) of an unfinished abbey; it has been virtually unaltered since 1068, with a slab for an altar, a tiny window for light, and the ceiling supported by massive columns with capitals displaying carvings of rams' heads.

For good views over the central southern moors take the short path from the road junction (at the signpost for Spaunton 1/4) leading above the Lastingham road to Lidsty Cross, erected for Queen Victoria's Diamond Jubilee in 1897. Or go to the churchyard at **Gillamoor** and survey the scene from a different but equally memorable viewpoint.

Cawthorn Roman Camp

East of Lastingham, between Cropton and Newton-on-Rawcliffe, a sign points into the woods where a 15–20-minute trail takes you around the site of this archaeological rarity. Roman soldiers from the ninth legion at York came here in

AD100 to practise constructing fortified camps as part of their army training. All that remains are long banks of earthworks showing a varity of fortifications.

ROSEDALE

Rosedale is a good base for walks in the dale and across the moors that surround it. Farndale and Rosedale are visually similar but their history is very different. From 1861 to 1929 Rosedale was busy with ironstone extraction and its population increased tenfold to 5,000 in a few years. The iron purity was 45 per cent – far higher than in the Skinningrove and Guisborough areas, justifying the building of a railway around the rim of the dale. Ironstone was sent to join the main rail network at Battersby *en route* to blast furnaces in County Durham; the railway snaked 11 miles over the moors but all that you can see today are the track-bed and inclines, grassed-over spoil heaps and a few arcades from old kilns.

The village of **Rosedale Abbey**, the only settlement of any significance in the valley, is named after a Cistercian house founded in 1158, of which all trace has vanished apart from a section of staircase, now incorporated into the church.

Pickering

While not actually in the National Park, Pickering, a busy market-town, is the southern terminus of the North York-shire Moors Railway (see p112) and attracts a lot of visitors. Seek out some of the attractive corners hidden in the compact terraces in the back-streets; the red-pantiled roofs are a particular feature. The main street leads up to the church of St Peter and St Paul, with its series of mid-fifteenth-century wall paintings. Plastered over for many years, the paintings were considered to be a distraction to the congregation. The vivid scenes from the Passion and incidents from lives of saints, including St Christopher, St George and the Martyrdom of St Thomas a Becket, have survived in very good condition.

Pickering Castle

(English Heritage, open Good Fri or Apr 1, whichever is earlier, to end Sept, daily 10 to 6; rest of the year Tue to Sun 10 to 4) Founded by William I, it is a good example of a Norman motte and bailey; remains of the keep known as the King's

Tower crown the motte, surrounded by a deep ditch. In medieval times the castle served as a royal hunting lodge for excursions into the Royal Forest of Pickering. Forest laws prohibited poaching and tree clearance, and people caught breaking the laws were tried and imprisoned here. The castle suffered damage in the Civil War and many of the stones were removed for building work.

THE EASTERN MOORS

East of Pickering, the terminus for the **North Yorkshire Railway**, the boundary juts out to include much-visited **Thornton Dale**, a self-conscious but undeniably pretty village on the A170 which skirts the north side of the low-lying Vale of Pickering. The central crossroads, complete with a green, market-cross and stocks, is overwhelmed by wall-to-wall teas and souvenirs. But a short walk away, at the Scarborough end of the village, everything is very neat, with carefully tended gardens, a brook, picturesque cottages and 12 seventeenth-century almshouses.

From East Ayton on the A170, you can head north along **Forge Valley**, a deciduous forest on both sides of the River

THE NORTH YORKSHIRE MOORS RAILWAY

THIS privately run railway offers one of Britain's longest and most scenic 'nostalgia' rides on steam or diesel-hauled trains. The 18-mile journey from Grosmont to Pickering takes about an hour each way, stopping at Goathland, Newton Dale Halt and Levisham (note that Levisham village is a mile away from the station), each station presented in period style, with antique advertising signs and old-fashioned porters' trolleys on the platforms. From the window you see the fields and wooded gorges around Beck Hole and Goathland, and occasional crags on the moorland slopes enclosing Newton Dale. The red and cream carriages are mostly old British Rail stock dating from the 1950s. The terminus stations have shops selling railway miscellania. The Loco Shed at Grosmont (open late-Mar to early-Nov, daily 10 to 5.30) is something of a train-spotter's dream, with a model railway layout, a viewing window on to the repair area, a shed full of engines and early carriages (where you can usually find

Derwent, designated a national nature reserve. Traces of ancient woodland remain: alder is found in the valley, ash and elm on the slopes, and oak higher up on the dry ground. In spring, the primroses, bluebells and anemones carpet the woods. Further north the road emerges into the open and reaches **Hackness**, where the late-Georgian splendour of Hackness Hall (not open), the seat of Lord Derwent, with its artificial lake can be glimpsed beyond a high wall fronting the village street. The Norman church has an eighth-century Celtic cross and fifteenth-century oak font-cover.

Vast Forestry Commission plantations fill much of the area west of Hackness; attempts have been made to turn the area into an amenity: a variety of tree species have been introduced and colour-coded forest walks and trails, visitor facilities and ready-made picnic sights are designed to make it user-friendly. Those who love this region purely for the landscapes of its moors and dales should steer well clear. Between Hackness and Thornton Dale, **Dalby Forest** has also been jazzed-up for visitors; access is by means of waymarked walks and a somewhat soporific forest drive of nine miles; toll machines (open at all hours) charge you for the privilege. A detour from Staindale Lake (a reservoir) into **Bridestones Nature Reserve** is worth taking; beyond a natural wood of

an inspection saloon, built in 1871 for the Stockton and Darlington Railway), and a siding with more of the same.

The line opened in 1836 as the Whitby and Pickering Railway, operating for its first 11 years as a horse-drawn tramway. But accidents happened; the 1–in–49 incline at Beck Hole was too steep for horses or even steam traction. So, in 1865, a new 'deviation' line was constructed by blasting a passage out of solid rock. The railway closed in 1965, but was re-opened by a group of enthusiasts eight years later, and is now the North York Moors' top tourist attraction. The disused line, engineered by George Stephenson, which runs parallel to the existing one, is now a Historic Rail Trail for walkers.

Services run from late-March to early-November, between three and seven times a day in each direction; check before you travel if you want to be sure of a ride on a steam train (some locos are diesel-powered). Grosmont connects both with British Rail (Whitby–Grosmont–Middlesbrough) and the local bus service from Whitby.

oaks and larches, you reach the moors and the mushroom-shaped Jurassic sandstone rocks known as the Bridestones.

Levisham

Levisham is another place to see typical moors' cottages prettily set around a village green. The Horseshoe Inn is a very popular meeting-place at the top of the main street. The village lies in fine walking country and routes lead north-west to the **Hole of Horcum**, a great natural amphitheatre scooped out by the erosive action of glacial meltwater and a popular place for hang-gliding; you can also reach it from the A169 between Pickering and Whitby.

If you continue north on the A169, the high-security fencing of the Ministry of Defence establishment on **Fylingdales Moor** soon comes into sight on the east side of the road. Towering above is the Raytheon ballistic missile early-warning system, comprising a prominent truncated pyramid and some 2,500 radar antennae. In 1991 this memorably hideous structure replaced the Radomes – three gigantic white spheres nicknamed 'the golf balls' – which had become the subject of one of the best-selling postcards of the North York Moors.

Goathland

The only village actually on the North Yorkshire Moors Railway between Grosmont and Pickering, Goathland is nearly a mile long from tip to toe. It must have more acreage of grass verge than any other village in the National Park, the whole of it kept trimmed by moorland sheep. Reached from the eponymous hotel, the **Mallyan Spout waterfall** drops into West Beck; flat rocks provide natural picnic places in this beautiful gorge.

South-west of Goathland (merely signposted as the 'Roman Road' from the road junction by the church), **Wade's Causeway** is reckoned to be the best-preserved stretch of Roman road in the country. Discovered in 1914, it extends $1\frac{1}{4}$ miles over majestically empty scenery, with its metalling of flat stones upon gravel, raised in the centre for drainage. The road originally ran from Malton via Cawthorn Camp and Esk Dale to Goldsborough (near the coast, just south of Kettleness) where there was a Roman signal station. Folk legend added the name: Wade was reputedly a giant from Mulgrave Castle who built the road as a footpath for his wife Bel to aid her 20-mile walk to market. The road is open to walkers but closed to cyclists and horse-riders.

North of Goathland, **Beck Hole** is a pretty hamlet with a pub and a handful of cottages and 'one-in-four' road-signs at either end. A waterfall, Thomason Foss, gushes into a pool within a wooded ravine at the end of a ten-minute path signposted from Beck Hole.

ESK DALE AND THE NORTH

The River Esk rises in the Cleveland Hills and flows along the broadest and most populated of the dales to reach the sea at Whitby. On its northern side, Bronze Age burial mounds are dotted across the moors; to the south a series of ridges protrude like the fingers of a hand; Glaisdale, Great Fryup Dale, Little Fryup Dale, Danby Dale and Westerdale make up the spaces in between. Villages are unspoilt rather than picturesque.

To the west and in the main dale, the railway-junction village of **Grosmont** grew up to house ironstone miners; today its prime role is as the northern terminus for the North Yorkshire Moors Railway (see p.112). **Egton** has long-established connections with Catholicism; Father Nicholas Postgate celebrated mass in secret in the seventeenth century, in a building by the road between Egton and Egton Bridge. In 1679 he was executed at York, at the age of 82, for baptising a child into the faith. Today the village is a place of pilgrimage, with a large Catholic church erected in 1866 and dedicated to St Edda. If you can time your visit to coincide with the Egton gooseberry show in August, you will see prize specimens that weigh-in at over two ounces each. At the bottom of Limber Hill on the road to Glaisdale, look out for **Duck Bridge**, a slender packhorse bridge, erected about 1386. It was named after a certain George Duck who was responsible for its restoration some 400 years later.

At **Danby**, in the heart of Esk Dale, you will find the main National Park information centre; **Danby Lodge Moors Centre** (open Apr to Oct, daily 10 to 5, Sun 12 to 4; Feb, Mar, Nov, daily 12 to 4; weekends only in winter; closed Dec and Jan).

Beacon Hill, a couple of miles east of Danby, has a stunning 360-degree panorama. You can survey the dale and central moors, the sea to the north and east and the Durham Pennines far away to the north-west. **Roseberry Topping**

115

(1,057 feet) is another summit to make for. From the top of this hook-shaped hill, scooped out by past ironstone- and whinstone-quarrying, you look out to the Tees Transporter Bridge in Middlesbrough, the steelworks at Redcar and the uplands of the Pennines. The easiest approach to Roseberry

CAPTAIN JAMES COOK

IN AN age of discovery, Captain Cook's navigational exploits put much of the Southern Hemisphere and Pacific on the map. He was one of the most prolific and successful explorers of all time and is commemorated by the monument erected on Easby Moor in 1828 on the centenary of his birth.

Born in 1728 in Marton, now a suburb of Middlesbrough, James Cook was the second of eight children. His father was a farm labourer and in 1736 was appointed foreman to Thomas Scottowe, of Airey Holme Farm near Great Ayton; an obelisk is all that remains of his father's home, which was moved to Melbourne in Australia, stone by stone, for the state centenary celebrations. The whole family moved to Great Ayton and, somewhat unusually for a farm-labourer's son, the young James Cook attended school. Within a few years he was working on the farm.

In 1745 he began an apprenticeship to William Sanderson, a friend of Scottowe's who ran a store dealing in haberdashery and grocery products on the sea-front at Staithes. Cook soon discovered that his ambitions lay elsewhere, and with Sanderson's help became apprenticed to John Walker, a Quaker ship-owner at the rapidly expanding sea-port of Whitby. Walker operated colliers which shipped coal from the Tyne and Wear ports to London. He was a kind man who liked his industrious apprentice. Cook rapidly gained sea-faring knowledge and experience, and in 1755 enlisted as an able seaman with the Royal Navy at Wapping.

At that time, most recruits were press-ganged into service, and a seaman of Cook's quality and keenness was a rarity. His promotion was swift. He was given command of a small sloop and went on to become master of the 64-gun HMS *Pembroke*, which in April 1758 left port for Halifax, Nova Scotia, during the war with France. The British were attempting to capture French colonies in America. Cook assisted in the survey of the St Lawrence River enabling Wolfe's forces to sail to Quebec and take the town for the British. In 1762 he returned to England and married Elizabeth Batts, but the couple spent little time together: after a five-year expedition to the

Topping is from a minor road to Gribdale Gate, a couple of miles east of **Great Ayton**, a large village where Captain James Cook spent a part of his childhood (see p90). The fullest record of Cook's achievements is at Marton (now swallowed up by Middlesbrough's suburbs), where the

Newfoundland coast, he embarked on the three great exploratory voyages of his life. These were to be the pinnacles of his achievement and kept him away from England for ten of the final twelve years of his life.

The first of these voyages took place between 1768 and 1771 on the HMS *Endeavour*, a type of collier vessel known as a 'Whitby cat' - a sturdy ship with a flat bottom which made it easy to refloat if it was grounded, and required little ballast. The purpose of the expedition was to make for Tahiti to carry out astronomical observations; the Admiralty gave him secret, additional instructions to seek for a great southern continent that was thought to exist, or failing its discovery to explore New Zealand. The continent remained undiscovered but they were the first Europeans to set foot in New Zealand; he also chartered the east coast of Australia.

For the second voyage (1772–1775), covering 60,000 miles in total, he took two Whitby cats, the *Adventure* and the *Resolution*. They came across icebergs as they sailed further south but the great Antarctic continent eluded them; no one had ever been as far south as this. The voyage included visits to the Friendly Isles (Tonga), and numerous Pacific islands, all charted for the first time.

The *Resolution* was again employed for the third voyage (1776–1780), accompanied by the *Discovery*. They set sail to search for a North-West Passage connecting the Pacific and Atlantic; their explorations of the northern Pacific led to the discovery of Christmas Island (on a Christmas Eve) and Hawaii. When the ships anchored at Kealakekua Bay in Hawaii in 1779 the crew had a warm reception: the islanders took Cook to be Lono (or Orono), a white deity, and showered him with gifts. But food supplies ran short and the inhabitants were glad to see Cook and his men leave. Damage to the rigging of the *Resolution* drove them back to the island where their reception this time was overtly hostile. Cook discovered that a boat had been stolen from the *Discovery* and decided to take the king hostage until it was returned, but as he ventured into the crowd he was clubbed and stabbed to death.

ambitious **Captain Cook Birthplace Museum** (open all year, Tue to Sun 10 to 6 and Bank Hol Mon; winter, Tue to Sun 9 to 4; closed Christmas and New Year) in Stewart Park features life-size recreations of Cook's childhood haunts, his days working at a shop in Staithes and the quayside at Whitby – all with atmospheric sound effects. You can also see personal belongings, Aboriginal artefacts and other items collected on his travels, and read extracts from his log.

There are a couple of places officially outside Yorkshire, but which merit a stop-over if you're here. **Ormesby Hall** (National Trust, open Apr to end Oct, Wed, Sat, Sun and Bank Hol Mon 2 to 5.30; also Thur in July), just north of Marton was built between 1740 and 1750 and has a highly decorated interior with Adam designs and plasterwork. The stable-block attributed to John Carr of York is a fine eighteenth-century building now leased to the Mounted Police.

Guisborough is an ancient market-town, now a much expanded commuter base for Teesside, with housing estates built right up to the National Park boundary. It has a good local museum and gallery but not much else to keep you there. **Gisborough Priory** (English Heritage, open Good Fri or Apr 1, whichever is earlier, to end Sept, daily 10 to 6; rest of the year Tue to Sun 10 to 4) close to the town centre is largely ruined down to foundation level. But the east end (late thirteenth-century) of the nave stands to its full height of 97 feet, and provides a magnificent frame for the view over farmland beyond. The priory was an Augustinian foundation, established by Robert de Brus in 1120.

On the A171 between Guisborough and Whitby, you pass **Scaling Reservoir**. You can have a good day out here bird-watching, fishing or sailing on the largest expanse of water in the National Park; the Scaling Dam Sailing Club office here issues permits for fishing and sailing.

THE COAST

Great cliffs of shale and sandstone dominate the coast between Scarborough and Saltburn. This is famous fossil-seeking country and dinosaur footprints have been discovered south of Ravenscar. The marine layers, which constitute all of the cliffs north of Ravenscar, contain great quantities of fossilised crustaceans and even a few marine reptiles such as the ichthyosaurus. Visit the Whitby Museum at Whitby to see some of the best specimens, discovered when coastal alum quarries operated from the 1600s until the 1870s.

From the main roads parallel to the coast you only get occasional glimpses of the scenery. To enjoy the full glory of the cliffs, you need to explore small tracks and take in sections of the path that run the length of the coast (the final part of the Cleveland Way). **Sandsend** and **Runswick Bay** have the best sandy beaches.

Hayburn Wyke to Whitby

Heading north from Scarborough and into the National Park via the Cloughton-to-Ravenscar road you pass a sign for Hayburn Wyke Hotel pointing down a steep drive. The ten-minute walk from the hotel car park (fee payable for non-residents) leads down a track and into woods to **Hayburn Wyke** itself. The stepped paths you see in the woods date from the Victorian era when day-trippers piled off the coastal train at this popular stop. Now it is secluded and rather wild in character, the trees and stream coming down to a boulder-strewn cove backed by high cliffs. About a mile inland, just south of Staintondale, you can visit **Staintondale Shire Horses** (open May to Sept, Sun, Tue, Wed, Fri and Bank Hol Mon 10.30 to 4.30; tel (0723) 870458) The size of these horses is remarkable; time your visit to coincide with one of the twice-daily harnessing demonstrations. Cart rides, rustic bygones and farm teas are other bonuses.

Ravenscar, further north along the coast, is hardly a village at all. Built in the 1890s, the hotel towering on immense cliffs and the handful of houses scattered around were the beginnings of a resort that was to rival Scarborough and Whitby in popularity. But the ground was unstable and the beach too far to attract developers, so the planned estates of villas and visitors never materialised. The walk on to the coast path from this road reveals dizzy drops with no fence in front of the spectacular undercliff far below.

Look out for a turning by a sail-less windmill a short distance inland, which leads down a steep lane over **Stoup Brow** to a small car park handy for **Stoup Beck Sands**; the beach is covered at high tide, but if you catch it when it's low, the walk along the shore is the best way to approach Robin Hood's Bay.

Robin Hood's Bay

One of the gems of the Yorkshire coast, the fishing village is so closely huddled together that the claim that it was once possible to pass a roll of silk from house to house the length of the village, without once going outside, seems entirely plausible. It was a very popular and cleverly organised smuggling centre where the customs men had little success. Many houses had secret recesses in walls and beneath the floors for hiding contraband. The place is named after Robin Hood because legend has it that he kept boats here in case he needed to make a quick getaway.

The quaint collection of stepped alleys, crooked walls and tiny backyards are fun to explore, each cottage jostling for a view over the red roofs of its neighbours. At the bottom of the narrow main street a slipway dips to the sea; but at low tide the village fronts a vast beach of sand and rock-pools. Inevitably the picturesque appeal of Robin Hood's Bay means a deluge of tourists for much of the year. Cars must be left above the village.

On your way down, visit the old chapel which now operates as a bookshop, café and **exhibition centre** (open all year, daily), and at the bottom of the Bay in Albion Hall, Albion Street 'Music in Miniature', a display of tiny tableaux depicting music-making through the ages. John Wesley (the founder of Methodism) recorded 11 visits to the village in his journal between 1753 and 1784.

Whitby

Whitby (itself excluded from the National Park) has retained a considerable sense of place and its genuine character as a working fishing port. The River Esk divides the town into two parts linked by a swing-bridge which has to be swung aside to allow boats to pass through. By the quay on the west side, fishermen mend their nets, booths advertise fresh halibut, cod, oak-smoked kippers and more, and plenty of fish restaurants serve the daily catch. The old lifeboat-house opens most days in summer: its free museum has photographs of rescues and disasters of the past; 1861 was one of Whitby's blackest years, a catalogue of storms and shipwrecks – even the lifeboat itself was a victim: all but one of her crew were lost when the sixth rescue attempt of the day left the men in a state of near exhaustion.

Much of the water-front is lined with amusement arcades and cafés sporting garish plastic signs, but find your way up the back streets to the town's most famous viewpoint marked by a statue of Captain Cook. A whalebone arch commemorates the long-defunct whaling industry. Between 1753 and

1833 over 2,700 whales were brought back as well as a few seals and polar bears; boiler houses on the harbour turned the whale-blubber into oil. The arch effectively frames the view of the river, the old town and the abbey ruins high above the opposite bank.

The older part of Whitby is mostly concentrated in a few narrow streets on the east side. It is a touch genteel with shops geared to the tourist trade. You can find plenty of nostalgia bits and pieces, home-made fudge, glass-ships in bottles and upmarket ethnic products or pick up sailing artefacts from one of the many antique shops. And don't miss the aromatic store called Shepherd's Purse selling exotic teas and spices. Whitby's jet workshops no longer operate on the scale they did in the last century, but you can still buy jet ornaments from a handful of outlets.

A flight of 199 steps leads up from the east side of town to the abbey ruins (see below). **St Mary's Church** stands alongside, its tower Norman and much of its fabric medieval but a building remarkable for its Georgian furnishings. A cheerfully hotch-potch arrangement of box pews surrounds a triple-decker pulpit of 1778; the ear-trumpets hanging from the pulpit were installed for the benefit of the wife of an early nineteenth-century incumbent. The churchyard, much blasted by sea winds, provided the opening scene for Bram Stoker's novel *Dracula*.

● **Whitby Abbey** (open Good Fri or 1 Apr, which ever is the earlier, to 30 Sept, daily 10 to 6; Tue to Sun 10 to 4) The Abbey's history is fraught with troubles. Originally founded in 657 by St Hilda, it was destroyed by the Danes in 867. Refounded by the Benedictines in the eleventh century, it grew to quite a sizeable community, housing both nuns and monks, and became a respected seat of learning. Not much remains of the monastic quarters but the medieval abbey church retains much Early English arcading and a soaring east front dating from 1220. After dissolution by Henry VIII in 1539, the roof-leading was removed and the building left merely as a daymark for sailors. By 1830, the lantern-tower, nave, south transept and west front had collapsed, and in 1914 the final stage of its demise came about when two German battle-cruisers shelled the coast and devastated the west front.

Between the Abbey ruins and St Mary's, a 20-foot sandstone cross commemorates the story of the monk Caedmon. He was reputedly very shy and would never sing with his fellow monks; one night he dreamt of an angel who asked him to sing for her. On waking he found he had acquired a beautiful voice; from that moment he regularly sang and wrote verse – his *Song of Creation* is the earliest known poem in the English language.

• **Captain Cook Memorial Museum** (open Apr to end Oct, daily 9.45 to 4.30), Grape Lane. James Cook lived in this house with his master John Walker during his apprenticeship (see p.116). Two of the downstairs rooms have been furnished in the simple manner typical of the Quakers. Other rooms house exhibitions on Cook's days in Whitby and London, details of his voyages, models of his ships and details of the scientific advances made on these expeditions. Next-door the **Whitby Archives** is a free photographic exhibition showing old views of the town and vicinity.

• **Museum of Victorian Whitby** (open all year, daily 9.30 to 5 (later in summer); Jan and Feb times and days vary tel. (0947) 601221) Arranged over two floors, life-size reconstructions of aspects of nineteenth-century Whitby include a fisherman's cottage, a jet workshop, a kipper smokery and a cooper's. The exhibition is well-captioned but unfortunately the lighting is too poor to read most of them.

• **Whitby Museum and Pannett Art Gallery** (open May to Sept, weekdays 9.30 to 5.30, Sun 2 to 5; winter, Mon and Tue 10.30 to 1, Wed to Sat 10.30 to 4, Sun 2 to 4) In a park a little out of the town centre, this old-fashioned, municipally-run museum is an absorbing local treasure-house. There is a small charge for the museum, but the gallery is free. The exhibits are packed close together in glass cases that relate to the area; items include jet ornaments, a Roman dedication stone found at the site of a signal station at Ravenscar, a model of Whitby Abbey before the collapse of the lantern-tower, model ships, a witch-post from Egton intended to ward off evil spirits, and a notable fossil collection.

SANDSEND TO BOULBY CLIFF

Sandsend

At low tide acres of firm sand stretch all the way from Whitby to aptly named Sandsend, a resort village sheltered by the bluff of **Sandsend Ness**; the sea-front development is unexceptional, but a combe running inland is lined with older cottages. You lose sight of the sea heading west to the hilltop village of **Lythe**, where the church contains a strange accumulation of masonry from a tenth-century burial ground.

Kettleness, a couple of miles from the main road, is a tiny windswept hamlet close to the cliff edge and the only coastal point between Sandsend and Runswick Bay which can be reached by car. The villagers had a narrow escape in 1829 when much of the settlement, including the alum works, slid into the sea.

Runswick Bay

Approached down a long 'one-in-four' hill, Runswick Bay clings precariously to the cliff – like a tiny version of Robin Hood's Bay without the commercialisation. The village is an appealing cocoon of passages and winding paths, white-washed cottages and postage-stamp gardens. You can walk along the sandy beach to **Hob Holes** at low tide.

Continuing north, the next access point to the coast is at **Port Mulgrave**, a straggly village with a few nineteenth-century cottages that survive from its days as an ironstone centre. The rock was quarried on the cliff-top and lowered to the jetty for shipping to Jarrow-on-Tyne. From here you can take the 1¼-mile cliff path to Staithes – an easy walk with great views.

Staithes

The outskirts are drab but the centre of this authentic old fishing village has changed little in 200 years. A densely built main street snakes down past non-conformist chapels and a maze of alleys running parallel to a sinuous creek. The most painted and photographed scene is the view from the footbridge over Staithes Beck. Houses cluster against the towering headland of **Cowbar Nab**, with its foreground of lobster pots and wide fishing boats known as cobles. The design of these boats has stayed fundamentally the same since the Vikings brought them over. Offshore fishing is important but to a large extent Staithes has been eclipsed by Whitby. In the eighteenth and nineteenth centuries the village economy was also dependent on alum, jet and smuggling. A lifeboat station on the Cowbar side tells of Staithes' uneasy relationship with the sea; over the years 13 houses have been lost through coastal erosion, and the Cod and Lobster Inn on the sea-front has been washed away and rebuilt three times: in 1953 the entire stock of the cellar floated out.

Driving towards Loftus, you can't miss the vast works of Boulby Mine, which produces potash for the chemical industry and rock salt for road- gritting; its main shaft goes down 3,000 feet (the deepest of its kind in Europe) and workings extend several miles out to sea. Access to **Boulby Cliff**, three-quarters-of-a-mile north-west, is by foot only; measuring 666 feet it is the highest point on the east coast of England.

WHERE TO STAY

EASINGTON

Grinkle Park
Easington, Saltburn-by-the-Sea TS13 4UB
TEL (0287) 640515 Fax (0287) 641278
A comfortable and relaxing place to stay. Part of the Bass group, it is geared towards corporate entertaining but the staff make sure the individual traveller gets a good welcome and is well looked-after.
££ *All year; 19 rooms; Access, Amex, Diners, Visa*

GOATHLAND

Whitfield House
Darnholm, Goathland, Nr Whitby YO22 5LA
TEL (0947) 86215
You can enjoy simple accommodation and good country cooking in this old stone farmhouse; peaceful setting, not far from the village.
£ *Mar to Oct; 9 rooms*

HAWNBY

The Hawnby Hotel
Hawnby, Nr Helmsley YO6 5QS
TEL (04396) 202
A very popular, friendly, old drover's inn in a lovely secluded village high on the moors. Six double rooms with their own bathrooms have been redecorated in Laura Ashley fabrics.

££ *Mar to Jan exc Chr; 6 rooms; Access, Visa*

INGLEBY GREENHOW

Manor House Farm
Ingleby Greenhow, Nr Great Ayton TS9 6RB
TEL (0642) 722384
The accommodation is simple but adequate with shared bathrooms in this pretty northern farmhouse. Plenty of good English food and a welcoming atmosphere after a day's walking.
£ *All year exc Chr; 3 rooms*

LASTINGHAM

Lastingham Grange
Lastingham YO6 6TH
TEL (07515) 345/402
An attractive, well-run hotel in a peaceful setting. Some bedrooms are slightly old-fashioned, but comfy, with flowers everywhere and lovely views.
££ *All year, exc Jan, Feb and Dec; 12 rooms*

PICKERING

White Swan
Market Place, Pickering YO18 7AA
TEL (0751) 72288
Original brick-and-stone inn with oak antiques and a blazing fire in the snug bar. Food and a comprehensive wine list are strong points.

£ *All year; 13 rooms; Access, Visa*

ROSEDALE ABBEY

White Horse Farm Hotel
Rosedale Abbey, Nr Pickering
TEL (07515) 239
This large stone farmhouse
offers a homely atmosphere and
good solid northern food.
Bedrooms are well decorated and
spacious, some with fabulous
views.
£ *All year exc 24–26 Dec; 15
rooms; Access, Amex, Diners, Visa*

SCALBY

Wrea Head Country Hotel
Scalby, Scarborough YO13 0PB
TEL (0723) 378211 Fax (0723)
371780
Close to the suburbs of
Scarborough but in large grounds,
the building and proportions of
the rooms are heavily Victorian.
Bright colours make the rooms
cheery.
££ *All year exc 23–28 Dec; 21
rooms; Access, Amex, Visa*

WHERE TO EAT

GOATHLAND

Mallyan Spout Hotel
Goathland
TEL (0947) 86206
A friendly country hotel, a short
walk from the waterfall after
which it is named. Excellent bar
food with generous portions of
fresh Whitby fish, local cheeses
and home-made conserves and
chutneys. More expensive
restaurant meals.
*All week 7–8.30, Sun 12.15–1.30;
Access, Diners, Visa*

STADDLEBRIDGE

The Tontine
TEL (060 982) 671
The dimly lit but atmospheric
dining-room offers an
unchanging, but classy menu with
the emphasis on game and fish and
much use of truffles and foie
gras. There is a cheaper bistro
downstairs.
*Rest. Tue to Sat 7–10.30, bistro all
week 12–2.30, 7–10.30; Amex,
Access, Diners, Visa*

STAITHES

Endeavour
1 High Street
TEL (0947) 840825
A cottagey-style restaurant that
has built up a fine reputation for
its high-quality seafood; prices to
match. Meat and vegetarian dishes
also available.
*Mon to Sat 7–9.30 (lunch by prior
booking only)*

STOKESLEY

Chapters
27 High Street
TEL (0642) 711888
Modern bistro in a converted
coaching-inn in the centre of the
village. The fairly pricey menu is
French and Far Eastern in style,
with the emphasis on fish. Skilful
cooking of well-presented and
generous portions includes duck,
chicken, turbot and salmon.
*All week 12–2, 7–10; Access, Amex,
Diners, Visa*

WHITBY

Magpie Cafe★
14 Pier Road
TEL (0947) 602058
A very popular, cosy café overlooking the harbour, so go early to avoid the queues. Home cooking of freshly landed Whitby fish and salmon from the Esk is great value; also special mixed fish platters, large salads and children's helpings.
All week 11.30–6.30; Access, Visa

Trenchers
New Quay Road
TEL (0947) 603212
A purpose-built café with a quayside location, fixed seating, plastic menus and loud pop music. Very fresh fish is fried deftly in excellent batter with crisp chips. Also available chargrilled steaks, sandwiches and sumptuous ice-creams.
All week 11–9

EAST YORKSHIRE

- Sleepy villages in pretty chalk countryside, linked by quiet country lanes
- Spectacular sea-cliffs and outstanding bird-life
- Bucket-and-spade country with famous resorts
- Mansions, windmills and the historic city centre of Hull
- Haunting sea-eroded landscapes of Holderness including Spurn Head

SAND, sea and a series of light-hearted, pleasure-minded towns designed to profit from both have long been the main attractions of East Yorkshire. Scarborough, Bridlington and Filey compete for trade among the dramatic cliffs which march to their climax at the 400 beetling feet (130m) of Flamborough Head. Hornsea and Withernsea do their best further south, in a flat, beach-hut and caravan-dotted landscape which sums up – attractive or awful according to taste – a quintessential type of British holiday.

Behind this well-known and sometimes 'trippery' coast, the area offers a notable contrast in the quietest of all Yorkshire's varied countryside. The Wolds (from the Old English 'wald' meaning moor or downland) and the sea-eroded plain of Holderness are reminders of B-road Britain. Sometimes beautiful and often atmospheric, their landscape is less exceptional than the Dales and Moors and man's additions have generally been modest.

This makes for a 'Southern' feel, regularly remarked on by newcomers to the tidy villages and also owing something to geology. Stone is the missing 'Northern' ingredient – the material which forms the essence of the West Riding towns and the limestone villages of North Yorkshire. The East is chalk, useable only for barns or outbuildings, so redbrick dominates local architecture. Even the magnificent mansion of Burton Constable was obliged to use cement-render for its dressed 'stone' quoins because the real thing would have bankrupted the sixteenth-century Constable family.

Burton Constable illustrates another reason for the tame, well-tended air of the fields and farms: great estates governed almost everywhere until comparatively recent times. Sir Tatton Sykes, a Victorian member of the dynasty still established at Sledmere House, built no fewer than twelve churches on his enormous acreage, as well as restoring another eight. Sunk Island, which literally rose from the Humber through the action of wind and tide, was promptly claimed by the Crown and decorated with almost-identical Victorian farmhouses.

East Yorkshire has its drama, though. The northern stretch of coastline is impressive enough for most visitors, from Scarborough's powerful castle to the bird-shrieking cliffs of Bempton, close to Flamborough Head. From the nests of the puffins and shags, the Yorkshire coastline drives inland, backed by the obvious eastern escarpment of the Wolds, past Driffield and Beverley to the Humber bank, arriving suitably close to the county's greatest man-made spectacular, the Humber Bridge.

Everything to the east of this should be examined with care: according to geologists, it will not be here in 10,000 years' time. In another drama, slow but satisfyingly eerie, the North Sea is eating away at Holderness, reclaiming the ground it lost when glacial overspill from Yorkshire's rivers poured over the chalk cliffs at the end of the last Ice Age.

The present loss of land, spectacularly visible among the cliff-edge holiday homes in places like Mappleton, averages some seven feet a year. Out to sea and in the Humber estuary, the waves hide the lost towns of Ravenser, Monkwike, Dimlington, Frismersk and Orwithfleet. Without modern coastal defence techniques (and possibly in spite of them) erosion will eventually swallow the lovely churches of Patrington and Hedon, the follies of Grimston Garth and Wassand's Mushroom Cottage – even the great port of Hull itself.

Although anciently founded as the King's Town on the River Hull, the city of Hull is a different, and relatively novel, addition to East Yorkshire's tourist list. Wonders have been performed in the aftermath of Nazi bombing and the decline of the traditional staple industry of deepwater fishing. The central docks, noble buildings and curious alleys like The Land Of Green Ginger, have been spruced up particularly well; a dead-end has become an end in itself. This could be the motto of much of the old East Riding (whose administrative boundaries have been a lamentable source of confusion and controversy for the last 20 years). More than anywhere else in Yorkshire, you are likely to find yourself straying off the beaten track – and often wondering why the track-makers have stayed away.

SCARBOROUGH TO WITHERNSEA

Scarborough

Scarborough is often known as the Queen of the Yorkshire coast, and with good reason. Its setting – twin sandy bays divided by a fine headland with castle ruins – lifts it above the usual kiss-me-quick seaside resort. The crowds throng here, causing regular summer weekend traffic jams; but the elegance of the town's hotels, terraces and parks survives the pressure.

129

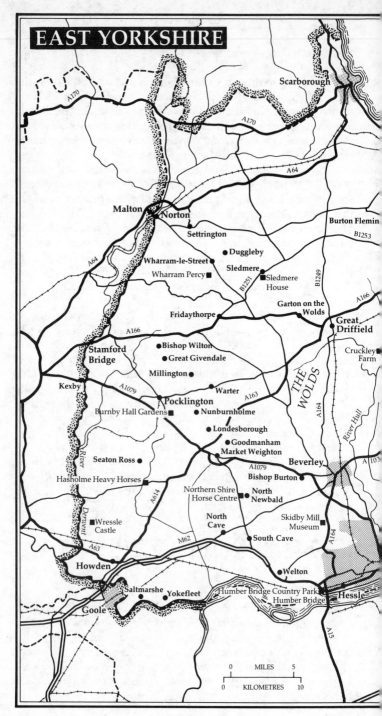

EAST YORKSHIRE

Scarborough

A170

A170

A64

Malton Norton

Settrington

Duggleby

Wharram-le-Street Sledmere

Wharram Percy Sledmere House

Burton Flemin

B1253

B1251

B1249

A166

Garton on the Wolds

Great Driffield

A64

Fridaythorpe

A166

Stamford Bridge

Bishop Wilton

Great Givendale

Millington

Cruckley Farm

THE WOLDS

A164

Kexby

A1079

Warter

A163

Pocklington

Burnby Hall Gardens Nunburnholme

River Hull

Londesborough

Goodmanham

Market Weighton

Beverley

A103

Seaton Ross

A1079

Bishop Burton

Hasholme Heavy Horses

A614

Northern Shire Horse Centre

North Newbald

Wressle Castle

North Cave

Skidby Mill Museum

A164

M62

South Cave

River Derwent

A63

Howden

Welton

Saltmarshe Yokefleet

Humber Bridge Country Park

Humber Bridge

Hessle

Goole

A15

MILES 0 5

KILOMETRES 0 10

130

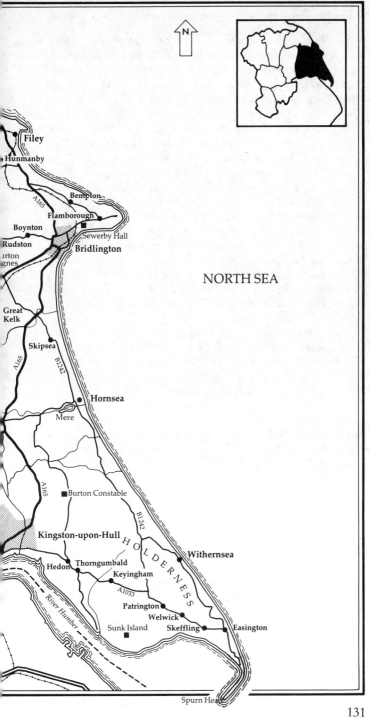

N

NORTH SEA

Filey
Hunmanby
A165
Bempton
Flamborough
Boynton
Sewerby Hall
Rudston
urton
gnes
Bridlington

Great
Kelk
Skipsea
A165
B1242
Hornsea
Mere

A165
Burton Constable
Kingston-upon-Hull
HOLDERNESS
B1242
Withernsea
Hedon
Thorngumbald
Keyingham
A1033
Patrington
Welwick
River Humber
Sunk Island
Skeffling
Easington
Spurn Head

Britain's oldest cliff lifts, clanking on cables and ratchets up an alarmingly steep gradient, link the **South Bay** beach to the upper town's shops, cafés and hotels, museums and theatres. Pottering anywhere round here is delightful. The North Bay has become a focus for modern attractions, easily reached by car or bus. Try the open-topped service along the sea-front.

At the Scalby Mills end of the North Bay you cannot miss the white pyramids of the **Sea-Life Centre** (open all year, daily 10 to 6; July to Sept 10 to 8; closed Christmas Day) which may, if negotiations with the US Air Force succeed, be joined by the geodesic domes of the Fylingdales early warning centre, newly redundant with the building of a new installation at the moorland base, see p114. Those who have been on unsuccessful sea-angling trips may see what they missed in huge aquaria. Conservation and education go with the fun. There is a café and gift shop.

A miniature railway runs between this end of the bay and Peasholm Park, passing through a concentration of holiday amusements. **WaterSplash World** (open end May to mid-Sept, daily 10 to 6; July to Sept 10 to 8) has rapids, water cannon, two exceptionally long flumes and 80-degree water, welcome after the rigours of the North Sea; at neighbouring **Kinderland** (open Easter to Sept, daily 10 to dusk) adults' excuses not to join in are undermined by climbing frames and roundabouts specifically designed to take their weight.

Peasholm Park, a venerable attraction built by previous generations, is still going strong. Its assortment of sports, picnic places and open-air music also includes the unique miniature naval battles on Peasholm Mere, involving ten scaled-down warships, three with Scarborough Park staff huddled inside to man the controls. Model aircraft on guided wires add to the excitement of 250 electronically controlled explosions, while the lake's nonchalant ducks (well-used to the twice-weekly performances in summer) contribute a surreal air, occasionally sitting on the battle's submarine when it surfaces to torpedo a merchant ship. Contact Scarborough's tourist office for times.

A different sort of boating activity is to be found at **The Mere** (off the A64 York road) on board the *Hispaniola*, a replica pirate ship which sails to Treasure Island where children can dig for buried doubloons (contact tourist office for details).

At the southern end of **North Bay,** the windy ramparts of the twelfth-century castle ruins on Scarborough's headland make a pleasant walk, particularly if combined with a visit to

St Mary's church just below. Anne Brontë's grave is here; the erudite may spot the mistake in her age on the headstone (28 instead of 29), which survived expensive re-lettering of the stone ordered by her sister Charlotte, who had discovered four other errors.

You are now well placed to walk into the 'cultural' end of Scarborough, in contrast to the North Bay's more typical holiday attractions. Take in the lively **harbour** en route, then mount the cliffs via several small alleys, pleasant shopping streets or the cliff lift below the amazing Edwardian Grand Hotel (four storeys on the landward side, 13 facing the sea). Just beyond the station is the **Stephen Joseph Theatre** in the Round (box office: (0723) 370541), which has the distinction of mounting the première of every new play by Alan Ayckbourn, a resident of the town for the last thirty-five years. He moved here from London to work as a stage-hand/actor/writer and his first play was staged here in 1959. The small building in Valley Bridge Parade also has a bistro with regular exhibitions.

Wood End Museum in The Crescent (open all year, Tue to Sat, 10 to 1, 2 to 5 and Bank Hol Mon; from Spring Bank Hol to end Sept, Sun 2 to 5) is as much of interest for its history as its contents. It is a competent display with the emphasis on the local natural world. The building was the Sitwell family's villa – the west wing has an almost complete collection of their books – and appears in various guises in work by Sir Osbert, Edith and Sacheverell, notably as the haunted Bellingham House in Osbert's *A Place of One's Own*.

Along The Crescent, **Scarborough Art Gallery** (open all year, Tue to Sat, 10 to 1, 2 to 5 and Bank Hol Mon; from Spring Bank Hol to end Sept, Sun 2 to 5) has a good collection of local paintings and some fine landscapes by Atkinson Grimshaw, the Victorian 'moonlight' painter. Complete your tour by walking down Vernon Road to the prettily domed **Rotunda Museum** (open all year, Tue to Sat, 10 to 1, 2 to 5 and Bank Hol Mon; from Spring Bank Hol to end Sept, Sun 2 to 5). It was one of the first purpose-built museums in Britain when Scarborough Philosophical Society opened its doors in 1829. The delightful interior with its curved mahogany display cabinets, gallery and two spiral staircases outshines the collections of archaeology and local history which it houses.

From here a short walk south along the sea-front (or, better still, along the sands at low tide) takes you to the Spa whose waters first brought fame and fortune to the town. As early as 1667 they were being described by a Dr Robert Wilkie as 'A most sovereign remedy against Hypochondriach Melancholly and Windiness'. Windiness – of the meteorological variety – can be a hazard on the slightly mournful Victorian promenade of the Spa, but its halls (when not in regular use for conferences) provide traditional seaside entertainments. Max Jaffa ruled here for years.

Filey

South of Scarborough, the A165 leads via **Osgodby**, with its mellow Georgian hall (private), to the much smaller resort of Filey. Looking south across the broad sweep of **Hunmanby Sands**, the town is protected by its interesting natural break-water, **Filey Brigg**. The Devil is supposed to have begun this narrow spit of rock as a road to Norway, although prosaic geologists prefer to argue that the overlying clay was simply washed away by the sea. It is a good spot for birdwatchers who regularly chalk up rare migrants on the Brigg.

Filey town is in some ways a miniature Scarborough, with the old village relatively unscathed at the northern end of the strand, separated from **St Oswald's** handsome church by a small ravine. A pleasant walk leads steeply down Church Street and across the iron footbridge which spans Ravine Road. From **Coble Landing** at the foot of the ravine you can watch Filey's fishermen haul their traditional boats – cobles – up the beach to sort their catch. While you're here, perhaps negotiate a sea-angling trip. Fishing's importance in Filey's history is recorded at a charming small **folk museum** (open May to Sept, Sun to Fri, 2 to 5) at the top of Queen Street. Two twelfth-century fishermen's cottages have been knocked through to display local memorabilia in domestic surroundings.

Nearer the sea, the area of white-stuccoed terraces around **The Crescent** marks a tentative nineteenth-century attempt to emulate Brighton; but although Filey became and has remained popular, it never reached the seaside first division. A relatively peaceful atmosphere has been one benefit, and the town is not wholly dependent on tourism. Its fishermen run a thriving choir and much of Filey turns out for the nine-day Edwardian Festival in June/July. You may also find a high concentration of walkers here; the town is the terminus for three long-distance paths, the **Wolds Way** to North Ferriby near Hull, the **Cleveland Way** to Sutton Bank and the **Centenary Way** (marking 100 years of county councils) to York. (Details and route maps are available from the tourist information bureau in John Street.)

The Flamborough cliffs

Past **Hunmanby**, with its double lock-up (one for humans, one for stray cattle), take the B1229 left to **Bempton**. The dramatic 'bird cliffs' here are famous as a natural series of tower-blocks for seabirds that are crammed together like families in Singapore or Hong Kong. You do not have to be an ornithologist, or even the slightest bit interested in birds, to appreciate the extraordinary sight, now protected by the RSPB, which provides good access. Until 1954 the cliffs were also busy with 'climmers': steely-nerved local people who dangled on ropes to collect up to 130,000 guillemot eggs a year for restaurants, collectors and, suprisingly, patent-leather workshops in the West Riding where the yolks were used in the production process. Early conservation law finally intervened but the climmers' names, like Moses Downgate, remain as the titles of ledges and pillars of rock.

When you've had enough of watching the gannets (the English mainland's only breeding colony), puffins, kittiwakes, razor-bills, guillemots and shags, head into **Flamborough** village with its twin roads dividing to the North and South Landings. The little stone cottages gather round a memorial to the Two Brothers' maritime tragedy in 1909 – a reminder that Flamborough and its lifeboat (currently threatened with redundancy) have a famous place in the annals of the sea. The boat, with its old-fashioned slipway, is on the small beach under the chalk cliffs at **North Landing**. **Robin Lythes' Cave** a 50ft-high smugglers' haunt nearby, is worth a look. Forays can be made along the beach, and from quieter **South Landing**, but be very careful indeed to check on tide movements and times.

Flamborough headland has a toposcope, equidistant between John O'Groats and Lands End (both 362 miles away), marking an unusual naval engagement between British and American ships in 1779, which ended in defeat for the home side. The 85ft-lighthouse towers nearby. In the village's part-Norman church is a curious effigy and inscription to the splendid Sir Marmaduke Constable (of the family which built Burton Constable), who fought at Flodden at the age of 70 and died, allegedly, from swallowing a toad while drinking. The unfortunate reptile is carved, along with part of a skeleton, on the great man's tomb.

The headland is defended from the land by an older monument, **Danes Dyke earthworks**, neither a dyke nor Danish, but a good place for a walk along the nature trail that winds through Iron Age mounds. Its air of sturdy independence is encouraged by the story that Flamborough paid taxes to Denmark rather than London until the sixteenth century – in the form of a single gold coin attached to an arrow which was fired, once a year, out to sea.

Bridlington

The assets of **Bridlington**, the next stop on the journey south along the coast, are self-evident: a wide sweep of sand, seaside shops festooned with plastic dinghies, fishing nets, and buckets and spades, donkeys on the beach and a backdrop of cliffs. The lifeboat nudges from its cavernous shelter on the Prom, with a good RNLI souvenir shop (lifeboat-shaped everything, from soap to ballpoints). Music filters from the Royal Spa halls on the sea-front.

Bridlington is more of a Bank Holiday, tripperish resort than Filey and much less varied than Scarborough. But it is especially popular with young families who stroll through the attractive streets or mill around happily on the well-cleaned beach. The resort was originally two communities, the Old Town around **Bridlington Priory**, and the **Quay**, where fishing smacks still anchor. The **priory** was much-battered in the Dissolution of the Monasteries, but substantial sections, including the entire nave, were absorbed into the present parish church of St Mary. The only separately surviving monastic relic, the **Bayle** or gatehouse, houses a small, largely local history **museum** (open Easter to Sept, Tue and Thur 2 to 4, 7 to 9; Wed 2 to 4). From here, an enjoyable walk takes in Kirkgate, High Street and Westgate, passing a series of handsome seventeenth-century and Georgian town houses.

A mile to the north of the town, **Sewerby Hall** (grounds open all year; house Easter to end Oct, Mon to Fri 10 to 6, Sat 1.30 to 6) is a fine mansion (1714–20) with a delightful walled garden and an interesting museum and art gallery. Exhibits and displays on the Bempton climmers and the Hull-born aviator Amy Johnson, who presided over Sewerby's launch as a public museum in 1936, are unusual and informative. The small **zoo** should please children, who will also enjoy the **model town** of Portminian in Sewerby village, some 200 miniature buildings populated by 2,000 tiny Portminians.

A lot goes on in Bridlington in season: Sewerby's grounds play host to circuses, medieval jousts and jugglers; the British national windsurfing championships regularly come to North Bay; and the Spa offers minor party or union conferences, national domino or table tennis tournaments and celebrated orchestras or rock bands. All the usual resort activities abound.

South of Brid (as everyone calls it), the flatlands begin, a landscape which depresses some (especially off-season) but appeals to others with its strange air of melancholy mixed with commercialised fun. **Skipsea** does its best to relieve the contours with the impressive earthwork remains of the Norman stronghold built by Drogo de Bevrere, but it is an exception.

Hornsea

The major resort on this stretch of coast, off the A165 on the B1242, is **Hornsea**, which heroically advertises itself as Lakeland by the Sea. Deprived of the fine settings which frame Scarborough, Filey and Bridlington, Hornsea falls back on its **Mere**, Yorkshire's largest freshwater lake. This is another favourite place for ornithologists, especially during the spring and autumn migrations, when honking waterfowl swoop from the sky for a brief stop-over. Many other species spend the winter here.

The long, sandy beach with its breakwaters takes second place, for most visitors, to the 28 acres of **Hornsea Pottery Leisure Park** (open all year, daily 10 to 6). Distinctive Hornsea mugs, jugs and other souvenirs are now only part of a complex which covers veteran cars, live tropical butterflies, a model village, birds of prey giving flying displays and a Minidale Farm, which offers the smaller domestic animals like rabbits and mice their place in the limelight. The connection between these exhibits is tenuous, but together with shops, minicars and minibikes there is no shortage of things to do.

The town's **Holderness Museum of Village Life** (open Easter to end Sept, daily 10 to 5) is a deserving past winner of Britain's Small Museum Award, housed in an old farmhouse at 11 Newbegin, with rooms and outbuildings carefully restored to nineteenth-century specifications. Agricultural devices abound. **St Nicholas's church** stands at the old centre of town, with one or two pleasant buildings nearby including the brick-built Old Hall (private). Large beach pebbles were used in the building of the church, which was severely damaged in a storm in 1733; the incident caused much local consternation about the Almighty's wrath, said to have been aroused because the clergy had allowed smugglers to store contraband in the crypt several months earlier. The former railway line to Hull, which once ferried thousands of trippers to Hornsea, is now a footpath and cycleway through quiet countryside – particularly appealing to cyclists because it is so flat.

Withernsea

The alarming reality of sea erosion is especially evident at Mappleton and Great Cowden cliffs on the B1242 south of Hornsea. A few miles further south, the small town of **Withernsea** is a classic minor North Sea coastal resort, with the pleasurably lugubrious air of places dedicated to enjoyment against the odds. Generations of shivering children have defied the wind and cold waves, built their doomed sandcastles and suffered the severe regimes of landladies' boarding houses. After doing your duty on the beach, visit the town's genuinely unusual attraction: the 127ft-high **Lighthouse Museum** (open Easter to mid–Sept, weekends 11 to 5; July and Aug, daily 11 to 5) with its 144 steps to an excellent panorama. Contents include stirring lifeboat stories and large displays in memory of the locally born actress Kay Kendall, whose sister created the museum. The family's distant connections with Captain Cook account for a separate room on him, and the whole operation is pleasantly cosy.

THE NORTHERN WOLDS

The Sykes' domain

A single family stamped their mark on the Northern Wolds, an area dominated by farming where the landscape can be austere, even dreary in dull weather. The drive connecting a string of villages from **Duggleby** to **Burton Fleming** is a lesson in intensive agriculture, with few pretty interludes in either the countryside or the workaday villages.

The area was moulded by the Sykes family, prosperous Leeds merchants who turned to agriculture in the 1700s, applying their rigour and energy to making the chalk downs more productive. Their efforts reached an apogee with nineteenth–century Sir Tatton, whose ideology is supposed to have included a ban on his tenants growing pointless flowers around their cottages, rather than useful vegetables.

Sir Tatton was largely responsible for the heavy Victorian architecture encountered again and again in the area surrounding his family's mansion and many monuments at **Sledmere**, the main estate village to which neighbouring communities still seem to turn, psychologically, like pilgrims acknowledging Mecca. The eighteenth-century classicism of the family's **Sledmere House** (open Easter to end Sept, Tue to Thur, Sat and Sun and Bank Hol Mon, 1.30 to 5) comes as something of a relief (although it was much rebuilt after a catastrophic fire in 1911). The many fine rooms include a good Turkish pastiche. The grounds are formally laid-out and there are souvenir shops and a café and a tradition of regular events such as traction-engine rallies and concerts. The **Waggoners' Memorial** is the best of assorted monuments which dot the village; its enjoyable carved friezes tell the story of the haywain regiment raised by Sir Mark Sykes to help army transport in the First World War. A couple of miles south-east on the road to **Garton on the Wolds** you can pay homage to Sir Tatton at the grotesque Victorian tower erected to his memory by grateful tenants, its clumsy bulges relieved by two endearing carved panels of Sykesian scenes.

Wharram Percy

A few miles from Sledmere, an excellent opportunity to penetrate the highly farmed countryside comes at **Wharram Percy** where the site of a medieval village is being excavated, slowly, by English Heritage. Little remains among the turfy hummocks where the houses stood, and the ruined church beyond the inevitable Victorian pair of farmworkers' cottages is a graceful shell. But the narrow valley, with its larks singing and clouds of Marbled White, Ringlet and Common Blue butterflies in summer, has an evocative atmosphere. It is a fairly steep, 20-minute walk from the car park signposted just off the B1248.

From the Wharrams you can potter down the Wolds escarpment and through quiet estate villages like **Settrington**, weaving your way eventually to **Norton** (wholly overshadowed by neighbouring **Malton**, see p 171) and **Stamford Bridge**. Contemplate the erstwhile bloody battleground here from one of several genteel cafés, examine the politely bilingual commemorative stone (English and Norwegian) and, if energetic, follow the tranquil riverbank walk downstream to **Kexby** (eight miles, returning through Low Catton).

Rudston and Burton Agnes

The other main treasures of the North Wolds lie well to the east, reachable rapidly by the A166 to Bridlington, or more pleasantly by map navigation on assorted B and unclassifed roads. Follow these first to **Boynton**, where the hall's Tudor brickwork can always be admired from a pleasant footpath starting by St Andrew's church, south of the B1253 which bisects the village. In the church a turkey on the lectern commemorates a disastrous event for poultry: William Strickland of Boynton Hall sailed with Cabot to America, brought back some turkeys and is credited with starting the fashion of eating them on Christmas Day.

A short drive west along the B1253 brings you to the large village of **Rudston**, which takes its name from an outstanding 25ft-high glacial **monolith**; it has the same depth below ground according to researchers, generations of whom have been fascinated by it since the eighteenth century. The centre of much speculation, but little certain knowledge, the enormous rock stands right by Rudston church, topped with an undignified lead cap to prevent erosion. The **church** is admirable too, with a delightful memorial to the writer Winifred Holtby who lies buried in the churchyard under the inscription on a carved book, poignant for one who died at 36, 'Give me work till my life shall end, And life till my work is done'.

The writer's childhood home, Rudston House, is private but can be peeped at from the road to the lovely Elizabethan mansion of **Burton Agnes** (open Easter to end Oct, daily 11 to 5), which comes with the bonus of a Norman manor house, excellently preserved between the redbrick mansion and the church. The ogee-topped gatehouse is the most satisfying of all this catholic complex of ancient buildings and the stables and barns have also been put to good use: an exhibition on 100 years of prams, enough to terrify small children; an adventure playground to cheer them up, and a good café and souvenir shop. The main house has interesting rooms and the grounds are delightful.

Crossing the A166 here, narrow lanes with passing places take you through **Great Kelk** to **Cruckley Farm** (open 25 Apr to end Sept, daily 10.30 to 6), a working establishment which welcomes visitors and offers a thorough guided tour; there is a small café, too. From here, you can venture south into Holderness, or turn north to **Great Driffield**, which seems almost a metropolis after the dozing B-roads all around. Its merits are mostly as a shopping and market centre for local people but the canal head, just behind the railway station, is a lovely spot, with well-restored old warehouses, a dock crane and the prospect (after further restoration of the old link to the River Hull) of gentle cruises into the hazy distance.

THE SOUTHERN WOLDS

Beverley

'So splendid! So precious!' wrote Sir John Betjeman of **Beverley**, a slogan which the town has somewhat coyly adopted as its marketing slogan. But who could disagree? Beverley is an exceptional market-town, most strikingly approached through the **North Bar**, a remarkable piece of medieval brickwork constructed well before kilns were capable of producing uniform shapes. The only survivor of five gateways in the mostly vanished town wall, the bar has a prominent portcullis groove – a reminder of how medieval towns could effectively batten down their hatches. Charles I and his two sons (later Charles II and James II) stayed in adjoining Bar House while Royalist troops besieged Hull.

Beyond North Bar, elegant Georgian shop frontages line **Saturday Market**, a spacious square with the traditional market-cross, smartly adorned by eight columns of solid stone supporting an elaborate roof. A large weekly market with a wide choice of goods, from fruit and veg to fabrics and wool, is still held here on Saturdays, spilling over – via Toll Gavel street, where taxes were paid in the Middle Ages – into smaller Wednesday Market (now a street name only; Wednesday's market has gone). Pedestrianised streets leading off the market-squares make Beverley an exceptionally pleasant place for strolling or shopping.

The town is most famous for two outstanding churches: the **Minster**, with the size and grandeur of a cathedral, and the less well known **St Mary's**. The Minster's wonderful medieval stonework, considered to be the finest example of Gothic architecture in Europe, is enhanced by its setting, proudly apart from nearby streets. Inside, there are superb examples of the medieval wood-carvers' and stonemasons' crafts, notably 68 misericords, figures representing the agonies of lumbago and stomach-ache and the ornate Percy tomb, so delicately carved that it is hard to believe it is made of stone. The adjoining screen was made for the shrine of St John of Beverley, an eighth-century Bishop of York who retired to monastic life. His reputation for miraculous powers drew streams of pilgrims to Beverley after his death. A seven-ton bell, **Great John**, commemorates him too. Look out in the chancel for the rare **Anglo-Saxon Frith stool**, one of only three in England, which entitled someone who sat on it to sanctuary for thirty days. This plain stone seat was positioned near the high altar, where only the most desperate layman would dare approach.

St Mary's is just north of the town centre, built between the twelfth and sixteenth centuries, and a delight. It is best known for its carvings, including bosses and misericords, and for the brightly painted panelled ceiling depicting forty English kings. Look out, too, for a group playing musical instruments carved on one of the pillars, in recognition of the guild of musicians who contributed to the church's building.

Beverley is best appreciated by strolling among its Georgian brick terraces, although there are few buildings to single out. However, it is worth going into the **Guildhall** in Register Square. Behind the nineteenth-century classical façade is the much older Court Room which dates from around 1760. Judges must have enjoyed a great sense of their own importance under the magnificent stucco ceiling depicting Justice amid swirls of Rococo patterning.

Those with children, whose interest in Beverley's architecture is likely to be limited, will find welcome relief at the **Museum of Army Transport** (open all year, daily 10 to 5; closed 3 days at Chr) in Flemingate on the edge of town (plenty of car-parking space). Every conceivable means of services transport is displayed in this two-acre hall, from the smallest folding motorbike to the huge Blackburn Beverley bomber aircraft. You can explore the inside of this leviathan and feel queasy peering down the parachutists' hatch. Next to it is a rather feeble children's assault course; much more rewarding are the armoured cars you can clamber in, the curious pink camouflage of desert jeeps and the impressive mobile bakery.

You are seldom far from a pleasant pub or café in Beverley, but if near Hengate, seek out the **White Horse** – informally known as Nellie's. Concessions to modernity have been made with the recent opening of its former men-only bar to women, but the flagstone floor, coke fire (all year round) and gas lighting remain along with the draught beer.

On the western edge of the town is **Westwood pasture**, 500 acres of common land which was given to the townspeople in the twelfth to fourteenth centuries for recreation. It now includes a golf course and racecourse. Beverley's freemen still have grazing rights here for part of the year, too.

Due south of Beverley on the A164 is **Skidby mill museum** (open May to Sept, Tue to Sat, 10 to 4, Sun and Bank Hol 1.30 to 4.30) with its working sails – unmissable in a county full of windmill stumps – the only ones left in East

Yorkshire. Corn is still ground on a dozen days every summer when the stoneground flour may be bought. There is a small museum and craft workshop attached.

The Southern Wolds around Beverley are children's story-book countryside, beautifully ordered and patterned with lovely villages, almost all with large, central ponds. **Bishop Burton** on the A1079 is a good example with an excellent church, unusually housing a bust of John Wesley. The road leads on and dramatically down the Wolds escarpment to **Market Weighton** (pronounced Weeton), where a church-yard monument marks the death in 1820 of William Bradley. He was 7ft 9in, weighed 27 stone and, like a proper level-headed Yorkshireman, turned these dubious assets to brass as a fairground freak.

Just to the north, **Goodmanham** has a revered place in Britain's Christian history; in AD627 King Edwin and his pagan high priest Coifi were converted to Christianity here by St Paulinus, who used the famous metaphor comparing man's life to a sparrow as one briefly flew through the warmth of the Royal longhouse. The Norman church is said to stand on the site.

Pocklington

Pocklington is a lively town whose streets and paved alleyways are a pleasure in themselves, with plenty of shops, cafés and pubs (that unusually include a Bavarian beer cellar). It also has two genuinely original attractions. **Penny Arcadia** (open 1 May to 30 Sept, daily 12.30 to 5; June to Aug, daily 10 to 5) in the Market Place has over 100 old penny-in-the-slot machines (some quite saucy). The museum is organised on the basis of a one-and-a-half-hour tour, with a film show, theatre perfor-mance – a kind of music-hall turn – by one of the staff and tour (with old pennies available) of the arcade machines. This will be put on even for solitary visitors. In the evening the place becomes Pocklington's Ritz cinema.

A few minutes away, off the Hull Road, **Burnby Hall Gardens** (open Easter to early Oct, daily 10 to 6) house Europe's biggest collection of water lilies in two lakes created by the late Major Percy Stewart, a local schoolmaster and author of books like 'Round the World with Rod and Rifle'. An energetic but disorganised collector, he piled up rhino horns, moose heads and similar trophies which gaze from the walls of a small modern museum with attached café. **Burnby Hall** itself is a comfortably ugly building occupied by the

143

local district council; the interest lies in the gardens and lakes (where you may, if you are lucky, see water lily experts carrying out their unique form of gardening in wet suits). Like Penny Arcadia, the whole operation has a satisfying air of eccentricity.

North-east of Pocklington the B1246 takes you past Kilnwick Percy (glimpse the fine hall, now a Buddhist centre, from the side-road to the left) to the pretty village of **Warter**, set in a wooded valley with a curious range of architectural styles: a row of thatched cottages, sporadic Victoriana and several villas reminiscent of London's Bedford Park. Like a lot of Wolds villages, Warter has a delightful little post office and store which will appreciate your passing trade. Turning left takes you to Millington Wood picnic area, **Great Givendale** and the cottages of **Bishop Wilton**, peacefully lining either side of a beck. The four-mile stretch from **Millington** to Bishop Wilton is also a delightful walk, using part of the Beverley-to-York long-distance path, the **Minster Way**.

Londesborough

Turning south from Warter takes you through **Nunburnholme**, another peaceful and pretty group of cottages straggling along a chalky stream, to Londesborough, one of the most interesting estate villages in Yorkshire. Still entirely tenanted, this friendly hamlet was once the Yorkshire home of Lord Burlington, architect of Chiswick House. The fragmentary remains of his mansion (demolished in 1819 and partly reused at Chatsworth) may be sought out by the determined. Your first stop should be the village shop for a copy of the excellent local history. Chatting to locals should gain you access to the concert hall (the former estate laundry) with its murals painted by two German prisoners of war using brushes made from their own hair, and directions to footpaths including part of the long-distance Wolds Way which give glimpses of Burlington's abandoned urns and terracing.

Two miles east up the A163 a large sign marks **Kiplingcotes Racecourse**, the oldest-known course in the world. It is only used on 3 March, when the Kiplingcotes Derby, held annually since 1519, takes place. At other times there is open access to the public. Seven miles from Londesborough across the A1079, the otherwise unexceptional village of **Seaton Ross** has an extraordinary cottage whose entire front forms a giant sundial, the Roman numerals competing with a vigorous Albertine climbing rose. The surrounding flood plain of the Derwent is a tranquil place to lose yourself, slowing down for pheasants and asking directions, when lost, from affable elderly gents out walking their dogs. At **Holme-on-Spalding Moor**, **Hasholme Heavy Horses** (open Easter to end Sept, weekends and school hols, daily 10.30 to 5) is a splendid, working farm genuinely using some 30 horses for routine chores. **The Northern Shire Horse Centre** (open Easter to end Sept, Sun to Thur, 10 to 5) at **North Newbald**, only seven miles to the east, is a more conventional farm museum, with close access to assorted animals.

HULL AND THE NORTH HUMBER BANK

Hull

Kingston-upon-Hull, to accord the city its full and sonorous name, is a place that has been transformed in recent years. From a drab, declining, fishing port, it has become a lively, clean and historic centre, turning its strongly maritime character to excellent account. Arriving via the M62 (and A63) or by train, you sniff the ozone well before the final three miles, passing masts and funnels, cold stores and cranes, along the flat Humber bank from Hessle.

This approach road has the aldermanic title of **Clive Sullivan Way**, typical of an important strand of Hull's modern history - vigorous municipal socialism. Another marker of this is the sign listing the city's foreign twins, so many of them that you need to enter and re-enter Hull several times to take them all in.

Devotion to mass rehousing after the wartime blitz has left the city's outskirts generally unappealing, but in **East Park**, off Holderness Road, you can find an antiquated 'splashboat' dating from the 1930s, which swooshes down a metal ramp into the park lake like an imitation lifeboat, its crew of holidaymakers screaming with pleasure and fright.

A walk around the **Old Town**, visiting a series of particularly good museums, is the best way to enjoy Hull. Parking is well-signposted and the streets around **Holy Trinity parish church** are largely pedestrianised and unhurried. Note Hull's distinctive white telephone boxes; the telephones here have always been run by the council and for years were the only independent system in Britain.

The Old Grammar School (open all year, Mon to Sat, 10 to 5, Sun 1.30 to 4.30) on South Church Side houses the newest museum in an outstanding civic tradition started by Tom Shepherd, a famous – or notorious – curator whose presence had people guarding their antiques in the way that other people lock up their daughters. Appointed in 1900 to Hull's then solitary, small museum, he was given the terse instruction: 'Come at ten, leave at four, attend to any inquiries but do not spend money'. His reputation for amassing exhibits by other means grew to the extent that he was greeted publicly by a Leeds professor in the 1930s: 'Ah, Shepherd – and how's thieving?'Shepherd's main museum, regarded as the best in provincial Britain, was blitzed on 25 June 1943 but re-excavated, in a fascinating piece of modern archaeology, in the late 1980s. Any surviving pieces were removed and then the whole site concreted over. Fire-blackened exhibits may be seen at several of the museums, some with traces of a black, sticky substance which puzzled the diggers. It turned out to be melted ladies' stockings from a department store, previously blitzed.

The grammar school tells the story of Hull imaginatively and is itself a well-restored piece of history. Five minutes' walk away, the **Hull and East Riding Museum** (open all year, Mon to Sat 10 to 5, Sun 1.30 to 4.30) at 36 High Street, Old Town, broadens the picture, with particular strength in the prehistoric history of the Wolds: the 2,000-year-old Hasholme boat, the Wetwang chariots and other ancient exhibits; preservation techniques are also well-explained. The generally fresh approach of the Hull museums continues at Streetlife – **Hull Museum of Transport** (open all year, Mon to Sat 10 to 5, Sun 1.30 to 4.30), also in the High Street, which is newly opened and makes the most of everything from sedan chairs to trams.

The Town Docks museum (open all year, Mon to Sat 10 to 5, Sun 1.30 to 4.30), in Queen Victoria Square, does a similar job for Hull's fishing history; exhibits include scrimshaw: the art of sculpting and engraving whalebone. Hull's large and well-stocked information bureau is also here, tel. (0482) 223344. The former house of the great emancipator William Wilberforce is a pleasant walk across the Old Town. It is one of a row of handsome Georgian houses renovated after a period of neglect.

Art enthusiasts will also know of the **Ferens Art Gallery** (open all year, Mon to Sat 10 to 5, Sun 1.30 to 4.30) in Queen Victoria Square, close to the Town Docks Museum, and may want to see the strong modern collection at **Hull University's galleries** in Middleton Hall, Cottingham Road (open during term time, tel. (0482) 465192). Otherwise, cross the busy A63 and potter down by Hull's foreshore. Among the pubs and cobbled streets is another museum, but this is one which even the weariest child may enjoy: the **Old Spurn Lightship** (open all year, Mon to Sat 10 to 5, Sun 1.30 to 4.30) rides at anchor in Hull Marina, a fascinating floating exhibit with crew's quarters, dazzling light and little kitchen galley all on show. The city's maritime heritage trail can also be picked up here.

THE HUMBER

Leaving Hull westwards, the dual carriageway has a magnetic attraction for those bustling off to Leeds or the motorways north and south. Resist the pull, and take a detour to the **Yorkshire Water Museum** (open all year, daily exc Mon) at Springhead pumping-station, just off Willerby Road, Hull, which has much ancient machinery displayed around a majestic beam-engine. Then make your way through **Hessle**, a proudly independent little town with smart Georgian houses, to the **Humber Bridge**.

This graceful tribute to modern engineering skill strides majestically out from the Humber bank, dwarfing the sail-less tower of **Hessle whiting mill** (no formal opening arrangements, but if closed collect key from the nearby café); the preserved machinery and small exhibition on chalk-quarrying and the process of grinding the stone into whiting powder (for rendering material, painting games-pitch lines and other uses) is part of the **Humber Bridge Country Park**. There is a café here and good parking for the bridge. The bridge is well worth a drive in spite of its hefty toll. To avoid this, and if you have the time and do not suffer from vertigo, walk the one-and-a-half miles across to **Barton** and its local museum. You can take a bus back in summer from the south bank car park.

The bridge's 1,410 metres (4,626ft) comfortably secure it the title of the world's longest single-span suspension bridge, and its other statistics, including 44,000 miles of wire, are fully listed in the Humber Bridge Country Park centre.

Westwards north of the A63 are three pleasant villages, **South** and **North Cave** and, above all, **Welton**, surprisingly close to the start of the industrial fringe of the Humber at Brough. A beck chatters under little bridges alongside Welton's village green and into a pond inhabited by greedy ducks. The handsome houses date from the earliest days of Hull commuting, the best three sharing out the traditional names of a rural English community – Welton Hall, Welton Manor and Welton Grange. The grandest house of all, Welton House, was pulled down after the Second World War but the mausoleum of the Raikes family, wealthy Hull merchants who lived in the house, survives in the pretty surroundings of **Welton Dale**, just over a mile to the north-east of the village. **St Helen's church** is an interesting mixture, from Norman traces to six fine stained-glass windows by William Morris. After contemplating the grave of Joseph Found, who married and survived eight wives, dally at the pleasant Green Dragon Inn, where Dick Turpin was finally arrested in 1736 (bathetically, for shooting a cock and threatening a local man while drunk).

Howden and Goole

As you drive, the M62 is flanked by immense, monotonous crop fields to the south although you'll find little Humber villages like **Yokefleet** and **Saltmarshe** are unexpectedly snug, with nothing notable to the north, either, until the grand tower of **Howden Minster** comes into view. Once famous as the centre of Britain's airship production (the R101 was made here), the little market-town needs an injection of self-confidence. The partly ruined **minster**, one of the largest parish churches in Britain, overlooks a fine centre but one which could do with much more renovation. The **Bishop's Manor**, part of the former summer palace of the warlike Bishops of Durham, has shown the way with an excellent restoration. It is on a small circular tour of the centre described in a good leaflet, available in local shops.

Three miles north-west, **Wressle Castle** is a smallish ruin which none the less wins the palm as East Yorkshire's best medieval castle remains. To the south, surprisingly large ships dock at Goole, which has a competent local history museum at the library in the Market Square.

Holderness

Those who still find Hull an 'end-of-the-worldish' sort of place are in for a shock when they head east across the swivelling bridge over the **River Hull** (prepare for long jams if it is open to allow a ship through). Although signs point to European destinations – ferries to Scandinavia, Germany or

Holland – much of Britain also lies beyond the city's eastern boundary.

The gateway to the seldom-visited triangle of Holderness is distinctly unpromising. A horrible road, four narrowish lanes usually busy with lorries bound for the docks, grinds past Hull prison, tatty shops and high dock walls. One small compensation, for those nostalgic for their childhood model-kits, is the Humbrol factory on the left, the source of all those tiny tins of model-makers' paint.

The grimness ends with your first sight of Hedon, gathered round one of this area's great churches, known as the King of Holderness. **Hedon** has interesting traces of its days as a port, linked to the Humber by canals, but the area's prime attraction lies a few miles north at **Burton Constable** (open Easter and May Bank Hol; Sun only in June and July; mid-July to Sept, Sun to Thur, grounds 12 to 5, house 1 to 5). This first-division stately home is a marvellous Elizabethan hall with splendid eighteenth-century landscaping and fine interiors (including a Chinese room and a collection of scientific instruments). The grounds have further displays of carriages and agricultural implements, as well as a café and souvenir shop.

Driving south-east, you enter that increasing rarity in Britain: distinctive, but little-known, countryside. Celebrated by the poet Philip Larkin, who loved exploring here while librarian at Hull University, and by novelist Winifred Holtby, the monotonous contours belie some lovely, miniature cameos: a winding lane latticed with cow parsley, or a village street of warm, old redbrick, often made older-looking still by the 'salling', or erosion of the seasalt-laden winds.

Sunk Island and Spurn Head

In **Keyingham** a sign points intriguingly to **Sunk Island**, a reclaimed community of prosperous farms whose history is an epitome of the story of Holderness. The road in runs straight and narrow to a featureless horizon – you almost sense the curvature of the earth, as if you were at sea. Identical farmhouses float amid clumps of trees and the cranes of Immingham and Grimsby's dock-tower stand beyond the Humber, dim in the haze.

In Henry VIII's day, you would now have been well below the surface of the river, which washed across this area uninterrupted until a small sandbank appeared in 1560. Tidal erosion, linked with the shifting mud and shingle of the Spurn peninsula, gradually raised Sonke Sand, as it was known, until it became large enough for a Carolingian adventurer, Colonel Anthony Gilby, to colonise it in 1669.

The island has doubled in size since then, finally joining the mainland in the 1830s as mud and successive embankments blocked the remaining channels. Always Crown property, by virtue of ancient laws governing the rare phenomenon of land rising out of the sea, it has survived neglect, drastic Victorian modernisation (accounting for the architect Samuel Teulon's 'identi-farms') and a catastrophic 'Land-fit-for-Heroes' experiment after the First World War when it was planned as a returning servicemen's colony, each with their allotted acres of land. The **Humber Bank Heritage Centre**, an excellent display on Sunk Island's history and characters, including the 'Mud Admiral' Robert Drewery who invented a tide-powered sludge-removing boat, is kept in the former Holy Trinity church. The key is available from the vicarage next door, or from Peter Wykes at Wood Farm, tel. (0964) 630611. An interesting way back to Hull is via **Stone Creek** (stop for a look around) over Cherry Cob Sands to splendidly named **Thorngumbald**, via one very short zig-zag of unmade road at Stone Creek itself. The curious structure on the left is an old army wireless tower, designed to pinpoint wartime invaders for nearby gun batteries, whose embrasures are slowly being over-run by nature.

East from Keyingham, the exceptional spire of **St Patrick, Patrington**, can soon be seen, a parish church of rare perfection known as the Queen of Holderness. The wealth of resources put into the building, with stone brought by barge to Stone Creek and then carted overland, reflected the fact that the Archbishop of York was Lord of the Manor until the Reformation. The church is also exceptionally satisfying inside. Patrington village is neat and modest in comparison.

Welwick dozes around another interesting church that is part finest Tadcaster limestone, part humble local cobbles. The change in building material was an indirect result of Bubonic plague, which destroyed the villagers' prosperity in mid-construction. Note a triumph of optimism in this billiard-table part of Yorkshire: a building at the eastern end of the village is called Hill Top House. **Skeffling** has medieval crosses in its small churchyard and **Easington**'s substantial church stands next to an interesting thatched and timber-framed tithe barn. The spiky gas installations just north of the village have a place in history, too: the very first therms of North Sea Gas were piped ashore here.

The road through Holderness ends at **Spurn Head**, an apparently fragile (but actually immensely resilient) finger of land hooking out into the Humber mouth. Like Sunk Island, and for the same atmospheric reasons, this is a strange piece of land, which visitors seldom forget. The Yorkshire Wildlife Trust will relieve you of £2 at the gate, or somewhere along the two-mile wartime road to the point of the spit: a patchy concrete highway which is regularly damaged and sometimes breached by the sea. Spend as much as you can at the small souvenir and wildlife bookshop just beyond the gate; the Trust maintains the peninsula extremely well.

Spurn Head is particularly famous among ornithologists, with regular sightings of rare migrant birds. Pebble-hunters roam ecstatically along the north shore of the spit and the huddle of buildings at the point, two lighthouses, coastguard cottages and the lifeboat station, are good places to watch the big ships creeping in and out of the Humber ports. Here, between the wind and waves, Yorkshire comes to an end.

WHERE TO STAY

FLAMBOROUGH

Manor House
Flamborough, Bridlington
YO15 1PD
TEL (0262) 850943
This early nineteenth-century house has been well restored and furnished by its owners who collect and sell antiques. One of the Wolsey Lodge group, the emphasis here is on informality and friendliness. Both rooms have their own bathrooms. Dinners by arrangement only.
£ *All year, exc Chr; 2 rooms; Access, Visa*

HUNMANBY

Wrangham House
10 Stonegate, Hunmanby
YO14 0NS
TEL (0723) 891333
This eighteenth-century house, formerly the vicarage, has cosy public rooms and pretty bedrooms. Welcoming owners make it an excellent base for the area.
£ *All year; 13 rooms; Access, Amex, Diners, Visa*

SCALBY

Wrea Head Country House
Scalby, Scarborough YO13 0PB
TEL (0723) 378211
About three miles north of Scarborough, this Victorian stone house is set in peaceful grounds on a hillside. The décor and furnishings are quite flamboyant and you are assured of a comfortable stay.
££ *All year, exc 23 to 28 Dec; 21 rooms; Access, Amex, Diners, Visa*

WALKINGTON

The Manor House
Northlands, Walkington, Nr
Beverley HU17 8RT
TEL (0482) 881645
The Manor House is a luxurious
place to stay, with very
comfortable bedrooms full of
detail and excess. Food is also an
important feature of staying here;
the elaborate menu is beautifully
presented.
££ *All year, rest closed Sun; 5
rooms; Access, Visa*

WINTERINGHAM

Winteringham Fields
Winteringham DN15 9PF
TEL (0724) 733096
This 400-year-old farmhouse has
been transformed by the owner's
decorative flair. Some Victoriana,
some French style, it is more of a
restaurant-with-rooms than a
traditional hotel. But the setting,
in the small village of
Winteringham, is convenient for
Hull and you will certainly be
comfortable and well-fed.
££ *Closed Chr, first half of Jan, first
week Aug; rest closed Sun; 6 rooms;
Access, Visa*

WHERE TO EAT

SCARBOROUGH

Lanterna
33 Queen Street
TEL (0723) 363616
A crowded informal trattoria,
offering a limited menu, with
carefully cooked popular dishes
such as spaghetti carbonara,
scampi fritto or escalope
Milanese, as well as various fish
dishes.
Tue to Sat 7–9.30; Access, Visa

SOUTH DALTON

Pipe & Glass
West End
TEL (0430) 810246
Welcoming family pub, with a
charming garden, offering
soundly cooked bar food from
Yorkshire pudding with onion
gravy to grilled fresh fish; soup
and sandwiches are also available.
*Tue to Sun 12–2, 7–10 (not Sun
eve); Access, Visa*

YORK
AND AROUND

- The ancient walled city of York: a year-round tourist city with a good choice of places to eat, from fine restaurants to tea-rooms and pubs
- York Minster, the largest medieval Gothic church in England
- A remarkable variety of archeological remains and historic buildings
- A wide choice of museums that include the National Railway Museum and the Jorvik Viking Centre
- Market-towns, beautiful stately homes and peaceful villages in the surrounding Vale of York

York Minster

YORK

ONE of England's most beautiful historic cities, York also has its own thriving university, which adds another dimension to the buzzing life and culture. On summer nights the city takes on a continental feel with lots of people milling round the streets, window-shopping, or heading for a lively bar or pub. Parliament Street's wide pedestrianised area is a popular meeting-place where you can stop for impromptu street performances: a string trio or the occasional gimmick salesman. The shops, restaurants, bars and cafés have to cater for the student purse as well as the tourists; the result is plenty of everything. You seldom have to walk more than 100 yards between cafés and even less around Bootham Bar, the Minster and the Shambles. Music bars, jazz clubs, the Arts Centre in Micklegate, and the Theatre Royal give visitors a wide choice in the evenings, and every four years, in July and August, the Mystery Plays form part of an Arts Festival (last held in 1992); there is an annual early music festival too.

Shopping choice is just as good. The streets around the Minster have everything, from shops selling expensive Scottish cashmere, designer clothes, antiques or delicious chocolates, to cheaper clothes, bric-a-brac and books: new or secondhand. The daily market is a mêlée of noise and colour; prices are reasonable and barrows are laden with food, vegetables, clothes, toys and anything else available.

If you visit York during Bank Holidays, a summer weekend, or during the festivals it will be crammed. Tourists and locals flock into the centre, milling through the ancient streets, sometimes just sitting and watching others flow past. A tour of the walls can be quite hair-raising at these times: bottlenecks can easily form round a push-chair on the narrow stretches. If you haven't time to visit the whole of Yorkshire, York is not to be missed. There are few cities where you can enjoy such a complete picture of history through the ages, shop and browse, eat and drink well and generally enjoy yourself.

The first thing to do on arrival in York (if you are a driver) is to abandon the car. Much of the city centre has been pedestrianised and the best way to explore the city is on foot. A park-and-ride scheme operates from the Tesco site on the Tadcaster Road (A64), just south of the city centre. It operates daily, 7.30am to 7.30pm, with four stops, ending up at Tower Street in the city centre. Most out-of-centre hotels and B&Bs have car-parking space, and so do the larger, central hotels.

The many public car parks are frequently full (some are limited to three hours). Taxis are a good way of getting to and from the centre and you may need them after a day's walking along cobbled streets.

York's railway station is a main Inter-City junction and close to the centre, so the city is an ideal weekend destination without the car. With almost more museums than restaurants (and there are plenty of those), you could spend a week in York and still not have seen everything. But if you have only a couple of days to spare, keep one for browsing around the Shambles, Stonegate and the Minster, as well as a walk along sections of the city walls. The National Railway Museum, Jorvik Viking Centre and York Story are three of the most stimulating museums to make time for. A sung service at the Minster is a memorable experience, a concert even better. But perhaps best of all, set in the ruins of St Mary's Abbey, a Mystery Play would complete the York experience.

City walls tour

By the end of a visit to the city, the words Eboracum, Eoferwic and Jorvik will become familiar; they are the Roman, Anglo-Saxon and Viking names for York. The multi-tiered history of this remarkable city becomes clear as you wander through the streets. A good way to start an exploration of York's history and get an idea of the city's layout is to take a tour of the city walls. This can either be done on your own or with a human or taped guide, though beware: the path on the top of the wall can be vertigo-inducing in places and narrow enough to create bottlenecks. The excellent tape can be rented very cheaply from the tourist office in Exhibition Square.

Although you can see fragments of the Roman fortress walls, it is the medieval ones that remain intact. The wall can be joined at a number of gates or 'bars'; the taped tour begins at **Bootham Bar**, closest to the Minster and the site of the gate of the original Roman fortress. A flight of steps opens out into the old portcullis, from where the wall leads off.

A short walk east from here gives fine views of the smooth green lawns and neat borders of the Deanery Garden, with the Minster rising majestically behind. On the west of the wall the line of the medieval moat that used to surround the city is clearly visible under the grass. Approaching the gate of **Monk Bar**, you can see the shapes of houses moulded into the curve of the wall, and at various stages of the tour you can also

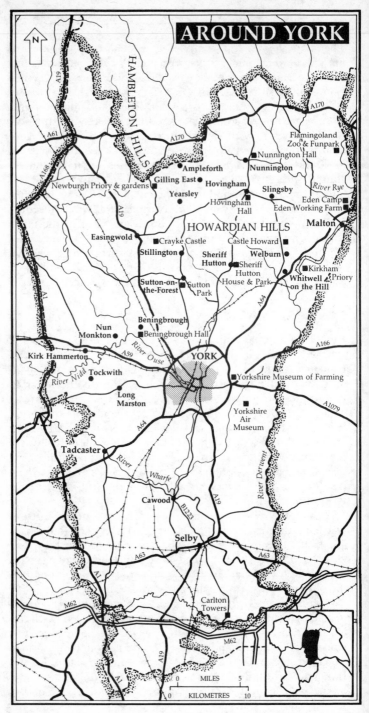

AROUND YORK

N

HAMBLETON HILLS

A19

A61

A168

A170

A170

A19

A1

Flamingoland Zoo & Funpark

Nunnington Hall

Nunnington

Ampleforth

Gilling East

Newburgh Priory & gardens

Hovingham

Slingsby

River Rye

Eden Camp

Eden Working Farm

Yearsley

Hovingham Hall

Malton

HOWARDIAN HILLS

Easingwold

Crayke Castle

Castle Howard

Welburn

Stillington

Sheriff Hutton

Sheriff Hutton House & Park

Whitwell on the Hill

Kirkham Priory

Sutton-on-the-Forest

Sutton Park

Beningbrough

Beningbrough Hall

Nun Monkton

A59

River Ouse

A166

Kirk Hammerton

YORK

Yorkshire Museum of Farming

River Nidd

Tockwith

Long Marston

A64

Yorkshire Air Museum

A1079

Tadcaster

A1

River Wharfe

River Derwent

Cawood

B1223

A19

Selby

A63

A63

A1

M62

Carlton Towers

A19

M62

| MILES | | 5 |
| 0 | | |

| KILOMETRES | | 10 |
| 0 | | |

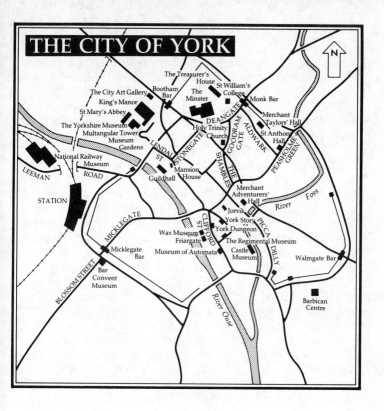

THE CITY OF YORK

admire unusual medieval structures such as the brick **ice-house**, the wonderful timbering of the **Merchant Adventurers' Guild Hall** and the **Red House**.

The car park for the large Sainsbury's store at the north-east of the city, easily visible from the walls close to the Oval corner turret, is in the area known as Jewbury. The Jews lived here, just outside the city walls, and were attacked in 1190 by their fellow townsfolk, masquerading as Christian crusaders. In reality the 'crusaders' were rebelling against the repayment of loans. The Jews fled in terror, seeking refuge in Clifford's Tower where they chose to commit suicide rather than convert to Christianity.

At a couple of points during a tour of the walls, natural elements take over their defensive role. The River Foss served this purpose, although the marshy grounds, islands and pools that were once here have now been filled in and the site is being developed. The Foss provided further natural defence close to the castle from where the natural barrier created by the confluence of the Ouse and the Foss could be overseen.

Walmgate Bar on the east side of the city is one of the few gates that has retained its barbican. The cattle-market was sited nearby but has been covered by the huge new sports and leisure complex of the **Barbican Centre**.

Bootham Bar and **Micklegate Bar** were often festooned with the heads of unfortunate citizens who had either fallen from favour or perpetrated some dreadful deed. Lord Scrope (died 1414), the Duke of York (died 1460) and the Earl of Northumberland were some of the distinguished victims.

Micklegate was part of the major route between London and Scotland and has continued to be one of the most important streets of the city over many centuries. York's leading citizens have lived here since the Middle Ages when the street's proximity to the riverside quays suited the merchants. Royal visitors used to enter through Micklegate Bar, with the exception of Henry VIII, who insisted on entering through Bootham Bar, nearest the Minster, perhaps making a point about his new status as Head of the Church of England. Micklegate retained its importance over the years and was certainly considered the most fashionable street in the eighteenth and nineteenth centuries. It remains an attractive street today, with some fine eighteenth-century and medieval buildings. A number of good second-hand bookshops and antiques emporiums are a pleasure to browse in and when you have had enough of that, Blake Head Bookshop and Vegetarian Café, half-way up Micklegate, is a cheerful place for coffee or lunch.

To complete the circuit of the walls, you pass the rows of Victorian terraces built for the railway workers by George Hudson who introduced great prosperity to York with his expansion of the railways in the mid-1830s.

York Story and the Guildhalls

Having established an idea of the geography of the city, a good place to visit next is the **York Story Museum** (open all year, daily 10 to 5). Housed in the skilfully converted medieval St Mary's church, the exhibition takes you through a thousand years of York's history with the aid of video, informative display panels, murals and reconstructed scenes.

The Merchant Adventurers' Guild Hall (open Apr to Nov, daily, 8.30 to 5; Nov to Mar, daily 8.30 to 3) in Piccadilly and the **Merchant Taylors' Hall** (infrequent openings; the hall is often booked for private functions) in Aldwark are buildings that form part of the town's commercial history. The guilds' role as regulators of the companies and trades have altered somewhat since medieval times and the exhibitions in their fine old halls explain their present-day function. The Merchant Adventurers' timbered Great Hall is hung with the banners of medieval guilds and portraits of York dignitaries; the ancient Undercroft was used as a hospital until the nineteenth century. The Merchant Taylors' Hall has a four-teenth-century arch-braced roof within the seventeenth-century exterior; it is still used by the Company of Merchant Taylors.

St Anthony's Hall on Peasholme Green is now part of the research department of York University but you can visit during working hours and see the huge 81-ft long hall which was used as a meeting-place for over sixty of the city's lesser guilds, whose finances didn't stretch to having their own halls.

York Minster

The Minster rises over the city, and its bold outline can be seen from miles around in the Vale of York. The cathedral in the Minster Close has been an important religious centre since the fourth century. The word 'minster' comes from the Latin Monasterium, corrupted into the Old-English 'mynster'. Its foundations surmount the fortress of Roman times; what you see now is an enormous Gothic structure.

This beautiful building has a remarkable history of survival: three fires, two world wars and a most alarming discovery, in 1967, that the central tower was threatening to collapse. The brilliance of the engineering work, carried out between 1967 and 1972, can be appreciated by visiting the **Foundations Museum** (accessible from the south transept); a concrete collar was inserted at the base of the central tower to preserve the cathedral for at least another 500 years. Also here is a fascinating model which shows the extent and layout of the original Roman fortress headquarters, as revealed beneath the Norman cathedral foundations. You can then inspect the actual remains of both these structures as they intersect.

The Treasury contains a collection of church and domestic silver, dating from the eleventh century and priceless items such as the Horn of Ulf (given to the Minster in the time of King Canute). The **crypt**, entered from the south choir aisle, dates from Norman times and is the earliest part of the present

Minster. A cavernous space supported by columns, it contains the font which stands on the site of the seventh-century wooden church built for King Edwin of Northumbria. Queen Ethelburga, Edwin's wife; Paulinus, the first bishop of the See of York; Hilde, Edwin's great niece, later to become the Abbess of Whitby, and Edwin himself are all featured on the font cover. Bright modern paintings of King Edwin, Paulinus and St Hilde hanging behind the three altars were commissioned by the Dean and Chapter and the Yorkshire Arts Council in 1979.

The most recent damage to the Minster occurred in 1984 when lightning struck the south transept. It was thought by some to be an 'act of God' as retribution for contentious statements made at that time by the Bishop of Durham. The fire destroyed the south transept roof and vaulting, the heat cracking but, miraculously, not breaking the glass of the Rose Window; this, along with its original thirteenth-century stone tracery, has been beautifully restored and reinforced by the York Glaziers Trust. Some historians speculate that the glass in the Rose Window could originally have been grisaille (a silver-grey glass in geometrical patterns interspersed with colour) to complement the Five Sisters Window in the north transept, which is the largest and finest of its type in the world.

There are, literally, thousands of other things to look out for in the Cathedral. The subjects for the replacement roof bosses in the south transept were chosen by local children to depict the most important modern events; a cleverly slanted mirror lets you identify Armstrong landing on the moon without cricking your neck. The off-centred stone choir-screen displays the stylised figures of English kings from William I to Henry VI which sport an interesting variety of expressions.

The fabulous octagonal **Chapter House** (separate entry off the north transept), in Decorated Gothic style, is unique in that it has no central supporting pillar. The variety of carvings round the capitals are also remarkable: look out for the sniggering monkey with his hand over his mouth and some scary-looking birds squatting on the heads of panic-stricken individuals. The Dean and Chapter publish their own guidebook to York Minster, which is on sale at the Minster Bookshop; the only areas not covered in this guidebook are the Foundations Museum and the Treasury for which there is a guide included with the entrance fee. You could spend hours in the cathedral in order to see everything, or do it in stages, dropping in for half an hour whenever you pass.

The Minster requires a large administrative band of people to help carry out its various functions and many of them live and work in the cathedral close. The main services are Anglican but other denominations frequently hold services here and together with its use as a centre for arts and music, it functions very much at the centre of the community.

The Minster Close

In an attempt to recreate a kind of peace around the Minster, Deangate has been permanently closed to traffic. **St William's College** (open all year, Mon to Sat 10 to 5 (4 in winter), Sun 11 to 5; closed 24 to 26 Dec and Good Fri) houses an exhibition entitled 'The World of the Minster'. The fifteenth-century building is a fitting location for the excellent audio–visual display explaining clearly the role of the Minster and its part in the community. Access to the courtyard is free but there is a charge for visiting the medieval rooms and the exhibition. Next door to the college, the **National Trust tea-rooms** are a light and quiet place to refresh flagging energies.

Another interesting building in this area is the **Treasurer's House** (National Trust, open Apr to Oct, daily 10.30 to 5, last admission 4.30). The earliest parts of the house date from the sixteenth century when it was probably built for the Treasurer, but after the confiscation of the Minster's treasure in 1547, William Cliff, the then treasurer, declared himself redundant. Frank Green bought the house in 1897 by which time it had been altered, added to and finally divided into a number of separate dwellings. He was an idiosyncratic individual – a perfectionist and almost obsessively tidy: you can see the studs he had fixed in the floor to mark the precise spot for each piece of furniture. Just opposite the entrance to Gray's Court (the section at the back of the Treasurer's House), on the corner of Chapter Street and Ogleforth, look out for an exceptional little house with gables and mirrored, mullion windows and an overhanging upper floor.

City centre

Most of the centre of York is for pedestrians only during daytime hours. The lack of traffic makes wandering round extremely pleasant and gives the visitor plenty of time to appreciate the plethora of historic features in every street. **Stonegate** is one of the richest. It was the Via Praetoria in Roman times, leading to the heart of the fortress town, but was later named Stonegate when the stones for the construction of the Minster were hauled down it. The sign of the most ancient pub in the city, the Olde Starre Inn, hangs boldly the width of the street and a few doors down is the red carved figure of the printer's devil, crouching above the entrance to Coffee Yard. (In medieval times the trades used to concentrate in particular areas, sharing special needs as well as keeping an eye on the competition). The printer's devil is a real devil, but the name was given to the most junior apprentice in the shop. Stonegate opens out into **St Helen's Square** where the haunting wail of the evening newspaper-seller, crying 'Press' in a weary Yorkshire drawl, sometimes competes with a flute-playing student. The grand façade of the eighteenth-century **Mansion House**, thought to be designed by William Etty, is the residence of the current Lord Mayor. Next door, the fifteenth-century **Guildhall**, now completely rebuilt, was one of the many fine buildings destroyed on 29 April 1942, when the Germans delivered a devastating attack on York. A good place to stop and watch the action in the square is Betty's; though not cheap, it is a good place for a superior snack-lunch, tea or coffee.

Heading down towards the river from St Helen's Square via Lendal brings you opposite the entrance to the **Museum Gardens**, a lovely ten-acre park which stretches from Bootham Bar down to the River Ouse; the distinguished ruins of St Mary's Abbey, the Multangular Tower and St Leonard's Hospital, as well as the mature gardens, make this area popular with locals and visitors alike. The main attraction here, however, is the **Yorkshire Museum** (open Mar to Oct, daily 10 to 5; Nov to Mar, Mon to Sat, 10 to 5; Sun 1 to 5, last admission 4.30). This displays a remarkable collection of archaeology, geology, natural history and pottery. Exhibits are well-planned and start with the Romans' arrival in the north and the establishment of Eboracum. Their way of life, fashions, jewellery and cuisine are shown in detail. The Anglo-Saxon and Viking periods are equally well tackled, including an interesting cross-section of a Viking ship. Another section explains the building of St Mary's Abbey. The main ruins of the Abbey are in the garden, but further excavation in the basement of the museum has unearthed parts of the vestibule and entrance to the Chapter House. These sections have been faithfully reconstructed and, with taped monastic voices drifting around the ancient walls, you can get a good idea of what life was like in the ancient Abbey.

Many local finds are displayed and one of the most exciting pieces, and only recently acquired, is the Middleham Jewel.

The finest piece of English Gothic jewellery to be found this century, it is a diamond-shaped pendant with a large oblong sapphire in front, discovered in North Yorkshire in 1985.

Exhibition Square at the end of St Leonard's Place by Bootham Bar is a good central meeting-place with the Tourist Office, the Theatre Royal, the City Art Gallery and King's Manor. You can wander into the lovely cobbled courtyards of **King's Manor**, which is now part of York University. A proud statue of William Etty presides over Exhibition Square. Very much a revered son of York, where he also died, he was almost entirely responsible for saving the city walls. In 1825 the order was given to start demolishing them as it was considered that the city had outgrown the confines of its medieval past. William Etty canvassed frantically for their survival, for which he is remembered with gratitude. **The City Art Gallery** (open all year, Mon to Sat 10 to 5, Sun 2.30 to 5, last admission 4.30; closed 1 Jan, Good Fri, 25, 26 Dec) has many of Etty's works, as well as those of other English painters from the sixteenth to twentieth century, and European paintings from 1350 onwards.

From Exhibition Square, one of the other main streets of Roman Eboracum leads up from Bootham Bar to the Minster. The Via Principalis, **High Petergate**, is still one of the main approach roads to the cathedral, but the street is now full of souvenir shops, restaurants and tea-shops; to the east, off Low Petergate and approached through the snickleway (medieval alleyway) of Hornpot Lane, the now redundant tiny church of **Holy Trinity** rests in an unexpected haven of calm. Believed to date from 1082, altered and extended between the thirteenth and fifteenth centuries, it has uneven box pews and an oddly sloping floor. From the tiny churchyard the gate leads out into **Goodramgate** where you are jolted back into the present by a row of ugly '60s shops, which must be the most uncomfortable buildings in York. A few yards further down the street, a row of small fourteenth-century houses with overhanging upper floors, known as Lady Row, restores the equilibrium.

Across nearby King's Square, the **Shambles**, with the upper storeys of its Tudor houses overhanging, was originally the street of the butchers: Fleshammels. It is hard to imagine this narrow, curving street lined with wooden counters, meat covered with flies, and rats and dogs attracted by the open sewer running down the centre. Smells today are of home-made sweets and pot-pourri and crowds amble about and browse in tiny shop doorways. One of the city's Catholic martyrs lived here; St Margaret Clitheroe, married to a butcher, was pressed to death under stone weights for harbouring Catholics in the 1580s. Her rather disappointingly bland shrine can be visited at No. 35 (although other evidence suggests she lived in a house opposite). The daily open-air market is just beside the Shambles, reached either through one of the many snickleways, or via Little Shambles.

Castle Area

All that remains of the original castle are parts of the curtain wall, the towers of the castle bailey and, the largest ruin, **Clifford's Tower** (English Heritage, open Good Fri or 1 Apr, whichever is earlier, to end Sept, daily 10 to 6; Oct to Maundy Thur or 31 Mar, whichever is earlier, daily 10 to 4; closed 24 to 26 Dec, 1 Jan). This thirteenth-century limestone tower, the keep of the York Castle, was built to replace the wooden tower that was destroyed in 1190 when Jews fled to take refuge here (see page 000); the incident is commemorated at the base of the tower. Steep steps lead to the courtyard of the tower and a further climb on to the upper walls gives impressive views of the city.

The other buildings in the area within the original castle bailey – the Debtors' Prison, the Assize Courts and the Female Prison – are an imposing group, the latter two built by the prestigious York architect, John Carr (1725–1807). The two prison buildings have been converted into the large **Castle Museum** (open Apr to Oct, Mon to Sat 9.30 to 5.30, Sun 10 to 5.30; Nov to Mar, Mon to Sat 9.30 to 4, Sun 10 to 4). Dr John Kirk originally conceived the idea of the museum. He had collected everyday household objects such as keys, locks, fireplaces, and so on, and wanted to preserve a way of life he saw rapidly disappearing. These ordinary things are displayed along with the large household goods section. Exhibits include a vintage collection of early radios and television sets that leave computer-age children staring in disbelief. Close to the entrance of the museum, a Victorian street, Kirkgate (after the famous doctor) has been reconstructed with cobbles, street lanterns and all the old shops including a forge.

One of the newest additions to the museum is the York Helmet, discovered in 1982 during the Jorvik excavations. It is only the third Anglo-Saxon helmet ever found. There is almost too much to take in at one visit – if you have the time to take it slowly, stopping in the café for lunch or tea, or having a picnic out at the restored flour-mill (part of the museum but outside down by the river), it is a fascinating way to spend three or four hours. During school term-time the place can be packed with streams of children so try and start early if you want a fairly free run; long queues build up during holiday weekends too.

Just across the road from Clifford's Tower is a small area of parkland leading down to the river, and beside the park-gate in Tower Street is the **Museum of Automata** (open all year, daily 9.30 to 5.30). An introductory video opens up the world of mechanised objects and you can watch the figures in these inspired musical boxes perform their tricks. In the gallery of modern automata visitors are invited to play with the exhibits: turning handles and pressing buttons set the pieces in motion. Part of the pleasure is trying out the machines, so avoid peak times.

The **Regimental Museum** (open all year, Mon to Thur 9.30 to 4.30, Fri 9.30 to 3.30), also in Tower Street, is strictly for the specialist. A thorough collection of gleaming memorabilia of the 4th/7th Dragoon Guards and the Prince of Wales's Own Regiment is lovingly displayed.

National Railway Museum

Leeman Road (open all year, exc 24 to 26 Dec, 1 Jan, Mon to Sat 10 to 6, Sun 11 to 6) Displayed in the old York North Motive Power Depot, the popular museum tells the story of British railways up to the present day. The rise and fall of George Hudson and the effect of the railways on York is all well documented and clearly exhibited. In the South Hall, part of the old station, different trains are lined up along each platform: the extraordinary opulence of some of the royal trains, and the old mail trains, are only a tiny part of the whole huge exhibition which can keep visitors here for hours. In the Great Hall, the main display of numerous engines and rolling stock, all with full explanatory panels, are laid out over the two acres. Gleaming engines and the use of recorded steam train and railway station noises help recreate the full romance of the railways. A café spreads casually across a couple of the platforms and there are hot dogs and burgers on sale outside the South Hall.

Jorvik Viking Centre

(Open all year, Apr to end Oct, daily 9 to 7; Nov to end Mar, daily 9 to 5.30) This superb complex is a combination of a ghost-train ride and an archaeological theme park. It is built around the underground excavations of the Viking street of Coppergate. While above ground the modern Coppergate Shopping Centre buzzes with activity, below, visitors to Jorvik Viking Centre travel back 1,000 years sitting in a silently moving Time Car with the voice of Magnus Magnusson whispering history in their ears. Viking Coppergate is a meticulously reconstructed street, complete with models of the people, sounds and smells of those times. As you move through the ancient town all aspects of Viking life are portrayed, playing children, home hearths, shouting sailors, pungent spices or stinking fish, even a privy.

The car then travels forward in time to 1980 showing the archaeological excavations and how mere foundations and traces of things can reveal the colourful way of life just witnessed. The exhibition continues with a walk through the reconstructed laboratories of York Archaelogical Trust, where models diligently analyse their finds.

The museum is one of York's most popular attractions. Its often huge queues seem to disappear miraculously about an hour before closing time – a good time to pick.

Other museums

In a small area around Clifford Street and Castlegate is another clutch of excellent museums.
● **Fairfax House** (open Mar to Jan, Mon to Sat 11 to 5, Sun 1.30 to 5; closed Fri), Castlegate. This fine eighteenth-century house, with the interior designed by Carr of York, was saved from collapse by the York Civic Trust and restored to its former glory in the early 1980s. It had become part of a cinema and latterly a dance hall with all its best decorative features plastered or painted over. This must have acted as an effective preservative because the result of the restoration job is outstanding. In addition, Noel G Terry donated his excellent collection of eighteenth-century English furniture and clocks for display in the house.
● **Friargate Museum** (open all year, daily 10 to 5), Lower Friargate. A lot of trouble has been taken to make this museum interesting and educational. The waxwork figures range from Alfred the Great to George V, creating a kind of visual history lesson. An annually changing themed area may represent a country, its culture and people; other display groups of the British royal family, world state leaders and famous sportsmen and women are changed regularly. The museum is run with a keenness and imaginative humour that is infectious, with little tests to keep even the most sceptical visitor alert.

- **York Dungeon** (open Easter to 31 Aug, daily 10 to 5.30; Sept to Easter, daily 10 to 5), 12 Clifford Street. Not a musuem for the squeamish or nervous. Many of the exhibits are extremely grim and alarmingly realistic; the effects are heightened by evocative sounds and the appropriate settings. The tour takes you along narrow passages in musty, dusty cellars where unexpected changes in light and ground-level leave you insecure and all the more vulnerable to the gory torture scenes eerily illuminated in unexpected corners. Scenes range from vivid manifestations of death by boiling or drowning, to the pathos of the Minster Dog, Seamus, whose ineffectual barking can be heard from behind his bricked up prison. Even the attendants are deathly white.
- **Bar Convent Museum** (open all year, exc Jan, Tue to Sat 10 to 5 and Bank Hols), Blossom Street, charts the development of Christianity in York. It is an inspiring story of the faith and courage shown by a group of women, particularly its founder, Mary Ward. Born in Yorkshire, she had a vocation to dedicate her life to God, but did not want to be incarcerated in a seventeenth-century convent. There is an excellent 45-minute video taking you through the story of her battle with the Roman hierarchy and her final success in the setting up of Catholic girls schools all over Europe. The whole story is then repeated in a visual display throughout the house. The building itself is remarkable with a fine tiled courtyard, glazed over in the nineteenth century, and with a light room, now used as an excellent café, off to one side. The hidden chapel at the back of the house is much restored but has charm and serenity. The seventeenth-century priest's hiding hole and relic of St Margaret of York's hand, both in the chapel, can be seen on request.

NORTH OF YORK

The countryside to the north-west of the city is flat, with the River Ouse and the River Nidd threading their way across the Vale, meeting just to the south of Beningbrough Hall. Driving around this area you are quite likely to suddenly find yourself at a dead-end: the road ends usually in a village but sometimes it just peters out; the feeling is that of a forgotten land.

Due west of York on the B1224, a turning off by **Long Marston** in the direction of **Tockwith** takes you past the site of the battle of Marston Moor fought between the Royalists and Parliamentarians in 1644. Continue through a series of small, pretty villages, including **Kirk Hammerton**, until the road ends at **Nun Monkton**. A huge green dominates the village, cattle graze freely and there's a small pond and blue-and-white-striped maypole, all surrounded by attractive houses of various periods. It is very peaceful and a wonderful spot for a picnic. The public right of way at the end of the village leads down to the Church of St Mary's, past the very pretty Priory and down to the river. Set at the confluence of the Nidd and the Ouse, the village is a lovely spot with romantic views of Beningbrough Hall across the Ouse in the distance.

Beningbrough Hall

(National Trust, open Apr to Nov, Tue to Thur, Sat, Sun, Good Fri, Bank Hol Mon, also Fri in July and Aug, 11 to 5.30 house, 11 to 5.30 grounds, shop and restaurant) The easiest approach to Beningbrough is to drive eight miles north-west of York, up the A19, although you can weave round the pretty back-roads and approach it via the Aldwark Toll Bridge off the B6265. Set just above the general level of the Ouse flood-plain, this large, red-brick, Georgian house was left to the National Trust in 1958. It needed much restoration, which was eventually completed in 1971. Baroque and Gothic influences can be seen in the lofty hall, similar to but not as grand as that at Castle Howard. The architect, William Thornton, worked at both houses. The cantilevered staircase is one of the finest interior features, with an unusually delicate balustrade. Over a hundred pictures are on loan from the National Gallery and if you are particularly keen to see them, as well as the interior detail, avoid dull days as some of the rooms have no electric lights. A cosily furnished reading room is a good place to catch up on the history of the house.

Two enclosed formal gardens have been created in the previously overgrown grounds, one in the style of a seven-teenth-century knot garden. Beyond these small formal gardens is another picnic area. The old courtyard is surrounded by pale-pink brick buildings, one of which houses the Victorian Laundry. The Hall is a particularly good place to take children: as well as the restaurant/café with indoor and outdoor eating spaces and the picnic area, there is a well-planned adventure playground positioned at a discreet distance from the house so the shrieks of delight don't reach the other visitors.

Easingwold and around

The flat plain of York rises into the Howardian Hills to the north with the dark outline of the moors in the distance. Further north along the A19, Easingwold's cobbled market-square is dominated by the Town Hall, currently occupied by a printing firm, and surrounded with shops, a bank, and pretty houses. A number of pubs, a hotel and a couple of cafés makes this a good stopping-point.

East of Easingwold, **Crayke Castle** (not open to the public) occupies a lovely position with the village and fifteenth-century church below. A few miles north, **Newburgh Priory and Gardens** (open May to end Aug, Wed and Sun 2.30 to 4.45; grounds 2 to 6) is a beautiful house set back from the road; its ornate gate and railings are guarded by two little square lodges. The house, dating from 1145, has Tudor, Jacobean and Georgian additions and a fine water-garden. The 'Ducks Crossing' sign prepares you for the mass of birds straying across the road from the lake.

The drive from **Yearsley**, which belonged to Newburgh Priory estate until 1944, to **Ampleforth** gives the best view of Ampleforth School and its famous Abbey ranged along the foothills of the Moors. Founded by a Benedictine monk in 1802, it is now one of the largest Catholic schools in the country. The modern Abbey, designed by Sir Giles Gilbert Scott who was also the architect of Liverpool Cathedral and St Pancras Station, remains the magnificent centrepiece of the school. In nearby **Gilling East**, the castle has become a preparatory school for Ampleforth, but the golf course, gardens, hall and Great Chamber are open to the public during the summer. The magnificent, elaborate oak-panelled wainscoting, painted frieze and fine painted glass windows must make this one of the grandest school dining-rooms in the country, though the low tables and ordinary school tumblers look a touch self-conscious. The entrance is unmarked except by two stone gate-posts on the main road and is easy to miss.

The only drawback to the otherwise immaculate village of **Hovingham** is the B1257 road running through the centre. The main feature here is the Palladian Hovingham Hall (open by appointment only Apr to Sept, Tue, Wed, Thur 11 to 7; write to the Secretary, Hovingham Hall, York YO6 4LU), designed by Thomas Worsley in 1760 and still lived in by the Worsley family (the present Duchess of Kent was born here). All around the rest of the village the greens are neatly kept, the gardens exquisite and the houses look freshly white-washed or are covered with climbing roses. A meandering stream completes the picture.

Nunnington Hall

(National Trust, open Apr to Nov, Apr weekends, 2–6 May, June, Sept, Oct, Tue to Thur, Sat and Sun 2 to 6; July and Aug, Tue to Thur 2 to 6, Sat, Sun and Bank Hol Mon 12 to 6 (last admissions 5) In a wonderful setting on the banks of the River Rye, with an unusual walled garden, the house was donated to the National Trust in 1952 by Mrs Ronald Fife. It dates from the Elizabethan and Stuart periods. Some of the furniture came with the house, other pieces have been brought in. The Oak Hall with its fine panelling and three-arched screen to the Great Staircase were once painted over and the signs of stripping are still evident. A notable feature both inside, above the doors and fireplaces, and outside the house, is the use of the broken pediment (the upper arch is left unjoined), thought to be based on a design by the French architect Jean Barbet. Some of the upstairs rooms like the Oak Bedroom are on the gloomy side with very dark panelling, but there are some fine pieces of furniture and a collection of Varley watercolours. The attics have been restored and house the fascinating and exquisite Carlisle Collection of Miniature Period Rooms assembled by Mrs F M Carlisle over forty years and brought to Nunnington in 1981 from Grey's Court in York.

Nunnington village stretches up the hillside from the packhorse bridge over the River Rye. It is a quiet, peaceful place with a post office, said to be the smallest in the country, and houses ranged along high grassy banks with plants tumbling over drystone walls. The Royal Oak pub is tucked into the row of houses leading up to the thirteenth-century church; the oak lectern and west screen are both modern, carved by Mousey Thompson of Kilburn (see p105). A few miles to the south-east, the village of **Slingsby** spreads down from the main road with its centrepiece of a red-and-white-striped maypole on the village green. It is still used on Mayday and other festive occasions. The ruin close to the church, half-hidden by overgrown plants, is that of **Slingsby Castle** which was never completed and only ever used as a farm building. Turn off the B1257 at Slingsby and head for Welburn. This is the best way to approach Castle Howard.

Castle Howard

(Open Mar to Nov, daily 10 to last admission 4.30) The first sight of Castle Howard, set on the hillside above the lake, is breathtaking. As the name suggests, this eighteenth-century palace was built for Charles Howard, 3rd Earl of Carlisle. His descendants still live here. One of the extraordinary facts about Castle Howard is that it was designed by the playwright Sir John Vanburgh who had no previous architectural experience. The east and central sections of the house were gutted by fire in 1940 and renovation was only started over the last decade. There is an interesting exhibition showing all the work that has been carried out both inside the house and in the grounds: the clearing of all the waterways, fountains and reservoirs, and the renovation of the cascade and bridges. It is possible to spend hours here wandering around the lakes, the woodland garden, and the formal walled garden. You can walk around the grounds to the stables, designed by the famous Yorkshire architect John Carr, Vanburgh's romantic Temple of the Four Winds, and Nicholas Hawksmoor's splendid Mausoleum. It is a magical place, the only twentieth-century encroachments being the tea-room and toilet signs. At the end of the walled garden, close to the greenhouses, there is a well-planned adventure playground and by the entrance to the park the stables now house the Castle Howard Costume Galleries.

Malton and around

By-passed by the A64, the town is still a thoroughfare for a lot of heavy traffic. The livestock markets here are the third-largest in England: fatstock on Tuesdays and store market on Fridays. The area was settled in Roman times and the site of the old fort and outline of the ramparts can still be seen in Orchard Field off Old Maltongate.

The street names – Wheelgate, Yorkersgate, Maltongate and Castlegate date back to the Middle Ages when Malton was a walled town. At the bottom of Castlegate the County Bridge crosses the Derwent. This bridge used to mark the border between the North and East Ridings but now only denotes the boundary between Malton and its neighbour, Norton. The main square, **Market Place**, has a range of slightly faded buildings with some eighteenth-century façades; some are earlier. The Old Town Hall, now housing the Tourist Information Centre, and the **Museum** are on one side of the square, while the Milton Rooms, a building of little beauty used for local events, dances and concerts, takes up the opposite side. St Michael's church sits squarely in the centre. The Museum has an exhibition on Malton's Roman history and a section devoted to the development of the town. A fun alphabet of local trade and industry is illustrated with the appropriate products and tools.

The Square and Wheelgate are the two main shopping areas with various quirky shops tucked down the side lanes. The Lanes Shopping Mall, converted from the nineteenth-century Corn Exchange in Yorkersgate, has an odd mixture of little stalls including an antique shop, and a couple of boutiques, all built to resemble an old-fashioned shopping street. Market day (for everything but cattle) is Saturday when the whole square is transformed with bustling activity and crowded stalls.

Just outside Malton to the north, signposted off the A169, is **Eden Camp** (open 14 Feb to 23 Dec, daily 10 to 5). Built as a Prisoner of War Camp in 1942, it has been turned into an extraordinary War Museum. In each of the 29 former prisoner huts a wartime scene has been reconstructed with the help of models, sound effects and smells. Lighting and smoke are also used to good effect. The displays are extremely realistic in every single detail, portraying the Blitz, the U-Boat Menace, Bomber Command Operations Room and so on. Some of the huts are used for more practical purposes: 'Prisoners Canteen' (Naafi), Souvenir Emporium and Toilets. An assault course has been built for children to simulate army training. The aim of the museum is stated to be 'A Tribute to the People of World War ll – Lest we Forget'. It would be difficult after visiting Eden Camp.

At the other extreme, a few hundred yards down the same road, is **Eden Working Farm** (open daily 10 to last admission 4.30). Visitors can go into the 'pets paddock', participate in 'Feeding time for the Lambs' and make friends with goats, piglets, calves and poultry. A comprehensive exhibition, well displayed and labelled, tells the story of traditional farm crops from seed, through harvest to the product in the shop.

Back on the A169 about 4 miles north of Malton, there's a turning off to Kirby Misperton and **Flamingoland Zoo and Funpark** (open Mar to Oct, daily 10 to 5). Entrance is quite expensive and some of the areas look a bit run down, but it is a huge complex of white-knuckle rides, helter-skelters, water rides, performing dolphins and sealions, a small zoo area and slot-machine galleries, plus numerous fast food outlets. Set in low-lying area the Funpark has little protection on a windy day and not much shade from the sun.

A few miles south of Malton at **Whitwell-on-the-Hill**, Kirkham Priory (open 1 Apr to 30 Sept, daily 10 to 6, Oct to Mar, Tue to Sat 10 to 4; closed Dec 24 to 26, 1 Jan) is set in a peaceful, secluded position beside the River Derwent. The Priory was founded by the Augustinian Order in the twelfth century and enlarged over the next 200 years. The thirteenth-century gatehouse and cloister arches are very fine.

Along the back-roads to the west you come across **Sheriff Hutton** village with the remains of the castle looming over the wide main street. If you visit **Sheriff Hutton House and Park** (open Mon to Fri 10 to 4.30) anything could happen. While admiring the ornate Jacobean ceiling in the Bird and Baby room, sounds of a struggle may be heard in another room; muffled screams filter out from one of the out-houses and as you wander in the garden, you might see an SS officer at the window. You may burst in on Anthony and Cleopatra in the Ballroom before finally realising you're here with the E15 Acting School who are on one of their regular workshops. The house is interesting but, sadly, in a poor state of repair and the gardens and woods informal.

Joining the B1363 at the ancient village of **Stillington** where Laurence Sterne was vicar in 1745, and heading back towards York, you reach **Sutton-on-the-Forest**. **Sutton Park** (open Easter weekend, May to Sept, Wed, Sun and Bank Hol Mon, 1.30 to 5.30), in spite of a rather unpromising approach, turns out to be an attractive, red-brick Georgian house full of beautiful English and French furniture, paintings and a collection of porcelain. The gardens around are a lovely mixture of wild and formal, leading in tiers up to the front door. The atmosphere is one of charming informality.

SOUTH OF YORK

The area to the south of York is generally fen-like with the Rivers Derwent, Ouse and Wharfe flowing across it. Not far from the city to the south-east, off the B1228, is the **Yorkshire Air Museum** (open Easter to Oct, Tue to Thur 11 to 4, Sat 2 to 5, Sun and Bank Hols 11 to 4), for World War II veterans and enthusiasts. More worthwhile is the **Yorkshire Museum of Farming**, three miles down the A64 at Murton (open all year, daily 9.30 to 5.30, last admission 5). The main display in a huge converted barn is of nineteenth-century and early-twentieth-century tools so arranged as to emphasise the rural calendar. A reconstruction of an agricultural village from the Dark Ages should be finished in 1992 and there are also plans to introduce a working station with diesel locomotives taking visitors along half-a-mile of track from Layerthorpe station.

Selby

The town is built on the southern banks of the River Ouse and was reputedly the birthplace of Henry I. Riverside walks take you past the port and ship-building yards. It is apparently the only place in England where ships are launched sideways.

The huge **Abbey**, a prominent sight from all round the town, was founded in 1069 by a monk, Benedict of Auxerre. It is 300-feet long and 55-feet wide, giving it cathedral-like proportions; it is at present undergoing extensive restoration due to rising damp in the limestone parts of the building. The rot has been caused by the high water table in Selby and the lack of an effective damp-resisting course in the Abbey. You can still appreciate the fine Norman doors and the eight tall Norman arches in the nave. The East Window features the 'Stem of Jesse', the family tree of the Kings of Israel, and the fourteenth-century Washington Window, high up in the choir, which displays the Washington Family arms and is the model for the present-day American flag. John de Washington was a Prior at the Abbey in the fourteenth century and can be traced from the same family tree as George Washington.

Abbey Place, just outside the confines of the Abbey, has a little patch of shady greenery around the Cholera Burial Ground for victims of the epidemic in 1848–9. Benedict's Delicatessen and Tea Rooms here is a good place for a drink and a rest. Opposite the Abbey gates the Market Place is identified by the market-cross. Quite a restricted area, with the road running alongside it and up the main street, the market sometimes spills out behind the Londesborough Arms Hotel. Apart from the Abbey and the Port, there is little else to keep you in Selby.

Six miles south of Selby, **Carlton Towers**, the Yorkshire home of the Duke of Norfolk, is a vast Victorian Gothic house, and still a family home. The present building was begun in 1614 and completely remodelled between 1871 and 1877. Although it has been open to the public on Sundays and Bank Holidays (May to September) for the last fifteen years, there are plans to only open the house on selected occasions from 1993; tel (0405) 861662 for details.

Between Selby and Tadcaster on the B1223, the charming village of **Cawood** is a good place to stop for lunch. A couple of pubs offer food which can then be walked off along the banks of the Ouse, past the terraced brick riverside cottages and some rather grander seventeenth- and eighteenth-century houses. Visit the lovely Norman church at the far end of the village, very much part of the community, with lots of crafts and children's contributions on display. Cawood Castle, no longer inhabited and right in the centre of the village, was the residence of the Archbishop of York from AD930 until the thirteenth century.

Tadcaster

About ten miles west of York, this town has an understated appeal. Founded by the Romans, it is nowadays known for its breweries and the old rivalries of Samuel and his nephew, John Smith. Samuel Smith's brewery has remained independent while John Smith's merged first with Courage and was later sold on to Elders IXL. Visitors can visit Samuel Smith's brewery and tours take place all year, Monday to Thursday at 11, 2, and 7; telephone for reservations and bookings, (0937) 832225 x351. There are a number of pubs in town with loyalty to one or the other of the breweries. The main centre of town is very small with an odd collection of shops leading up from the bridge and some attractive eighteenth-century houses by the river or along the main street and in the square behind. The red-brick building with white columns that stands out next to the Angel and White Horse public house is the headquarters of Sam Smith's brewery. The market-place doubles up as the car park and, at the end of Kirkgate, **St Mary's Parish church** has some good fifteenth- and sixteenth-century stained-glass and a leafy graveyard stretching down to the banks of the Wharfe. The riverside walk to the Wharfe viaduct and weir a few hundred yards up-river is lined with willow and cherry trees.

A few miles south-west of Tadcaster, **Lotherton Hall, Park and Bird Garden** (tel. (0532) 813259 for the Hall, and 813723 for the Bird Garden; the gardens and parkland are open all year, daily dawn to dusk) is a modest Edwardian museum with good Oriental art and a mini zoo; it is particularly strong on birds and is popular with schoolchildren.

WHERE TO STAY

HAROME

The Pheasant
Harome, Nr Helmsley YO6 5JG
TEL (0439) 71241
This cosy, family-run hotel
makes an ideal base for touring
the North York Moors area as
well as visiting York. Beamed
restaurant and bar.
£££ *Mar to Nov; 44 rooms; Access,
Amex, Diners, Visa*

HOVINGHAM

The Worsley Arms Hotel
Hovingham, York YO6 4LA
TEL (0653) 628234
A lovely old coaching-inn in this
extremely pretty village.
Tastefully decorated and with a
good but quite expensive
restaurant; good value,
enterprising bar food.
££ *All year; 23 rooms; Access,
Amex, Visa*

NUNNINGTON

Ryedale Lodge
Station Road, Nunnington
YO6 5XB
TEL (043 95) 246
This low-slung hotel used to be
Nunnington station in the 1920s.
Set in the middle of open
countryside, there are great views
from the comfortable bedrooms.
Friendly owners and an excellent
restaurant.
££ *All year exc 2 weeks in Jan; 7
rooms; Access, Visa*

SHERIFF HUTTON

Rangers House
Sheriff Hutton Park, Sheriff
Hutton YO6 1RH

TEL (03477) 397
In a very rural setting close to the
Sheriff Hutton House and Park,
this is a very relaxed place, with
antiques, parquet floors and
paintings.
£ *All year; 6 rooms*

YORK

Middlethorpe Hall
Bishopthorpe Road, York
YO2 1QB
TEL (0904) 641241
Fax (0904) 620176
A beautiful William III house.
You can rely on the comfort,
civilised atmosphere, high-quality
furnishings, antiques and good
food. And you will pay
handsomely for it.
£££ *All year; 29 rooms; Access,
Amex, Diners, Visa*

Mount Royale
The Mount, York YO2 2DA
TEL (0904) 628856
Fax (0904) 611171
About ten minutes' walk from
Micklegate Bar on the A64, this
Gothic-façaded hotel is unusual.
Family-run for many years, the
atmosphere is homely and
welcoming. It is overflowing with
plants both inside and in the
lovely garden.
££ *All year exc 1 week at Chr; 22
rooms; Access, Amex, Diners, Visa*

Holmwood House Hotel
Holgate Road, York YO2 4BB
TEL (0904) 626183 Fax (0904)
670899
About fifteen minutes' walk to
Micklegate Bar, this is a very
well-decorated, pristine, bed-and-
breakfast hotel. Christina and
Roberto Gramellini run it with

care and sophistication and provide delicious breakfasts that include plenty of coffee. Rooms on the back are much quieter.

£ *All year; 12 rooms; Access, Visa*

Curzon Lodge & Stable Cottages
23 Tadcaster Road, Dringhouses,
York YO2 2QG
TEL (0904) 703157

Overlooking the racecourse, on the A64, a short bus-ride from the centre. A small homely bed-and-breakfast hotel with a cosy dining-room and comfortable fairly simple bedrooms. A couple of restaurants are nearby.

£ *All year; 10 rooms; Access, Visa*

WHERE TO EAT

HELMSLEY

Black Swan
Market Place
TEL (0439) 70466
One of Forte's nicest Heritage hotels in a striking Georgian house with beams and panelling and a sheltered garden. Plain-cooked traditional lunches with more expensive dinners. Well-kept real ale.
All week 12–2, 7–9.30; Access, Amex, Diners, Visa

NUNNINGTON

Royal Oak
Church Street
TEL (043 95) 271
A friendly pub with good views from the small terrace. Decorated with collections of farm tools, copper jugs and old keys. Hearty food includes steak and kidney casserole with herb dumplings. Well-kept Theakstons.
All week 12–2 (exc Mon), 6.30–9

YORK

Betty's
6–8 St Helen's Square
TEL (0904) 659142
The most stylish of this chain of tea-rooms (see entries under

Harrogate and Northallerton and Ilkley). Excellent-quality food with higher than normal prices. Speciality teas and rare coffees to complement the tea-breads and scones. Evening dishes include chicken provençale, scrambled eggs and smoked salmon.
All week 9–9; Access, Visa

Ivy Restaurant, Grange Hotel
Clifton
TEL (0904) 644744
Very professional restaurant in a high-quality private hotel, originally a Regency town house. The Roux-trained chef produces well-sauced dishes such as saddle of venison with juniper sauce, and beef with madeira sauce.
All week, exc Sat L, 12.30–2.30, 7–10.15; Access, Amex, Diners, Visa

Kites
13 Grape Lane
TEL (0904) 641750
A not always consistent restaurant down an alley up a steep staircase. Décor is 'early Habitat', with cramped tables. Eclectic food, with dishes such as lamb with sorrel sauce, cod with tomato and pepper salsa; substantial puddings.
Mon to Sat 6.30–10.30, Sun 12–2; Access, Visa

Melton's
7 Scarcroft Road
TEL (0904) 634341
A small restaurant in a Victorian
terrace about a mile from the city
centre. The chef is Roux-trained
and his inventive style of cooking
reflects their influence. Generous
portions and attention to detail.
Rack of lamb and sea bass baked
with fennel are particularly
recommended. Well-kept British
and Irish cheeses.
*Tue to Sat 12.30–2, 7–10; Access,
Visa*

19 Grape Lane
19 Grape Lane
TEL (0904) 641750
Down a narrow lane near the
Minster, this cramped restaurant
serves light lunches and more
expensive dinners. Simple
presentation of dishes such as
collops of beef, medallions of
hare, with traditional treacle tart
or Eve's pudding to follow.
Tue to Sat 12.30–1.45, 7.30–10.30

SOUTH
YORKSHIRE

- The best of industrial history
- Mines, steel and cutlery
- Beautiful areas of countryside hidden close to large industrial cities
- Rich in ancient and historic churches

TORN abruptly from the former West Riding in 1974, South Yorkshire spent its formative years with all the appearances of a local government runt. Its 'capital' was the declining steel city of Sheffield whose enormous furnaces and foundries along the lower Don valley were in a sorry state. The ravaged scenery, dominated by two fat, stained power station chimneys, epitomised the cliché of a Gateway to the Grim North for uninitiated travellers from the South.

The rest of the county appeared little better: Barnsley equalled coal, Rotherham meant steel and Doncaster more coal, albeit with the gentry making their way from time to time to the horse races.

Over the last two decades, the landscape has undergone dramatic changes. The domes of a commercial Xanadu – the Meadowhall shopping centre – gleam alongside the Tinsley stretch of the M1. A green swathe of willows, shrubs and even fig trees lines a much cleaner River Don beneath the flyover. A little further north, the motorway switchbacks through woods, past fields of browsing deer and the classical façades of stately homes.

As these indicate, the grim and gritty image of South Yorkshire was never the whole truth. Ancient copses and poppy-red cornfields dominate hundreds of square miles of South Yorkshire; magnificent mansions like Wentworth Woodhouse stand gracefully in largely unspoilt parkland. For every workaday Grimethorpe there is an idyllic, slumbering Hooton Pagnell. With the decline of coal and other heavy industries, this older South Yorkshire is gradually coming back into its own. But you are still an explorer; it remains astonishingly little-known.

The locals share most of the traits of their fellow-Yorkshire people, even round Tickhill and lovely Roche Abbey, where the county merges almost imperceptibly into Nottinghamshire. The mining communities are the last fortress of 'thee-ing' and 'thou-ing', a dialect absorbing to eavesdrop on in a local pub. Very few visitors spend much time in towns like Mexborough or Bentley although Sir Nikolaus Pevsner was exceptionally thorough, and ecstatic, in his architectural survey of the many pithead bath buildings. Local spectaculars in this area include the World Coal-Carrying Championships held every Easter Monday at Gawthorpe, near Wakefield. The races attract a lot of South Yorkshire hopefuls for the five-minute dash: 1012.5 metres (1107 yards) uphill, from the Royal Oak to the maypole, carrying a 50-kilo sack of coal.

The coalfield dominates the central swathe of the county, as well as the politics of the 'Socialist Republic of South Yorkshire', as it is affectionately known, but the outlying areas are also distinctive. To the east, where the oozy lowlands sink gently towards the River Humber, pretty pinkish-brick villages shelter behind flood-defence dykes, and naturalists head for the rare peat habitat of waterlogged Thorne Waste. The west of the county crumples up into the Pennine foothills, with their craggy scenery, mills and chapels.

Geographically, South Yorkshire divides dramatically between the airy escarpments of the southern Pennines, which include a large slice of the Peak District National Park (see Chapter 8), and the gentler lower valleys of the Rivers Dearne, Don and Trent. But administratively the county is quartered between Sheffield, Doncaster, Rotherham and Barnsley. These divisions, upon which local tourist arrangements are largely based, are best for an introductory tour.

SHEFFIELD

If strength comes from the hills, as a biblical psalmist supposed, Sheffield's sturdy history owes much to the seven hills upon which it is built. This city of valleys and miniature mountains – one of them crowned, like a Yorkshire alp, with an elaborate network of artificial ski runs – is big and busy. Its many shopping streets are spread out over a large area and are exhausting if taken too swiftly or without a plan. It is also notoriously devoid of public lavatories, a failing recognised by the wooden spoon trophy from several consumer groups. The city is rightly praised for its green surroundings, splendid parks and several good museums. The central hill, above the Rivers Don and Sheaf (which gave Sheffield its name), is a muddle encircled by traffic whizzing along the inner ring road. Many streets are pedestrianised, but beware of the many ferocious buses, which are exempt from traffic restrictions.

The best place to make for is the **Tudor Square** 'cultural complex', tucked behind the **Town Hall**, with its statue of Vulcan, the Roman god of weapon-forging and allied iron-mongery, a fitting symbol of the city's long expertise in cutlery-making, silver-plating and the forging of steel. Friezes on the Town Hall also depict the craftsmen, buffers, grinders and platers of the steel industry whose works are displayed in the excellent industrial museums (and whose skill lives on in a much-reduced industry). Steelworkers are also

181

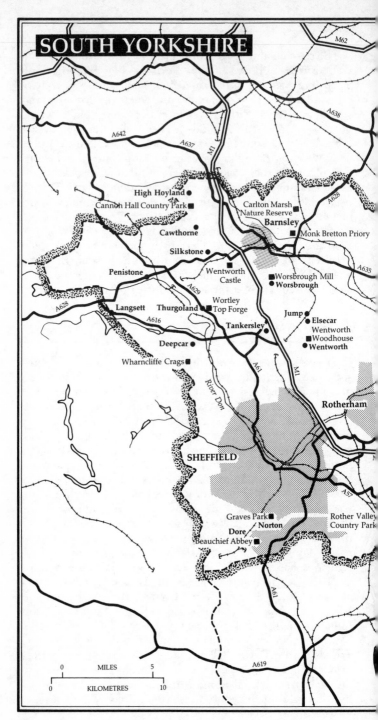

SOUTH YORKSHIRE

High Hoyland ●
Cannon Hall Country Park ■
Carlton Marsh Nature Reserve ■
Barnsley
Monk Bretton Priory ■
Cawthorne ●
Silkstone ●
Wentworth Castle ●
Worsbrough Mill ■
Worsbrough ●
Penistone ●
Wortley Top Forge ■
Langsett ■
Thurgoland ■
Jump ●
Elsecar ●
Tankersley ●
Wentworth Woodhouse ●
Deepcar ●
Wentworth ●
Wharncliffe Crags ■
River Don
Rotherham
SHEFFIELD
Graves Park ■
Rother Valley Country Park
Norton ●
Dore ●
Beauchief Abbey ■

0 MILES 5
0 KILOMETRES 10

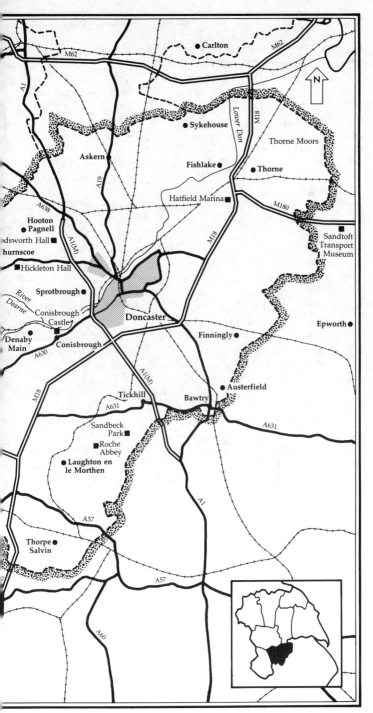

honoured by the striking brick portrait on a gable in **Snig Hill**, often erroneously described as 'the coalminer'.

Two first-rate theatres flank Tudor Square, the modern **Crucible** and the sumptuously restored Victorian **Lyceum**, whose corner tower is topped by the flying figure of Mercury. A good mixture of touring productions and repertory are on offer at both. On the Norfolk Street side of the square stands the **Ruskin Gallery** (open all year, Mon to Fri 10 to 6, Sat 10 to 5), one of Ruskin's many projects designed to bring culture to the masses. Unlike most of his other schemes, it was realised and still flourishes. Exhibitions include a wide range of items such as minerals, prints, books and paintings; admission is free. Close by in the Central Library Building in Surrey Street is the **Graves Art Gallery** (open all year, Mon to Sat 10 to 6). It offers changing exhibitions from the city's collection; admission is free. Also in Surrey Street, Tuckwood's Restaurant, the oldest in Sheffield, dispenses enormous grills and steamed treacle sponge. Work off your meal with a little urban hill-walking past the **Cathedral** and Cutlers' Hall down to the Georgian houses of **Paradise Square** where John Wesley often preached; or along the back of the Town Hall and through the ring road subway to **Arundel Street**. Here you can potter round a busy area of small cutlery firms, especially in the Dickensian cobbled yard of Butchers' Works at No. 72, where self-employed craftsmen continue to beaver away in their great-great-grandfathers' trade.

Sheffield has recently looked to sport as an engine of economic revival, and although the World Student Games of 1991 lost millions and passed most of the world by, some outstanding sporting facilities have been left in their wake. The central **Ponds Forge International Sports Centre** in Sheaf Street (open daily, tel. (0742) 799766) has a superb Olympic-standard pool as well as a 'tropical water world' complete with wave-machine and 'lazy river'; big sporting events are regularly held at the 25,000-seater Don Valley International Stadium. The **Ski Village** on Vale Road, Parkwood Springs (open daily 9 to 10.30) is the largest dry skiing complex in Britain; it has six pistes, the longest of which is 330 metres. **Trax** is the largest indoor go-karting circuit in Europe, in Olive Grove Road (open daily 9 to 10; over 14yrs only).

Industrial sights

● **Kelham Island Industrial Museum** (open all year, Wed to Sat 10 to 5, Sun 11 to 5; closed Mon and Tue exc Bank Hols).

The sense of a continuing tradition is strong at Kelham Island where the museum is the centrepiece. In Alma Street, well signposted from the city centre, a complicated but well-planned trail of industrial sites, some working, others preserved, and a cavern of huge mechanical relics, take you through the city's history, sometimes with memorable sound effects: the Crossley Gas Engine has a habit of backfiring with an earsplitting crash. The trail is extensive, so allow a whole morning or afternoon. The 'Lock, Stock and Barrel' exhibition of ancient guns, bullets and delicate silver powder-flasks shares a separate building opposite the entrance with a friendly café.

• **Globe Works**, Penistone Road (open all year, daily 10 to 5) You can experience the flavour of Sheffield's industrial past if you visit this splendid works, once a cutlery factory built on the site of the Workhouse. A visitor centre charts the development of the city's cutlery industry. Next door is a 'Made in Sheffield' shop, and in the stone-flagged basement you will find Ratteners Rest, a free house offering coffee, snacks and three-course meals (children are welcome in the dining area). Follow the trail along Green Lane as far as Ball Street, where you can see one of the oldest large industrial buildings in Sheffield. In the nineteenth century, Dixon's Cornish Place Works occupied four acres here, unbelievably once a favourite bathing spot on the River Don.

• **The Abbeydale Industrial Hamlet**, Abbeydale Road (open all year, Wed to Sat 10 to 5, Sun 11 to 5) The Hamlet is four miles from the centre on the main road to Bakewell (A261), which is signposted after the A61 Chesterfield road out of the city. Sheffield's most atmospheric industrial relic was one of the largest water-powered sites where scythes were forged on the River Sheaf. You can see the processes of making crucible steel for the scythes which were made in the tilt forge. The eighteenth-century workshops grouped round a courtyard, together with the manager's house and adjoining stables, look as if they could have been designed for a TV set.

• **The Shepherd Wheel**, Whiteley Woods, Hangingwater Road (open all year, Wed to Sat 10 to 12.30, 1.30 to 5, Sun 11 to 12.30, 1.30 to 5) Named after an eighteenth-century employer called Shepherd rather than any agricultural connection, the works are a fine example of early Sheffield industry. Driven by the River Porter, the water-powered grinding-works sharpened blades. Take the A625, signed to Chapel-en-le-Frith out of Sheffield and follow the signs.

Around Sheffield

• **Sheffield Manor and Turret House** (open May to Sept, Wed to Sun 11 to dusk) The delightful sixteenth-century Turret House – all that remains of a once extensive manor house – was home to Mary Queen of Scots for part of her fourteen years' captivity in the city. The worry and expense of guarding the Queen proved too much for the Sixth Earl of Shrewsbury: it broke up his marriage and family life, ruined his health and scuppered his chances of political preferment at Court. He would have liked the neat, small relic which is all that survives of his mansion, with its informative historical display and a garden large enough for children to run around.

• **Bishop's House** (open all year, Wed to Sat 10 to 4.30, Sun 11 to 4.30) Driving to the Bishop's House presents quite a challenge to the navigator; easier, perhaps, would be to take the 434/42 bus to Meersbrook Park from the centre of town. The museum, a picturesque timber-framed yeoman's house, has two rooms furnished in period style and others showing aspects of local history.

• **The City Museum and Mappin Art Gallery** (open all year, Tue to Sat 10 to 5, Sun 11 to 5) are in Weston Park, on the outskirts of the city. As you would expect, the museum has a comprehensive section on cutlery and the collection of Sheffield Plate is the largest in the world. The gallery concentrates on English art of the nineteenth century, with changing exhibitions of contemporary work.

BEZZLE AND CROZZILS

APART FROM the 'thee-ing' and 'thou-ing' – so strong here that local schools tried to stop pupils using the familiar 'tha' to staff in 1983 – South Yorkshire has its own particular dialect. Some of the terms only just cling to life, but they will not be lost to posterity because the county also produced one of Britain's greatest recorders of dialect terms.

Revd Joseph Hunter was born in Sheffield in 1783, moved to London to help preserve the Public Records and left the British Museum one of its principal archives of manuscripts, the Hunter Collection. Enormously varied, and with important collections of

Trails, walks and gardens

Two miles south-west of the city centre are the **Botanical Gardens** (open all year, daily), which lay claim to their own bear pit and more than 5,000 different plants. The eighteen acres of grounds provide plenty of scope for picnics; admission is free.

Sheffield claims, with justice, to have some of the finest and most accessible countryside surrounding any major city in Britain. The brief fringe of rural landscape between the city and the Peak District National Park has several attractions. At **Beauchief**, between the A621 and A61 south of Sheffield, the twelfth-century ruins of **Beauchief Abbey** stand in an agreeable park. Nearby at **Dore**, just beyond the Abbeydale Industrial Hamlet, you can contemplate the Dore Stone on the village green. It marks the spot where England was finally unified as a nation in AD 879. Also to the south, off the A61 at **Norton**, is **Graves Park** (open daily), which has a rare breeds centre, a sculpture trail dedicated to the locally born sculptor Sir Francis Chantrey and pleasant woodland. Admission is free.

The park also lies at one end of the 10-mile **Sheffield Round Walk**, threading together Sheffield's handsome tally of parks; well signposted, it is one of several 'long-distance' footpaths devised by the energetic city fathers. The route leads to Endcliffe Park, off the A625 to the Peak District. You can also tackle the **Rivelin Nature Trail**, east beside the A6101, along a riverbank dotted with abandoned grindingstones, and the **Five Weirs Walk**, through the shattered but

Shakespeariana, this also includes thousands of South Yorkshire dialect terms. Be bold, and try some out.

Agaterds – A-gate-wards – means to see guests on the first stage of their journey home. Bezzle is to drink water, beer or any other liquid immoderately. A crozzil is a half-burnt lump of coal, held over the fire next day. If it burns with a lilli-lo, it burns with a bright, flickering flame. A farantly man is plain-spoken if an equal, but condescending if a superior. To be halal is to be unusually shy. A manners-bit is a small portion of food left by the host, to show that he has got provisions enough. It had better not be moskered or fuzbally, though – blue-spotted with mould.

fascinating terrain of the Lower Don, the former heart of steel-making where restoration work is proceeding by leaps and bounds.

BARNSLEY

Barnsley is often dismissed as a town monopolised by coal-mining, whose inhabitants play soccer, eat enormous chops and drink a lot of bitter. Its centre, dominated by the striking 1930s **Town Hall** (pop inside to see a proud collection of council silverware) is indeed nothing special, but the enormous, fascinating **Market**, the largest gathering of traders' stalls in Yorkshire, is thought by many to be the best. Here you will find the local friendliness and wit in full flow. Most of the suburban areas are as undistinguished as the centre, but the 'nowt but coal' image is misleading – Barnsley makes 34,000 tennis balls for every Wimbledon, apple pies, and most of Britain's milk bottles.

A brief stop in Church Street is best. Here is '**King Arthur's Castle**', the spired and turreted HQ of the Yorkshire branch of the National Union of Mineworkers, with its neat flower-beds of red roses. Across the road, the **Cooper Gallery** (open all year, Wed to Sat 10 to 5.30, Tue 1 to 5.30) has a modest permanent collection of paintings and sculpture and different monthly exhibitions. The small shops in former cottages on Church Street are probably the oldest buildings in central Barnsley but not otherwise exciting; just down **Market Hill**, the shops and café in the Victorian Arcade are more picturesque.

Monk Bretton Priory and around

(English Heritage, open Apr to Sept, daily 10 to 6; Oct to Mar, Tue to Sun 10 to 4)
Barnsley's great architectural treasure, the twelfth-century ruins of Monk Bretton Priory, lie just over a mile to the east, huddled in a grimy landscape with a huge glassworks sitting on one horizon like a Dreadnought. The lawn-surrounded, soot-stained remains repay close inspection and the priory's turbulent history is comic. Its monks were particularly aggressive and, on several occasions, their religious superiors had to deal with them by armed force. The annual Barnsley Feast at Michaelmas (29 September) centres on the priory and fills it with longbow-shooting, ox-roasts and the like. Remember

not to eat the plentiful local blackberries, though, because the devil spits on them at Michaelmas to spite St Michael. The Mill of the Black Monks is an atmospheric pub in the former priory mill, parts of which are eleventh-century. In the summer live music can be enjoyed in the garden.

At Shaw Lane, Carlton, is the **Carlton Marsh Nature Reserve**, an unusual habitat with a meandering network of lonely paths. Explorers with time, and one of an impressive range of local footpath guides, can nose out other surprises like this. Monk Bretton, for instance, stands on the 30-mile **Dearne Way long-distance footpath**, which weaves through forgotten countryside beside the River Dearne.

If you want a less tiring attempt at exercise, Barnsley's modern **Metrodome Leisure Centre**, tel. (0226) 730060, offers fake beaches, waves, a swimming-pool and a pool-side café.

PENNINE BARNSLEY

East and north of Barnsley, the explorer has to work quite hard. The west and south are another matter; you still have that satisfying feeling of being a pioneer, but the rewards are more obvious. Over 80 per cent of Barnsley metropolitan district is green belt. The best of the countryside is in the triangle between **High Hoyland** to the north, **Langsett** to the west and **Tankersley** to the south; woods and fields dip up and down into hidden valleys suddenly interrupted by the grand old trees and spacious landscaping of country house parkland. High Hoyland is typically Pennine, with stone-built weaving and farming cottages perched on a hill. Down through the woods, **Cawthorne**, in contrast, is sheltered and pretty with the sterling **Victoria Jubilee Museum** (open Apr to Oct, Sat and Sun 2 to 5 and Thur by prior arrangement); a real village enterprise dating from 1889, it resembles a communal attic with its local collections of birds' eggs, moths and fossils.

Between these two villages is the free **Cannon Hall museum, country park and farm** (open all year except Mon, Good Fri, 25 to 28 Dec and 1 to 2 Jan; Tue to Sat 10.30 to 5, Sun 2.30 to 5). The house is plain architecturally but well stocked with a model local collection: arts, furniture, industrial products and displays on the 13/18th Hussars (Queen Mary's Own, traditionally recruited from Barnsley), which include a diorama of the Charge of the Light Brigade in which the regiment took part. The gardens are particularly well cared for and there is a good café and a children's farm for which admission is charged. The 70-acre grounds also include several lakes and a collection of exotic fowl.

South of Cawthorne, **Silkstone** is another pleasant village with an unusual feature: local sculptors are gradually setting up carved stone boundary marks at every entrance. Linked by footpaths the markers record historical events like the mining catastrophe of 1838 which killed 26 child workers (also commemorated movingly in the churchyard).

Wentworth Castle

(Open by arrangement, tel. (0226) 285426; gardens open in summer Tue to Thur)

Down the hill from Silkstone, you arrive at one of the great mansions of South Yorkshire, overlooking the M1 motor-way. It is now the Northern College of Adult Education. Like Wentworth Woodhouse (near Rotherham), this enormous house is a testimony to the limitless building energies of the Wentworths, South Yorkshire's leading family in the eigh-teenth and nineteenth centuries. You need an aircraft to take it in properly; luckily, the castle's guidebook spares you the expense, with an aerial picture showing how the original 1670 house has been boxed in, first by ever-more grandiose wings and a vast conservatory, then by one of the finest rhodo-dendron collections in Britain. The grounds of this astonish-ing place are open to the public and offer wonderful walks to follies like Stainborough Castle ruins. In May and early June, when the rhododendrons are in flower, Wentworth Castle is magical.

The industrial past

The swathes of countryside west and south of Barnsley also offer – in South Yorkshire's typical mixture of grit and green – a series of worthwhile industrial relics and museums. In the gentle valley of **Worsbrough** you pass the lake which is flanked by the long-distance **Liverpool-to-Hull footpath** and bridleway; this path is part of a walkers' 'Euro-route' due eventually to reach Istanbul! Content yourself for now with the water-powered **Worsbrough Mill Museum** (open Wed to Sun, 10 to 5.30 or dusk if earlier, and Bank Hol Mon), clanking away to make the stoneground flour that is for sale. This process has been carried out here (as the good exhibition records) since before the Domesday Book, which duly mentions the mill at Worsbrough. Footpaths, and regular guided walks, link the mill with the **Rockley Engine House and Museum**, which houses hefty relics dating back to 1652 and lesser remains like **Darwin Ironworks** and **Wigfield Open Farm** (open all year, weekdays, Apr to Sept 10 to 5, Oct to Mar 12 to 4), which explains farming and animals to the uninitiated.

If your appetite for cogs and sprockets is limited, however, the most atmospheric reminder of Victorian industrial days is **Elsecar**, an entire 'industrial village' built to serve the lordly Wentworths of Wentworth Woodhouse. This is perhaps best visited, logically, along with the house (see under Rotherham) but it can be swiftly reached from Worsbrough via the nicely named community of **Jump**. Legend has it that visitors to the original farming community had to jump a beck (or stream) to get there.

Elsecar's individual glory is Britain's last eighteenth-century Newcomen Beam Engine, which drained local mines until 1923. But the whole village is splendidly intact, with an absorbing trail to follow and a good pub, called the Beggar and the Gentleman, which still has a neatly engraved promise of gigs for hire, although the landlord is unlikely to honour it.

From here, cross over the M1 (junction 36), through **Tankersley**, pausing to appreciate the picturesque ruined hall and Cromwellian cannonballs and bullets in the church, before passing on to **Wortley Top Forge** at **Thurgoland** (open all year, Sun 11 to 5, other times by arrangement). The first Sunday in every month, during May to October, is a 'steam day'; for other special events and information contact Mr Chris Carnley, tel. (0226) 201848. The only ironworks in Britain to survive from the earliest, seventeenth-century industrial era, it originally made nails, then switched to production of railway axles, finally ending manufacture in 1910.

To digest your diet of industrial knowledge, head out to Barnsley's Pennine boundary beyond **Penistone**, a rugged community with a busy market on Thursday and Saturday, an interesting old Cloth Hall and a good choice of pubs. **Wharncliffe Crags** south-east of Deepcar are an especially good place to let off steam.

DONCASTER

The very name of Doncaster – from the Latin phrase meaning 'military camp on the River Don' – underlines the ancient origins of this handsome, though industry-scarred, town. Any stategist would naturally build here, on the north–south spine of Britain, with navigable access to the sea.

The town's distinguished past is recalled by some noble street frontages, especially around the **Mansion House**, tel. (0302) 734019, in the High Street (there are fine interiors too – visits are by appointment), and the Victorian **Corn Exchange**, all glass and wrought iron, in the market-place. The eye-catching **St George's Church** looks convincingly medieval but is the work, completed in 1858, of Sir Giles Gilbert Scott, whose architecture is complemented by windows made by seven different nineteenth-century stained-glass artists. Doncaster was a social centre for the local gentry based in great (and surviving) houses like Hickleton, Brodsworth and Cusworth. The races brought notables from further afield, especially for the St Leger, Britain's oldest classic horse race which was founded in 1776 and runs annually in early September. But geology undermined any chance the town had of remaining a tranquil Georgian market centre. Coal ran in rich, black seams for miles around. The pit wheels went up and the mineshafts went down.

Other industries arrived too, making Doncaster famous for butterscotch and steam engines – both the Flying Scotsman and Mallard, the latter still the holder of the world speed record for steam, were made here. Paradoxically, geology saved the town from becoming as black and smoky as some of its Yorkshire neighbours. The spur of limestone running north and south across the county takes in Doncaster, and was much-quarried to give light and delicate facings to local buildings.

If your visit happens to coincide with one of the 26 race meetings held annually, the **racecourse** is well worth a visit; the noise and excitement are infectious. Typically of South Yorkshire, the whole operation is run by a committee of the unshakeably Labour council, rather than the Jockey Club.

Outside the course, an ingenious bit of recycling by Doncaster's leisure department has led to some unusual flower-beds: flower-filled slipper baths previously in the town's public baths now adorn the central reservation of the dual carriageway.

Following the tap-ends brings you to the **Dome Leisure Centre** (open Mon to Fri 11 to 10, Sat 9 to 11, Sun 9 to 10.30). This excellent centre is a satisfyingly original piece of modern architecture of which Kubla Khan would have approved. Here you can swim in a wonderworld of lagoons, rainstorms, artificial currents and an outdoor whirlpool (the last barred to non-swimmers), or skate down an indoor alp or play bowls on an artificial village green. There are several cafés and although the pools (all leisure; nowhere for lengths) can get crowded, they are well supervised and the atmosphere is cheerful.

Museums

• **Museum of South Yorkshire Life** (open all year, daily Mon to Fri 10 to 5, Sat 11 to 5, Sun 1 to 5). More conventional fare is laid on here, housed in the graceful limestone mansion of Cusworth Hall, which looks straight down a steep hill to Doncaster in a manner which must have much-pleased its former owners, the Battie-Wrightsons. The sound basic collections are almost always complemented by temporary special exhibitions and a wide range of activities, particularly for children.

• **Town Museum and Art Gallery**, in Chequer Road (open all year, Mon to Fri 10 to 5, Sat 11 to 5, Sun 1 to 5), has another strong regional collection and is a centre of particular expertise in natural history, explaining in regular newspaper pieces about entirely new flies, beetles or plants being discovered in or around Doncaster. There is also a section devoted to the King's Own Yorkshire Light Infantry, and, like Cusworth, the museum is imaginative about special educational events.

• **Sandtoft Transport Museum** (open Apr to Sept, Sat, Sun 12 to 6). To learn all you have ever wanted to know about buses and trolleybuses means a twelve-mile journey out on the A18 Hatfield Road. This is Britain's largest collection and – joy for the nostalgic – it includes working trolleybus rides.

IVANHOE COUNTRY

The limestone which helped to see Doncaster's graceful historic buildings through the town's period of heavy industry also adds something extra to the surrounding countryside. There is a Cotswold feel here, especially to the villages scattered to the south-west.

Conisbrough

Conisbrough Castle (English Heritage, open Apr to Sept, daily 10 to 6, Oct to Mar, Tue to Sun 10 to 4) is one of the finest castles in Britain, with an outstanding keep – a great, sheer, almost windowless bastion of finely cut stone – built in the 1170s and epitomising power.

Built by Hameline Plantagenet, the castle received the funds, time and craftsmanship available to the half-brother of Henry II, the law-giving king who put England's over-mighty barons in order after the anarchic reign of Stephen. Never seriously attacked (and you can see why), the castle had the good luck to fall into decay before the Civil War. Neither side used it and so neither Cromwell nor Charles II bothered to have its remains dismantled. Even its decay is awe-inspiring; by the entrance, a colossal section of curved tower has fallen, in one broken-off piece, into the surrounding earthwork ditch.

Looking out from the top of the 95-foot keep over the River Don gorge, perhaps with one of English Heritage's regular archery or sword-fighting contests taking place in the courtyard, you can easily think yourself in the world of *Ivanhoe*, much of which is set at Conisbrough.

Sir Walter Scott wrote most of the novel at the Boat Inn in nearby **Sprotbrough** – still a lovely pub in a lovely village,

THE TOLL OF THE MINES

ONE OF the hardest jobs ever demanded of Britain's workforce, coal-mining has dug deeply into the psychology of South Yorkshire.

A type of monument almost unique to mining areas – the record of awful industrial catastrophes with scores of dead – is commonplace in South Yorkshire. Archives and displays at the Yorkshire Mining Museum (see West Yorkshire) repeatedly show forlorn newspaper photographs of women and children at the pithead waiting for men who will not return.

The Oaks Memorial, an obelisk topped by a statue on the A635 a mile south-east of Barnsley, records two explosions at the vanished Oaks colliery. The first, in 1847, killed 79 miners; the second, far worse, saw 334 miners and 27 rescue workers die in 1866. The iron bucket, in which two brave men were lowered after the 1866 disaster to return with one survivor, is displayed at the mining museum. Three of the Oaks victims are poignantly recorded with the inscription 'identity unknown'.

The Huskar Pit flooding of 1838 drowned 11 girls and 15 boys, the youngest only seven, a tragedy commemorated in Silkstone

perched above and along the wooded valley of the Don, with its associated canal, Sprotbrough Flash nature reserve, and pleasant tow-path walks. He had no known connection with the Sir Walter Scott coffee house in Church Street, Conisbrough, but it is a good place for a rest – an early eighteenth-century cottage and even earlier well. The castle information centre looks appropriately like a jousting tent and has a good exhibition, plentiful local guides and a small but well-chosen range of souvenirs. Conisbrough's **St Peter's parish church** is the oldest in the county, an eighth-century nave enlarged by the Normans, with a leper squint (to allow the feared pariahs to watch Communion).

The Miners' Memorial Chapel

A mile along the A6023 Mexborough road from Conisbrough in All Saints' parish church at **Denaby Main**, the chapel, tel. (0709) 862297, shows a different side of this area's history. This peaceful little section of the modern church is dedicated to the skill and craftsmanship of the industry. The walls are made from firebricks salvaged from closed pits, the ceiling is

churchyard and by one of the village's new boundary stones. All Saints' church at Darfield, in the Dearne Valley, has a memorial to another 189 of coal's victims – men and boys who died in the Lundhill pit catastrophe of 1857.

Forays into other local churchyards will turn up evidence of further disasters; sometimes a single collier, sometimes another devastating toll like the 143 miners killed at Swaithe Main, Worsbrough, in 1875. A gas explosion killed three men at Rockingham colliery in 1936. Two years earlier, at Elsecar Main, a miners' cage bringing men up from shift overshot and was hauled into the winding machinery, where the pithead wheels mangled arms and legs. Lesser injuries were commonplace between the wars; the doctor at Lidgett colliery, near Barnsley, had a parrot which greeted men suffering from crushed fingers and toes with the squawk 'Cut it off!'.

In the nineteenth century, when life was even cheaper, the bodies of dead miners were sometimes brought back home in coal carts that had been hastily swept out and lined with clean straw.

'cockered' – a method of erecting pit-props using wooden beams – and the windows show aspects of mining and its history. A thorough booklet, written in a recessional tone for the steady disappearance of the county's pits, is available.

Brodsworth Hall

The limestone escarpment to the west of Doncaster runs past South Yorkshire's 'newest' stately home, buried in the trees and shrubs of its large park. The lost Victorian domain of Brodsworth Hall is being prepared for public opening in Spring 1993 by English Heritage. Brodsworth has some of the 'time capsule' qualities of Calke Abbey in Derbyshire or Erdigg in North Wales, including a lavatory full of comfortable devices and an enormous kitchen which still had its cumbersome blackout screens in place when English Heritage took possession. The purchase of the contents alone cost £3,365,000. The building's uncompromising size is lightened by the Italianate style of its architect, Cavaliere Casentini. But it did not win him any other commissions: Brodsworth is his only English work.

Hooton Pagnell

Close to Brodsworth this luscious little village has a fine church and a lovely hall (not open, and disfigured by broken glass on its unwelcoming walls). The quaint post office sells a classic vicar's local history. **Hickleton Hall**, now a Cheshire Home and not open, can be admired from the A635, along with its solid outbuildings. A little foray over the Barnsley border to Thurnscoe provides an illuminating contrast: the cramped former pit village is less than a mile from the grandeur of Hickleton, the Earl of Halifax's former seat.

EAST OF DONCASTER

Although not exotic in the Oriental sense, the landscape east of Doncaster has a strange, lost quality which makes it very different from most of the rest of this busy county. It stretches from the flat, damp landscape of **Sykehouse** and **Fishlake**, reclaimed from swamps by the 'Dutch River' – the embanked system of drains based on the Don, devised by seventeenth-century Dutch engineers – to **Bawtry** in the south, the gateway to White Rose country, with its southernmost house still officially addressed as No. 1 Yorkshire.

Askern, due north of Doncaster, rivalled Harrogate as a gentlemanly spa town in the late-eighteenth century, but then fell victim to coal. Only the ornamental lake recalls the past.

The flat agricultural landscape is also relieved by man-made attractions like **Hatfield Marina**, just south of **Thorne**, where hardy souls sailboard, and RAF Finningley, at **Finningley**, which hosts the biggest air display in the country every September. You may be tempted to cross to John Wesley's Birthplace Museum at **Epworth**, the January Haxey Hood Ritual in **Haxey**, and the tightly knit little world of the **Isle of Axholme**. Just outside Bawtry, the village of **Austerfield** is an important stopping point for Pilgrim Father enthusiasts: William Bradford, one of the gallant Mayflower's complement and the first Governor of the pioneer's colony of Plymouth, was born and christened here. Pious Americans rebuilt the north aisle of St Helen's after a fire in 1897.

In places, it must be admitted, the landscape of this eastern beat of Doncaster shrinks to a sort of complete nothingness, but the desolation is a genuine attraction at the wilderness of **Thorne Moors**. This is one of Britain's most important peat habitats and a lot more accessible than its remote counterparts in Scotland. Great controversy rages here about extraction for garden peat; armed with stout wellies and a good anorak or overcoat, you can plash around happily and decide the issue for yourself.

Tickhill

Tickhill, just west of Bawtry, is a slumbering place which must dream of what might-have-been. An enormous royal castle stood here in medieval times. Now only the roofless gatehouse and sections of curtain wall are all that remain of the once formidable stronghold. It was deliberately slighted after the Civil War (during which both sides seized it) as an intolerable threat to order in the wrong hands. For a small town (or large village), Tickhill has a remarkable wealth of early buildings: the remains of a thirteenth-century Augustinian **friary**, a domed and pillared **buttercross** in the market-place, the tremendous thirteenth-century **parish church of St Mary's**, a medieval millpond and **parish rooms** housed in a fifteenth-century relic of the vanished St Leonard's hospital.

ROTHERHAM

Rotherham occupies a striking position on a hill above the River Don, a sadly polluted river but gracefully bridged by a span with four arches and the late fifteenth-century **Bridge Chapel of Our Lady**, one of only four bridge chapels in the country (see also Wakefield in West Yorkshire). This little building's lively history, which includes periods as an almshouse, a jail and a tobacconist's shop, is shared by the town in general. Once a market centre, dominated by the splendid – and surviving - **parish church of All Saints**, it might have become the Oxford or Cambridge of the North. Thomas Rotherham, a local man who became Archbishop of York, founded Jesus College here in 1483 but, alas, instead of developing into a university it was strangled in its infancy by Henry VIII in the 1547–8 suppression of the monasteries. Rotherham was fated instead to turn into the roaring, smoky home of glassmaking, potteries and steel forges during the Industrial Revolution. The ingenuity which might have gone into scholarly thought was harnessed instead to such practical Rotherham inventions as the screw-tap, humble feature of basins and baths, which was first made here in 1845 by Edward Chrimes; and the Bailey Bridge, used in war and disaster to replace broken bridges swiftly, designed by Sir Donald Coleman Bailey.

The town still has an industrial reputation, but although chimneys and factory sheds hum surprisingly close to the compact centre, a new and more attractive incarnation is taking place. Elegant buildings like the eighteenth-century lawyer's house in **Bridgate**, admired by Anthony Trollope when he was courting his Rotherham-born wife, Rose Heseltine, are attracting sightseers once more.

The square half-mile around **All Saints** has accordingly been scrubbed and polished, cars are excluded from many streets, and an interesting morning can be spent tracking down various small historical curiosities. The **Hollis Chapel** in Downs Row was the Nonconformists' first foothold in Rotherham, its congregation including Ebenezer Elliott, the 'Corn Law Rhymer' who composed the stirringly radical 'alternative' national anthem 'God Save The People'. The former Feoffees' Charity School in **The Crofts** is also a pleasant building, especially suited for contemplation since its conversion into a pub.

Clifton House and the Regimental Museum

● **Clifton House**, Clifton Lane, tel. (0709) 371602/372106, is a classic iron-founder's mansion, opulently built in 1783 on a hill from which its owner, Joshua Walker, could survey his grimy domain. It houses a strong municipal collection, complete with a reconstructed street and a notable quantity of the local Rockingham Ware pottery. The pride of this, the gargantuan Rhinoceros Vase which dominates the building's hall, is famous for inspiring heated discussions on what constitutes good taste. The house is surrounded by 56 acres of model urban park, with attractions that include crazy golf, an aviary and mini-zoo, a miniature railway, paddling pool and events held during school holidays.

● **The York and Lancaster Regimental Museum** (open all year, Tue to Sat 10 to 5) is housed in the convenient but hideous Library and Arts Centre, a hymn to concrete between Nottingham Street and Walker Place in the town centre. Displays, amid authentic guns, medals and other trophies of war, explain how York and Lancaster recruits rubbed along together without re-igniting the Wars of the Roses.

ROTHERHAM'S COUNTRYSIDE

Wentworth Woodhouse

A few miles north of Rotherham, on the B6091 Barnsley Road at Wentworth, this enormous edifice is one of the most astounding of Britain's stately homes. It has the longest façade in the country, 1,800 windows according to some diligent surveyor, and a vast park sprinkled with comparably oversized follies. The house is now privately owned, after a long period as a teacher-training college, but footpaths criss-cross the grounds and allow a close and satisfying view of the elaborate classical architecture.

The mansion is actually two houses – a gigantic parody of the Northern 'back-to-back', built virtually simultaneously by the Wentworth family with a cavalier disregard for cost and an eye to outdoing their cousins at Wentworth Castle (see p190). The 'Woodhouse' family won, hands down, first with the west-facing house of 1725–35, and then with the still larger east-facing range of 1734–50, which backs directly on to its predecessor.

Opening arrangements are likely, in due course, by the present owner who is attempting a faithful restoration after the years of hard usage by the local authority. But a thorough sense of the scale of the house can be swiftly gained by exploring the small area of garden open to the public beside the Hauge Lane Garden Centre (reached via Wentworth village).

The formal landscaping here includes a spooky bear pit, entered by a cobwebby tunnel and left by a gloomy, delicately curving stairway. The adjacent rock garden has lines of abandoned stone duck nesting boxes and there are colossal bits of wall and statuary everywhere. The whole thing looks as though it was built to last for thousands of years; but it has succumbed to time, and an eerie feeling of wilderness adds to the intriguing atmosphere.

Wentworth village itself is picturesque and has two good pubs, the George and Dragon and the Rockingham Arms. The splendidly Victorian Holy Trinity church was given by the Wentworth family, and the lovely but ruined 'Old Church', with its Wentworth Chapel, is well stocked with family memorials, vital for construing the intricate links between Wentworths, Fitzwilliams, Rockinghams and Staffords – names which recur constantly in South Yorkshire. Essentially, they were all the same huge tribe, which dominated the county in a way which only the National Union of Mineworkers has matched.

A map and leaflet are more or less indispensable if you want to spend a satisfying time tracking down Wentworth Woodhouse's four major follies: **Keppel's Column**, **the Mausoleum**, **Hoober Stand** and **the Needle's Eye**. The first, with its unusual bulge starting a third of the way up the 115 feet of gritstone blocks, can be best seen from Admiral's Crest, off Upper Wortley Road, quite close to Rotherham and with modern houses incongruously nearby. The Mausoleum, badly affected by mining subsidence, is hidden in private woods off Cotworth Lane, but the other two follies are close to public footpaths, which make pleasant countryside walks. Hoober's 100-foot pyramid is at Lea Brook and the Needle's Eye, supposedly built to win a Wentworth's bet that he could drive a horse and carriage through the eye of a needle, stands by the path from the Coaley Lane/Street Lane junction to Elsecar Green. A day or half-day spent in the remarkable fantasy world of the Wentworths should alter anyone's murky preconceptions of South Yorkshire for ever.

East to Roche Abbey

A good way to enter the quiet, unhurried world of medieval Roche Abbey is by taking the winding footpath there from **Laughton en le Morthen**, three miles away. This is a memorable outing on a fine day and Laughton itself is a lovely huddle of mullioned houses (and an old school), a small motte-

and–bailey castle and a church spire considered by many to be the finest in the former West Riding. The romantic will be distressed to learn that the delightful name means merely 'the place on the moors where leeks are grown'. Across country from here, towards Worksop, **Thorpe Salvin** is another charming village, with a fine church and the eerie ruins of a Tudor hall, recently shored up and best seen from Lady Field Road.

The green girdle south and east of Rotherham has a final, modern ornament in the **Rother Valley Country Park** (open all year, dawn till dusk), a swathe of restored, once–derelict land and well-planted countryside off the Mansfield Road between Killamarsh and Anton, which – perhaps startlingly – attracted more visitors in 1990 than any other single attraction in Yorkshire, apart from Flamingoland (see Chapter 6). It is a place for watersports, from canoeing to fishing, with plentiful picnic sites and two old mills at Bedgreave – one, described as the New Mill although dating from 1631, is a well-arranged and helpful visitor centre.

Roche Abbey

(Open Apr to Sept, daily; weekends only Oct to Mar)
Signposted to the right, down a steep, recently recobbled track into a narrow limestone valley (drive fearlessly to the bottom car park), the slender and graceful ruins of Roche Abbey decorate English Heritage's neatly cropped lawns alongside the stream which has been partly diverted to provide a rushing mill race.

The Cistercians settled in this hidden glen in 1147, led by two noblemen whose unpromising names, Richard de Bully and Richard Fitzturgis, belied the elegantly beautiful buildings they provided. Henry VIII dissolved Roche, along with the other monasteries, and much was destroyed, but the ruins are considerable, rising in places to three storeys and approached through a lovely gatehouse, with relics of 'monkish' rooms carved out of the limestone cliffs from which the abbey took its name. The landscape was given its final distinction by Capability Brown, whose genius was employed in the mid-eighteenth century to incorporate Roche into the grounds of nearby **Sandbeck Park**, the stately Corinthian-pillared pile of the Earls of Scarborough.

WHERE TO STAY

Our inspectors didn't find anything particularly special in this area, with the exception of the bed and breakfast cottage mentioned below. There are many good hotels and bed and breakfasts in the Dales, West Yorkshire and North Yorkshire; please refer to the 'Where to Stay' sections at the end of the other chapters for our recommendations.

EVERTON

Gable Cottage Guest House
High Street, Everton, Nr Bawtry, Doncaster DN10 5AR
TEL (0777) 817 601
A very welcoming bed and breakfast in this pretty cottage, parts of which are over two hundred years old. Each of the three bedrooms is neatly decorated and furnished in soft colours.
All year; 3 rooms

WHERE TO EAT

BARNSLEY

Armstrongs
6 Shambles Street
TEL (0226) 240113
Stylish town-centre restaurant complete with piano, mirrored bar and curving staircase. Mostly modern cooking features warm salads, puff pastry and fruit sauces; tempting, elaborate desserts.
Tue to Sat, exc Sat L, 12–2, 7–10; closed 2 weeks Aug, bank hols; Access, Visa

Restaurant Peano
102 Dodworth Road
TEL (0226) 244990
Adventurous cooking with Italian influences: great pasta made on the premises; meat, fish and game dishes with interesting sauces are sometimes accompanied by polenta or lentils. Home-baked bread; pleasing desserts.
Mon to Sat, 7–9.30, (L Tue to Fri by arrangement); Access, Amex, Visa

RIDGEWAY

Old Vicarage
Ridgeway Moor, off A616, on B6054 nearly opposite village church
TEL (0742) 475814
Superior cooking and prices to match at this Victorian house. First-class ingredients are used imaginatively and with great success: pot-roasted breast of pheasant on a spaghetti of celeriac, carrot and swede and rich plum pudding with two sauces. Well-chosen wines.
Tue to Sat, 7–11, Sun L 12.15–2.30 (L Tue to Sat by arrangement)

SHEFFIELD

Greenhead House
84 Burncross Road, Chapeltown
TEL Tel (0742) 469004
A monthly changing menu encompasses shellfish, game and excellent vegetables at this stone cottage on the outskirts of Sheffield. Popular with locals –

book early for Saturday. Friendly
service.
*Tue to Sat 7.15–9; closed first 2
weeks Apr, first 2 weeks Aug;
Access, Amex, Visa*

Henfrey's Restaurant, Charnwood Hotel

10 Sharrow Lane
TEL (0742) 589411
A smart dining-room requiring
jacket and tie (the adjoining
Brasserie Leo is cheaper and more
relaxed). Complex, accurate
cooking of luxury ingredients.
Good range of wines, fairly
priced.
*Tue to Sat 7.30–10, (L by
arrangement); Access, Amex, Diners,
Visa*

Fat Cat ★

24 Alma Road
TEL (0742) 728195
Pub serving wholesome food –
soups, casseroles, curries, fruit
crumbles – real ales, draught
ciders and drinkable wines. No-
smoking area; garden.
All week, L 12–2.30

Nirmal's

189-93 Glossop Road
TEL (0742) 724054

Good local reputation for skilful
curries, tandooris, Indian breads
and other Asian specialities. Daily
dishes extend the menu further.
Kingfisher or Tiger beer.
*Mon to Sat 12–2.30, all week 6–12
(1am Fri, Sat); Access, Amex, Visa*

Just Cooking ★

16–18 Carver Street
TEL (0742) 727869
Popular at lunchtime (attracting
long queues). Fresh, imaginative
salads, cold dishes and desserts
such as chocolate roulade are
recommended.
*Mon to Sat 10–3.30, to 7.30 Wed, 5
Sat*

TICKHILL

Forge

1 Sunderland Street
TEL (0302) 744122
Small restaurant with an
astounding array of mousses,
roulades, soufflés, sorbets, sauces
and fruit flavourings. Sweets
come laden with cream. Booking
neccessary.
Tue to Fri 7–9; Visa

THE PEAK DISTRICT

- Huge expanses of rolling, peat moors, limestone dales, simple stone villages and sheep farms
- Potholes and 'show' caverns
- One of Britain's most rewarding spa towns
- Arkwright's earliest mills, lead-mines, and abandoned millstones
- Wonderful walking country including the start of the Pennine Way

Millstones

THE DARK PEAK AND THE WHITE PEAK

Few regions display their geological make-up as obviously as the Peak. The area known as the Dark Peak, covering three-quarters of the region, comprises an inverted horseshoe-shaped swathe of sandstone and shales. Its characteristic landscapes are huge windswept wastes of heather-and-bilberry moorland. Dark, jointed crags line up along the eastern side to form a 12-mile wall, which has been weathered into gnarled ridges along the western peripheries; pasture land is olive-green, the peaty paths often squelchy, settlements are few.

The White Peak fills the void in the horseshoe: a tongue of carboniferous limestone in the south and centre of the Peak. Here the turf is light-green, the landscape mild; pleasant villages with houses of uniform stone are grouped around a village pond or green. Lichens speckle the whitish-grey drystone walls, stone barns merge into the landscape and the plateau grasslands slope off abruptly into exquisite steep-sided dales where the rivers sometimes vanish into the porous rock and caverns.

The Dark Peak rates among England's loneliest and emptiest tracts - punctuated by the occasional boulder, sheep or wind-blown farmstead. Take any journey west to east or north to south across the region (except in the extreme north), and you will see some exciting transitions from the one Peak landscape to the other. The National Park boundary snakes about in a strange fashion, avoiding major towns and much of the quarry-despoiled landscape of the White Peak.

Some of the towns just outside the National Park are worth visiting but it is the rural scene that most visitors come to see, and apart from a few viewpoints such as Monsal Head, you have to walk to reach the true beauty spots. Up on the plateau the stone villages – many of which were once lead-miners' settlements – are not conspicuously prettified, though second-home ownership and craft shops have arrived in some places. A handful of villages stand out for their village greens, halls, estate cottages, ponds, market-crosses, views, or general charm: Alstonefield, Ashford in the Water, Castleton, Eyam, Hartington, Ilam, Tideswell, Tissington and Winster make up our short-list. If you can avoid weekends and school holidays, you should have at least some of these places to yourself. North of Castleton the huge scarcely populated area is crossed by only a few main roads; these are some of the most scenic drives in the Peak. For rainy days, and an industrial education, there are a number of interesting museums on the fringes of the National Park.

BUXTON AND AROUND

Although Buxton had been renowned for its healthy, life-giving waters since Roman times, it was the fifth Duke of Devonshire, William Cavendish, who turned Buxton into a fashionable spa. John Carr was commissioned to build the Doric-style Crescent (1780–84) and a National Bath Building (now the tourist information centre) on the source of the spa water. After the railways came to Buxton in the 1860s, the spa reached its heyday. The Pavilion Gardens were developed, hotels and a pump-room sprang up and in 1905 the Opera House was the last major building still surviving to be erected before the spa's terminal decline. The Opera House, used as a cinema for many years, was revived in 1979 and the town began its renaissance with an annual arts festival, now a major event in the Peak calendar.

The Town Hall stands at the top of the Slopes – a large lawn dipping to a superb Georgian crescent and the old spa building. Buxton no longer functions as a spa but bottled Buxton Water now fills supermarket shelves nationwide. To the left, the neat lawns and shrubberies of the **Pavilion Gardens** stretch away beneath well-tended Victorian houses, period street-lamps and a conservatory-like pavilion. Beyond the Crescent, the Edwardian **Opera House** is fronted with an elegant glass and cast-iron canopy; close by, look out for the mosque-like dome of the **Devonshire Royal Hospital**, an Italianate parish church and the vast **Palace Hotel**.

● **Buxton Micrarium** (open end of Mar to early Nov, daily 10 to 5) Housed in the Victorian pumphouse, this is an extraordinary museum, the first of its kind, where microscopic images are projected on to screens, and captions light up to explain what you are looking at: a snowflake or a set of contrasting leaf sections perhaps. There are hundreds of exhibits and quite a lot to read.

● **Buxton Museum and Art Gallery**, Terrace Road (open Tue to Fri 9.30 to 5.30, Sat 9.30 to 5) The museum won an award naming it Archaeological Museum of the Year in 1990 for its 'Wonders of the Peak' walk-through-time display of the geological formation of the Peak District, early man, the Romans and after. Downstairs there is a room full of

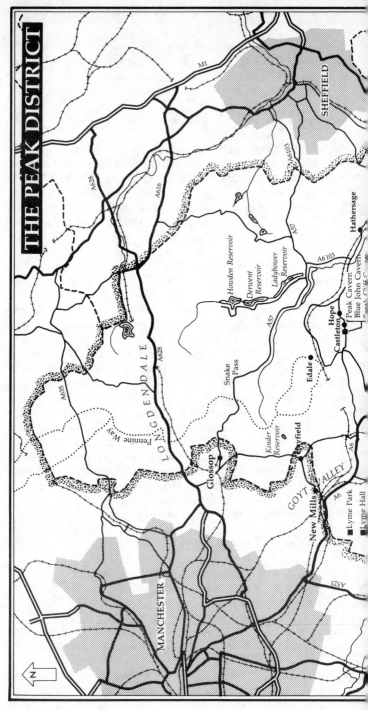

THE PEAK DISTRICT

SHEFFIELD

M1

A628

A616

A628

A6103

A57

Houden Reservoir

Derwent Reservoir

Ladybower Reservoir

Hathersage

A6103

Peak Cavern
Blue John Cavern

Hope
Castleton

A635

L O N G D E N D A L E

Snake Pass

Edale

Pennine Way

Glossop

Kinder Reservoir

...field

New Mills

GOYT VALLEY

A6

A6

Lyme Park
Lyme Hall

MANCHESTER

A523

N

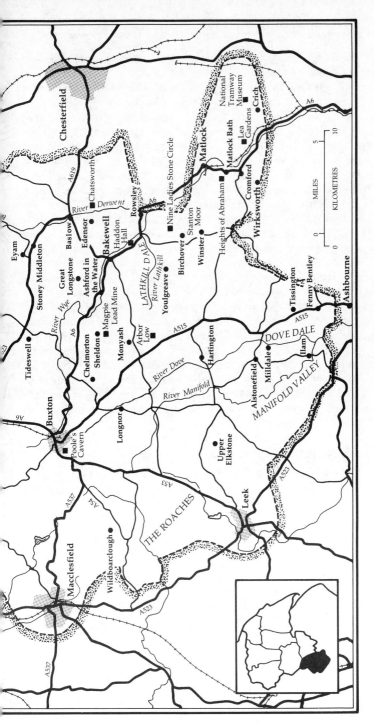

reminders of Buxton's spa days with Victorian souvenirs and sepia photographs.

• **Poole's Cavern and Grin Low Woods Country Park** (cavern open Easter to first week of Nov, daily 10 to 5; closed Wed in Apr, May and Oct) On the edge of town, it is well signposted and there's no fee if you just want to visit the country park. If time is limited and you can only visit one cave while you're in the Peak District, make for this one. Poole was an outlaw who allegedly used the cavern as a hideaway in the 1440s, but evidence of much earlier occupation is displayed in a small museum at the entrance. The limestone concretions are the most interesting features, with stalactites, fragile 'straw formations' and unique stalagmites coloured rusty orange by the seeping of water through iron ore dumped on the site of Grin Low Woods above. At one point you look 500 feet along the longest 'show' cave view in Britain. The country park is a mature woodland with a nature trail and a good view of Buxton from Solomon's Temple, a nineteenth-century folly.

A few miles out of town you cross the National Park boundary to enter the White Peak. **Longnor** stands on the brink of a series of hills that, for the Peak, are individually defined to an unusual degree. The village feels quite remote and is compact around a cobbled square fronted by four pubs and a craft shop. Across it flows the Upper Dove, which proceeds southwards to pass through the most famous of all Peak landscapes.

Hartington and around

The Upper Dove flows south across the hills bypassing Hartington. It is a pretty, if touristy village, with huddled cottages, a gargoyle-embellished church (best from outside), and a gabled manor house (now a youth hostel) tucked around the back. Gift shops, a defunct Town Hall, tea-rooms and hotels look on to a triangular market-square and pond, where a tiny shop sells produce from the adjacent Stilton cheese factory. To the south, the River Dove enters **Beresford Dale** and **Wolfscote Dale**, classic steep-sided valleys. These dales can only be seen on foot: take the path from the lavatory block at the edge of Hartington on the road to Warslow.

DOVE DALE

The dale starts south of the delightfully placed hamlet of **Milldale**, where the Dove is spanned by a double-arched packhorse bridge known as Viator's Bridge, its size immortalised in *The Compleat Angler* by Izaak Walton and Charles Cotton: 'Why! A mouse can hardly go over it; it is but two fingers broad'. The only way to see the dale is on foot. Two shallow caves, known as Dove Holes, appear about half a mile down the dale, followed by a succession of fancifully named natural land formations including the 40-foot-high natural arch known as Reynard's Cave and Dove Dale 'Castle' (a natural crag). Dove Dale has become so popular that it is no longer promoted by the tourist authorities and it can become fiercely over-crowded in summer.

Tissington

Located east of Dove Dale, Tissington has a carefully groomed appearance – broad grass verges, ducks on the village mere, tidy cottage frontages and a handsome Jacobean hall, home of the Fitzherbert family since Elizabethan times. It epitomises a delicious scene of rural England. The village prides itself on its well-dressing (see p218) – it is the only place in the Peak to have maintained the tradition without a break since the times of the Plague or even earlier. The five wells are reputed to have saved the inhabitants in a time of severe drought centuries ago and the tradition has been kept up ever since. Six yew trees flank the path to the church, which is crammed with Fitzherbert memorials; one truncates the arch with amazingly little regard for the symmetry of the building.

The village gives its name to the **Tissington Trail**, the path and cycleway along the old Buxton–Ashbourne railway which passes just to the east (see p 241). **Fenny Bentley** village, to the south and just off the A515, merits a short visit to its church, which possesses a sixteenth-century canopied and traceried screen, and a bizarre sculpted monument to Thomas Beresford and his wife (1473) showing the incumbents entirely wrapped in shrouds.

THE MANIFOLD VALLEY

A few miles to the west of Dove Dale, the Manifold Valley is more open and mellow than its neighbour. You can walk, bicycle or ride along the old Manifold Railway route. Public roads dip into the dale at several points, enabling you to drive along the valley from Grindon Mill to Ecton, where you can still see remains of the spoil heaps of the lucrative copper mines owned by the Dukes of Devonshire, the proceeds of which funded the building of Chatsworth House and Buxton's Crescent. Just below Wetton Mill, **Thor's Cave** perforates the most spectacular feature of the valley, a high towering crag, reached by a short, steep climb from the valley floor. The view from the cave mouth is one of the great sights of the Peak.

Ilam

An estate village of immaculate front gardens, tile-hung *cottages ornés* and chained bollards around a green. The village, church excepted, was created after the rebuilding of Ilam Hall in the early nineteenth century by Jesse Watts Russell, a wealthy industrialist. Above the village you'll find the Gothic pile, with a terrace overlooking idyllic parkland fringing the River Manifold. Parts of the hall, a spectacular mansion bristling with turrets and mock-battlements, were demolished in the 1930s, and the Italian formal gardens are not what they were, but a stroll through the grounds is pleasant enough; the hall itself is now a youth hostel and is not open to the public. The country park (free access) is owned by the National Trust and they have a shop and a restaurant in the Hall.

Between the Manifold Valley and Leek

Two features in this area are worth seeking out. **Upper Elkstone** on a minor lane west of Warslow, is a minute village with a church so small that you'll miss it if you blink. This simple chapel-like building of 1786–88 is crammed with box

---

ROYAL SHROVETIDE FOOTBALL

A RARE survival of medieval football, similar to the sport of Hurling played at St Columb Major in Cornwall: this free-for-all-style game takes place in Ashbourne annually on Shrove Tuesday and Ash Wednesday between 2pm and 10pm. Any number take part – usually hundreds on each side: teams are decided simply on the basis of which side of the Henmore Brook players live on 'Up'ards' or 'Down'ards'. The goals are three miles apart: the 'Up'ards' at Sturston and the 'Down'ards' at Clifton. Both are sites of mills that have since vanished. Before play begins, windows are boarded up

pews, topped by a tiny gallery and lit by simple arched windows. **Morridge** is a long escarpment forming the south-western bastion of the Peak District, with a wide, lonely road along its length: it is one of the best scenic drives in the National Park, with panoramas extending across the pottery towns and the Cheshire Plain.

Ashbourne

Home of Ashbourne Water and Royal Shrovetide Football, and graced with one of the most architecturally interesting streets in Derbyshire, Ashbourne is unlucky enough to suffer from heavy lorry traffic. Spanning its echoey, red-brick main street is the unusual 'gallows' type inn-sign for The Green Man and Black's Head, depicting a strange juxtaposition of negro head and huntsman. There are some excellent shops: the long-established Gingerbread Shop, selling cakes and parkin, Cheddar Gorge, a smart delicatessen with a wide range of cheeses and strange mushroom-shaped loaves, and Fosters Sporting Services, suppliers of fishing equipment since 1763.

Smart antique shops line Church Street, the buildings themselves worth attention. Much is three-storey Georgian, but the almshouses make a pleasing exception; look out for the tiny close of Owfield's and Pegge's almshouses. Further along are the town's most important buildings: the **old Grammar School** built 1583–1589 in stone, with a symmetrical, six-gabled façade; opposite, the **Mansion**, is a late-seventeenth-century residence, once the home of Reverend Dr John Taylor, who was often visited by his close friend Dr Johnson. The soaring 212-foot-high spire of the parish church provides

and the town looks like it is awaiting a siege.

A lunch at the Green Man Hotel and the singing of the Shrovetide Song ('It's a good old game, deny it who can, that tries the pluck of an Englishman') precedes the start of play. Players play towards their own goal, the painted, cork-stuffed leather ball can only be carried on foot (you can throw the ball but cannot grasp it), and the churchyard is out of bounds; otherwise there are no rules as such. The 'royal' title was added in 1928 when the Prince of Wales (later Edward VIII) started the game.

a splendid focal point for the street. Within its spacious, much Victorianised interior is a notable collection of monuments, including fifteenth- and sixteenth-century ones to the Cock-aynes and Bradbournes; most famous of all is the touching Carrara marble memorial by Thomas Banks to five-year-old Penelope Boothby (1791).

BUXTON TO BAKEWELL

Apart from the stretch of the A6 just east of Buxton that runs past the end of Monsal Dale, the main places of interest are off the main road. Old lead-mines dot the area between **Chelmorton** and **Sheldon**, perhaps none more striking anywhere in the country than the well-preserved remains of **Magpie Lead Mine**, visible from the road just south of Sheldon. The surface buildings you see are nineteenth-century but the mine was operational from 1682 (maybe earlier) until 1958; two chimneys, a Cornish-type beam-engine house and headgear. Most of the time you're unlikely to encounter anyone, apart from sheep and perhaps the occasional industrial archaeologist. A track leads to the site from the road. If you're interested in seeing inside the mine, contact the Peak District Mining Museum at Matlock Bath who arrange party visits, tel. (0629) 583834.

The village of **Chelmorton** consists of a long single street, lined with cottages, farms and barns, which reaches a dead end at the church and pub, closest to the spring of Illy Willy Water and snug beneath the towering form of **Chelmorton Low**, a green hill tipped by Bronze-Age burial mounds. In medieval times the open field system surrounded Chelmorton: one big open field encircled by an earth bank, with allocated strips

BAKEWELL PUDDING

WALK AROUND Bakewell and you will find two bakeries which claim to sell the authentic Bakewell Puddings: neither calls them tarts, and the large, unevenly shaped confections of flaky pastry with a dollop of jam in the middle bear little resemblance to the neat, mass-produced miniatures sold in supermarkets all over the country. Purists say the Bakewell Pudding must be eaten warm.

The invention of the Pudding was the result of a mistake in the

behind each farmstead running at right angles to the main road. When the days of enclosure came in 1809, these strips were dry-stone walled in exactly the same pattern, leaving us with a remarkable 'fossilisation' of a once widespread medieval farming practice: to see the full effect you need to view the village from higher ground.

North of the A6 near **Great Longstone**, **Monsal Head** provides one of the classic Peak views, over an enticing dale spanned by the viaduct for the old London-to-Manchester railway. The Buxton-to-Matlock section was closed in 1967 and part of the track now forms the Monsal Trail, a scenic walkway. It is a beautiful place for wandering by the trout-laden River Wye (see walk on p.246) and watching dippers flying above the water; part of the dale has been designated a nature reserve for its butterflies and limestone flora.

Tideswell

'The cathedral of the Peak' as the church has been dubbed, is the focal point of this large village. Lead-mining and the wool trade brought great prosperity to the village in medieval times, and much money was poured into the building of the church. Built almost entirely in the Decorated style of the fourteenth century, its Perpendicular tower was added later. The churchyard is the resting place for many of the corpses of the badly treated apprentices from Litton Mill.

Ashford in the Water

The busy A6 runs along one side of the village but the rest is pretty with a long meandering street, with eighteenth- and a few seventeenth-century cottages alongside broad grass

kitchen of the White Horse Inn (now the Rutland Arms) around 1860, when the cook's assistant's attempted to make strawberry tart. She mistakenly put the jam in and poured egg mixture intended for the pastry over the top. However, the guests enjoyed the result; Mrs Greaves the cook noted the recipe, which the assistant left in her will to a Mr Radford. He in turn passed it on to a Mr Bloomer to produce the Pudding on the premises for public sale; the original recipe is still in the safe of the Original Bakewell Pudding Shop.

verges. Of the village's three bridges, the most celebrated is Sheepwash Bridge, whose former function is self-explanatory, and the walled sheep enclosure can be seen on the opposite bank. Comprehensive rebuilding of the church in 1869–70 deprived it of any major period architectural features.

Bakewell

The only town within the National Park boundary, Bakewell has some pretty corners, but a walk through the centre is likely to be a struggle against traffic streaming through its highly necessary one-way system. Market day (Monday) brings a friendlier bustle – with a lively cattle market and lots of market stalls – and in August the town stages a major agricultural show, featuring livestock competitions, show-jumping, and horticultural exhibits.

Part of the town is tranquil and picturesque with ducks swimming on the river beside the fourteenth-century bridge, and the shapely church spire dominating the town. The central square has unfortunately become a traffic roundabout, fronted by the **Rutland Arms**, once stayed in by Jane Austen. But close by are a few other historic buildings, including the old **market hall**, now functioning as the main National Park Tourist Information Centre for the Peak, and the Old Town Hall of 1709 (to the left of the Rutland Arms), in King Street, where the Quarter Sessions used to be held.

Up by the church you come to a more secluded quarter. Stepped paths and crooked lanes lead to the church, heavily restored by Gilbert Scott the younger in the nineteenth century; his addition of a spire was a triumph. Look out for the monuments, which are some of the finest in the Peak: a knight and his lady in the south aisle, and the Vernon Chapel within the south transept, where you will find sixteenth-century memorials to the Vernon and Manners families of Haddon Hall.

Near the church and well signposted from the town centre, the **Bakewell Old House Museum** (open Easter to end Oct, daily 2 to 5) contains an absorbing exhibition of rural bygones, Victoriana, and Edwardian costumes and toys. The building, dating from 1534, is one of the oldest houses in town.

SOUTH OF BAKEWELL

Haddon Hall

(Open Easter to Oct, daily 11 to 6) Owned and still lived in by the Dukes of Rutland (family name Manners), Haddon Hall, one of the finest examples of an English medieval manor house, dates from between the twelfth and sixteenth centuries; the buildings cover many periods but are all built in the same weathered stone to create a beautifully unified composition. Castellations, towers and turrets are picturesque adornments rather than military fortifications. Clipped yews and rosebeds grace walled garden terraces which jut out above a packhorse bridge on a meander of the Wye. Inside, too, there is much to savour. Restoration revealed a set of fifteenth-century wall-paintings in the chapel. A fine oak roof of 1923–25 was put on the banqueting hall and minstrels' gallery, and intricately carved panelling adorns a magnificent long gallery.

Rowsley

Just east of Haddon Hall on the A6, Rowsley is a village in two halves: the old part centres around Caudwell's Mill and the handsome Peacock Hotel, the latter built in 1652 by John Stevenson. Across the bridge, industrial Little Rowsley is a railway-age development of red-brick – Joseph Paxton's picturesque chalet-style railway station of 1849 looks stranded in a wasteland of abandoned railway tracks. Visitors to **Caudwell's Mill** (open Easter or 1 Apr to end Oct, daily 10 to 6; rest of year 10 to 4.30 weekends only) can wander around this large turbine-driven roller-mill, built in 1874 with much of its machinery dating from about 1900. You can watch the rollers breaking wheat grain, flour being sifted and then buy the wholemeal flour.

Signposted off the main road at Darley Dale, **Red House Stables Carriage Museum** (open all year, daily from 10am (for details of rides and instruction tel. (0629) 733583) is an enthusiast's collection of horse-drawn carriages, including an early petrol-tanker and a stage-coach. From the adjoining stables, carriage-rides operate regularly in season, and carriage-driving instruction is also available.

Winster

West of Darley Bridge, high up on the plateau, Winster is a former lead-miners' village with a dignified main street lined with three-storey houses. At its heart stands an old market hall, now a National Trust information centre. The medieval lower floor is arched (originally these arches were open) and its seventeenth-century upper floor has mullioned windows. The Old Hall (now a pub), adorned with pilasters and a balustraded top, stands out among the numerous fine eighteenth-century houses. In June or July each year the Winster Wakes bring a carnival atmosphere to the village, with Morris dancing and children's sports among the attractions.

About a mile to the north of Winster, the small village of **Birchover** lies among working quarries. Above the village's Druid Stone Inn are the curious **Rowtor Rocks**, a natural outcrop into which a Reverend Thomas Eyre (died 1717) cut a staircase, benches and an armchair in which to meditate and prepare his sermons.

Stanton Moor lies just north-east of the village, a strange place pitted with old quarry-workings and studded with over seventy prehistoric burial mounds. Items excavated from here are in the Sheffield Museum; other archaeological sites around the moor include the **Nine Ladies**, a Bronze-Age stone circle some 50 feet across and standing in a birch wood. As its name suggests, there are nine stones, but the ladies are gnomish in the extreme; the tallest is a mere 39 inches. Legend has it that these were the tombs of nine ladies of Haddon, afflicted with the Plague, who danced a last dance on the moor with their dying fiddler; the fiddler's stone stands nearby. For directions to these sites see p 242.

From the B5056 west of Birchover you can see **Robin Hood's Stride**, a large rock outcrop prominent from the road. Just to the right of it, approached from a track, woods cling around Cratcliffe Rocks, near the foot of which is a

WELL-DRESSING

THIS COLOURFUL tradition, largely peculiar to the Peak District, draws visitors in ever-increasing numbers to the villages of the White Peak. Villagers prepare tableaux of biblical scenes and churches. They mount clay upon a board, and then cover this mosaic-style with whatever natural materials are suitable – petals, mosses, stones, lichens and leaves predominate; alder cones and seeds are used for the outlines.

Giving thanks for the gift of water has certainly been carried out in Mediterranean countries, and it is from these places that the practice may have been imported in Roman times when it took the form of a dedication made to pagan spirits. Missionaries taught that homage should instead be paid to saints. The practice later died out but was revived in Tissington, either after the Black Death, or in the

medieval hermit's cave – not that easy to find, it must be stressed – with a crucifix carved into the wall.

Youlgreave

Two quirky features can be found in the centre of this elongated village: a circular tank, known both as the Conduit Head and the Fountain, which supplied the first piped drinking-water in 1829 to villagers prepared to fork out an annual sixpenny subscription; and a youth hostel retaining the appearance of an old-fashioned co-operative store, with gold lettering and a beehive-motif plaque.

Youlgreave church has one of the best towers in Derbyshire – a 96-foot high structure added in the fifteenth century. The building lives up to its external promise: a spacious interior, sensitively restored by Norman Shaw in 1870. Look out for Burne-Jones's east window added in 1876 and four angels by William Morris in the tracery above.

LATHKILL DALE

A limestone dale of rare beauty, the finest part of Lathkill is a three-mile stretch from its source near Monyash to the confluence with the River Bradford at Alport. Much of the dale is now designated as a nature reserve for the flora and

seventeenth century after the Plague; the village avoided both disasters and the springs provided an unfailing source of pure water.

Tourist information centres have details of the well-dressing calendar for each year, but the approximate timings are: **May**: Tissington, Wirksworth, Etwall, Newborough, Endon, Brackenfield, Chester Green, Middleton-by-Youlgreave, Monyash; **June**: Ashford, Tideswell, Youlgreave, Old Whittington, Cressbrook, Chelmorton, Witton, Rowsley, Hope, Bakewell; **July**: Pilsley, Stoney Middleton, Baslow, Buxton, Heath, Cowley Mission, West Hallam, Dronfield Woodhouse, Cutthorpe; **August**: Barlow, Bradwell, Wormhill, Bonsall, Holmsfield, Great Hucklow, Taddington, Holymoorside, Eyam, Foolow; **September**: Hartington, Longnor, Wardlow

insect life. Walking along the river you can see the weirs, introduced to create hatcheries for trout, and lovely coppiced woodland planted in the 1800s half-covering some of the dale's old lead-mines. Also on the way are the remains of an engine-house and a pumping-shaft belonging to Mandale lead-mine.

Monyash

Just west of the source of the River Lathkill, Monyash was a market-town in medieval times and later became a quarrying and lead-mining centre for the High Peak. A small patch of clay on the limestone plateau is the geological reason for the siting of this remote village; the impermeable layer once supported five ponds, which proved to be a valuable water supply. The well is dressed in thanksgiving even though Fen Mere is now the lone survivor. All that is left from those thriving days is a big triangular green with the weathered shaft of an old market-cross at the centre, flanked by a sole pub.

South of Monyash, look for the sign to **Arbor Low**, without doubt, the most impressive archaeological monument in the Peak; its remoteness probably saved it for posterity. Dating from about 2000BC, Arbor Low is a classic henge feature. Late Stone Age or early Bronze Age, the six-foot high circular bank has two entrances enclosing a stone circle of nearly fifty stones, that in turn encloses an inner sanctum with a smaller group of stones. **Gib Hill**, just across the neighbouring field, is a conical tumulus thought to be of slightly later date standing about 17 feet high. Access to the site is through a farmyard, where a small admission charge is payable into an honesty box.

MATLOCK GORGE

'I can assure you there are things in Derbyshire as noble as Greece or Switzerland' wrote Lord Byron on one of his many visits to Matlock Gorge. The scene that excited the Romantics and brought in day-trippers on the canal and later on the railway was the sinuous gorge south of Matlock, hemmed in by tremendous cliffs. There is nothing much to see in Matlock, but a mile further south, at the hub of the gorge, **Matlock Bath** is of considerable curiosity value, a faded spa with something of the character of a mid-European *Kur* resort. Paxton's chalet-style railway station and cable cars crossing overhead reinforce the un-Englishness of it all, with tall nineteenth-century villas climbing the hillside; down at main road level there are tacky amusement parlours among the Victorian brick and wrought-iron, and the place fills up with Sunday afternoon bikers. The former Fountain Baths now function as an aquarium and hologram gallery.

• **High Tor and the Heights of Abraham** (Heights of Abraham open Easter to Oct, daily 10 to 5, later in high season; cable car may not run in high wind; access to cable car and High Tor grounds from Matlock Bath station) These are the two great crags on either side of the gorge. Both are fine vantage points, reached by zigzagging paths through steep woodlands. The Heights of Abraham, which has marginally the better view, is more like a park, with a Scandinavian-style café, a craft shop, a prospect tower and two caverns to visit.

• **Peak District Mining Museum** (open all year exc Christmas Day, daily 11 to 4; closes later in summer) Housed in the former pavilion building, this well conceived exhibition gives a comprehensive picture of mining in the Peak. There are mock-ups of the inside of a mine, pumping-engines, rock displays and features on historical developments.

A visit here ties in nicely with a tour of **Temple Mine** (open Easter to Oct, daily 11 to 4 or later; Nov to Mar weekends only, 2 to 4), just across the road. The mine visit is not recommended for claustrophobics, as the roof is low – if your height exceeds five feet you will need to pick up a helmet at the entrance.

Cromford

The proximity of quarries unfortunately means that during most of the week Cromford's main street suffers from the racket of lorries changing down a gear before grinding up Cromford Hill. Don't let that put you off, for the village is one of the cradles of the Industrial Revolution. Here in 1771 Richard Arkwright established the first water-powered cotton spinning-mill, the beginning of the end for the cottage hand-loom industry and the precursor of the industrial expansion of the cotton towns of Lancashire when steam power took over in the 1840s.

Arkwright used Bonsall Brook and Cromford Sough, a water-channel which can be seen passing through a sluice in a lane off the lower part of the main street. The houses he built for his mill-workers still dominate the village; of special interest is **North Street**, the first planned industrial street in

Derbyshire, completed in 1777. Arkwright's own homes are still here – Rock House and imposing Willersley Castle, both occupying hill-top sites; he is buried in Cromford churchyard. On the A6 to Matlock, just outside the village, is the huge **Masson Mills**, built by Arkwright in 1783 – six storeys of red brick, with Venetian windows and a cupola.

Guided tours are offered around **Cromford Mill** (open all year, Mon to Fri 9.30 to 5; weekends and Bank Hol 10 to 5; winter 10 to 4.30) and you can visit the exhibition hall where the history of the mill is explained. Close to the mill and opposite the church, horse-drawn barges operate in summer from the once busy wharf on the **Cromford Canal**. Completed in 1793 as part of a network connecting Cromford with the main industrial centres of the north-west, it was primarily used for the transportation of raw cotton, minerals and yarn. A long mile along the canal (there is car access here or you can walk along the towpath) are the wharf and railway workshops at **High Peak Junction**, now a visitor centre (open every weekend and daily in school holidays and Bank Holidays) with an exhibition about the railway, and some preserved goods trucks. The High Peak walking trail runs where the old railway track used to be.

The A5012 snakes along a deep valley westwards from Cromford; also named the **Via Gellia**, the road was made around the beginning of the nineteenth century for lead-ore traffic travelling from local mines to the smelting-mills. One mill later became the premises of Viyella textiles, that trade-name being a deliberate distortion of Via Gellia. The B5023 south from this road leads through Middleton and into Wirksworth.

Wirksworth

Now at the heart of a major quarrying area, once a centre of the old lead-mining industry, Wirksworth has, to a surprising degree, retained its gruff yet fragile character – irregular streets, sloping cobbled paths and quarry spoils in the background. The Barmote Court, the oldest in the country, was set up to settle lead-mining disputes and still sits twice a year, in April and October. A bowl made in the reign of Henry VIII for measuring lead-ore is still kept in the Moot Hall.

The town's most picturesque area lies in a gracious close around the church, below which are almshouses and the Old Free School founded in the late sixteenth century. George Gilbert Scott restored the medieval church in the 1870s, and stained-glass in the east window was added by Edward Burne-Jones in 1909. The town has a minor role in literary history as the Snowfield of George Eliot's *Adam Bede*.

Wirksworth's history, from Roman times to the present day features in a display in the **Heritage Centre** (open Apr to mid-June, Tue to Sun and Bank Hols 10 to 5; mid-June to Sept daily 10 to 5; winter, exc mid-Dec to Jan, Tue to Sun 11 to 4.30). Housed in a former silk- and velvet-mill building, you can pick up a town trail guide from here.

East of Matlock Gorge

• **Lea Gardens** (open mid-Mar to end July, 10 to 7) John Marsden-Smedley, a woollen manufacturer, created the four-acre garden in the early part of this century on a steep hillside, lacing a woodland with narrow paths and introducing rockery and Alpine plants and shrubs. Try to come here in May, when the rhododendrons and azaleas reach their prime.

• **National Tramway Museum**, Crich (open Mar to Oct, most days 10 to 5.30, or 6.30 at weekends and Bank Hol Mon; tel Ambergate (0773) 852565) Vintage vehicles take you on nostalgic rides along a mile of track laid out with period tram shelters, buildings and street furniture; you can also admire some forty exhibits.

ROWSLEY TO HATHERSAGE

The great natural wonder of this area is the twelve-mile-long edge of dark millstone-grit, the raw material of the vanished millstone industry, creating a wall along the eastern side of the Peak and providing a magnificent viewing-platform (see walk on p.245). Its main section runs from Birchen Edge, east of Baslow and reaches its highest point at Stanage Edge north of Hathersage. Below, the River Derwent winds through lush green scenery and broad-leaved woodlands, a placid contrast to the 'frightful river when the hills load her current' which Defoe saw on his visit here in the early eighteenth century; weirs and banking in the intervening years have mitigated the risk of flooding.

Chatsworth House

(Open daily, Easter to early Nov; house 11 to 4.30, gardens 11 to 5; farm and adventure playground Easter to end Sept, 10.30 to 4.30, playground open weekends in Oct; estate farm shop at Pilsley open daily exc Sun 9 to 5.30, 9 to 5 in winter)

Your first glimpse of Chatsworth is not one you will easily forget. The approach road crosses the green swathe of parkland landscaped by Capability Brown and goes over the much-photographed bridge across the Derwent; beyond rises the great mansion of honey-coloured stone, backed by the gravity-operated Emperor fountain, which, after heavy rain can send up a jet of water 290 feet, the second highest such feature in Europe.

The house, residence of the Dukes of Devonshire, is of Elizabethan origin but was comprehensively remodelled in classical style between 1678 and 1707, first by William Talman and then by Thomas Archer; Jeffry Wyatville added the north wing in the 1820s. The interior of the house is dark and palatial – huge rooms with painted ceilings, classical statues, rare furniture and fine paintings.

The formal gardens are a delight, occupying a hundred-acre site. A grand terrace, the Broad Walk, provides the central axis; above, a cascade tumbles down steps from the Cascade House (1703). A charming series of surprises awaits you as you follow paths past the rockeries, the surreal Serpentine Hedge, a tiny ravine leading up to a pond and backed by a grotto and banks of rhododendrons, and a 'willow tree' cunningly disguised as a fountain. Much of the garden's present form is attributed to Joseph Paxton, the head gardener in the nineteenth century; the central fanlight in one of the glass-houses hints at his later design for the Crystal Palace.

Paxton also collaborated with the architect J C Roberston in the design of the estate village of **Edensor** (pronounced Ensor), across the B6012 from the main entrance to Chatsworth. This was done with great panache, creating a series of picturesque *cottages ornés*, each in a different style, one beneath a tower, another with rustic eaves above an oriel window. The church is the focal point; Paxton is buried in the churchyard.

THE UPPER DERWENT VALLEY

The high eastern moors of the Dark Peak form a barrier between the National Park and the fringes of Sheffield, but suburbanisation has nevertheless crept into the Derwent valley villages. The A623 from here heads westwards past the large village of **Stoney Middleton**, on the brink of a landscape despoiled by limestone and fluorspar quarries. The church stands just off the main road giving little hint of its unusual octagonal interior added to the Perpendicular tower in 1759.

Eyam

There is much to enjoy walking around the streets of limestone cottages in Eyam (pronounced 'Eem'), north-west of Stoney Middleton, but the village has a grim history. In 1665 an Eyam tailor called George Viccars brought a box of cloth from London which was later considered to be the source of the deadly Plague virus in the village. His death on 7 September was the first of many entries made in the register of deaths. The vicar, William Mompesson, spearheaded a campaign of self-imposed quarantine for the villagers. Those who wanted to leave did so at the beginning; three hundred and fifty inhabitants remained. The news was carried to the Earl of Devonshire, the lord of the manor, who arranged for supplies to be left at given points on the village boundary. A total of over two hundred and fifty lives were claimed by the disease in Eyam. Sobering reminders of this bleak time can be found all around the village, hand-painted signs explaining each site.

Cucklet Church, a limestone cavern, is where an annual commemoration service takes place in the open air. The church contains an exhibition detailing the story of its Plague, as well as a chair that belonged to Mompesson, a cupboard thought to have been made from Viccars' ill-fated box and the register of Plague victims.

Hathersage

Once a mill village where needles were manufactured, Hathersage today has a straggly and suburban appearance, influenced by Sheffield to the east. But the village is also at the hub of some fine scenic variety. This was Morton village in *Jane Eyre*, and members of the real Eyre family (who lived at Moorseats, a house in Hathersage) are buried in the church, at the top of the village.

The A625 climbs eastwards on to the moors, gaining impressive views as it does so. At a bend in the road by a lone bus-stop a wild valley set in a deep basin and edged on one side by **Burbage Rocks** is briefly revealed on the left, dominated by the towering form of **Carl Wark**, an ancient hill-fort, thought to date from AD500 to 600.

CASTLETON AND AROUND

Castleton is considered to be at the geographical heart of the Peak District, on the borderland of a remarkable cave district in the limestone country, and the open moors of the Dark Peak to its north.

Castleton

A large village dissected by a mill brook, it is overshadowed by the gaunt ruins of Peveril Castle perched on the hill above it. Castleton is full of restaurants, B&Bs and souvenir shops, but the natural wonders and sense of place still win through. Cottages flank the brookside path leading to Peak Cavern, the largest cave entrance in Britain. Souvenir vases and trinkets made from a mauve crystalline flourspar called Blue John (found only in this area) are sold in some shops; the Blue John Craft Shop has a one-room museum (the Ollerenshaw Collection: open during shop hours) of Blue John and Ashford Black Marble ornaments.

Peveril Castle (English Heritage, open Good Fri or 1 Apr to 30 Sept, daily, 10 to 6; winter Tue to Sun 10 to 4) was begun by William Peverel (*sic*) supposedly an illegitimate son of

THE CAVES OF THE CASTLETON AREA

APART FROM the caving excursions into Bagshawe Cavern, all of the caves include guided tours with electric lighting, steps and hand-rails; each takes about 45 minutes to explore. Blue John, Speedwell and Treak Cliff caverns are situated a short distance west of Castleton.

Bagshawe Cavern (open weekends from 2pm, at other times by appointment; for details of tour times tel Hope Valley (0433) 20540 or 21298) is on the edge of Bradwell (not signposted). This is the cave to visit if you want to experience some of the elements of true caving: the 'adventure trip' and 'lower level trip' entail scrambling, wading and crawling through chimneys and natural features with names such as the Letter Box and Agony Crawl; old clothes and a torch are essential, and you have to book in advance. Additionally, there is an electrically lit 'show' cave with stalagmite and stalactite formations for anyone who can manage the 98 steps.

Blue John Cavern (open daily 10 to dusk) The tour passes outcrops of the mauve rock known as Blue John, and glistening 'flow rock' - formed by dripping water. There are no stalactite formations of any significance, but you experience some exciting moments when unexpected narrow depths of the cavern are revealed.

William the Conqueror. The ruins are only of minor intrinsic interest but the castle site, reached by a steep winding path, gives an excellent view of Cave Dale (behind the castle) and Castleton.

Hope and Edale

Hope is a large village on the edge of wild and remote scenery, yet oddly suburban in character. The church has some interesting carvings and the outside is adorned with splendid gargoyles.

The one-street village of **Edale**, to the north-west, is beautifully sited at the foot of the Kinder Scout moors and walkers pack its tiny street at weekends. **The Pennine Way** starts here, making a 270-mile course over the high backbone of northern England, finishing at Kirk Yetholm in the Scottish Borders.

Just west of Castleton, the A625 diverts along **Winnats Pass**, a spectacular limestone gorge. North on the road to

Peak Cavern (open Easter to early Nov, daily 10 to 5) In Castleton village itself, the awe-inspiringly vast cave entrance is beneath Peveril Castle. A former rope-maker's cottage, inhabited until 1830, huddles just inside the natural cavern, with surviving rope-making apparatus and a rope-walk behind. Peak Cavern, known as the Devil's Arse until Victorian times, is the largest cavern system in England; Victorian visitors used to be entertained by the village choir here. Only a fraction of the cavern is seen, but you can get an idea of its size; there are no significant stalactite concretions.

Speedwell Cavern (open daily 9.30 to 5.30) is the only cave visit in the Castleton area to feature an underground boat-trip. It takes you along a flooded tunnel that was blasted out of the rock by lead-miners. At the end of the tunnel you reach a narrow and phenomenally tall natural cavern – but the tunnel itself is merely straight and low, and is visually the least interesting of the local cave visits.

Treak Cliff Cavern (open Apr to Oct, daily 9.30 to 6; winter 9.30 to 4) is a short natural cavern that has been mined for Blue John. It has some very pretty stalactite formations; pieces of Blue John are placed over lights to show the rock's translucent quality.

Edale you can climb a long flight of steps to Mam Tor and see the glorious four-way view over White and Dark Peak landscapes; you can continue along the exhilarating path to the ridge at Hollin's Cross and Lose Hill (see walk on p.249).

THE HIGH PEAK

This is a vast, virtually unpeopled area, forming the northern half of the National Park. It is terrain for long, arduous yomps over peaty, elemental expanses. In good weather and light traffic, driving over it is exhilarating, with wide, empty horizons. Reservoirs and main roads are the principal intrusions on the primeval, rolling moor. Beware sudden turns in the weather which can plunge you into mist; signs indicate when the high-level roads are closed even when conditions lower down seem mild.

The Derwent, Howden and Ladybower reservoirs by the A57 constitute the Peak's most impressive lakelands: four miles of valley drowned between 1901 and 1945. Gloomy conifer plantations fringe the lakes, but it's still rewarding to explore on foot around here by heading up on to the hill-tops. A plaque on the dam commemorates those who died in the Dambusters raid in the Ruhr Valley in 1943; the Lancaster Bomber pilots practised the bouncing bomb technique here in the Upper Derwent Valley because of the similarity of its topography to the real target.

Westwards, the A57 takes a lonely course over the scenic **Snake Pass**, a road engineered by Thomas Telford. Austere-looking hills and bare moorland give you a good idea of the heart of the High Peak. If you descend from the Pass, **Glossop** is the first of a number of old cotton towns between the National Park and Manchester. To the north, only two other roads cross the moor: the busy A628 from Tintwistle, just north of Glossop, climbs up Longdendale past reservoirs and pylons, and the A635 west of Holmfirth.

NEW MILLS TO LEEK

This area is the most intricate and varied part of the Dark Peak, with green hills folded in complex fashion, remote hamlets and farmsteads and some vast panoramas looking westwards over Cheshire and into North Wales. Below, and quite separate in character, lie a series of towns – Pennine stone to the north, red-brick Midland further south.

New Mills

It is the location that makes this the most rewarding of the Peak mill-towns. From a plain town centre, signs point to the Torrs Riverside Park where, within a few yards, the gorge of the Rivers Goyt and Sett is revealed and you can set off on a rural walk beneath the cliffs, with houses crouched above decaying mills.

The New Mills Heritage Centre (open Tue to Fri, 11 to 4, Sat, Sun and Bank Hol Mon 10.30 to 4.30; free) has a viewing-platform over the gorge, as well as a local history display and a model of the town as it looked in 1884. Leaflets available here detail a two-mile 'bridges trail' along the river and the Peak Forest Canal. The canal opened in 1796 to connect the Peak Forest Tramway at Bugsworth with the Cromford and High Peak Railway at Whaley Bridge.

Right on the fringes of the National Park, **Hayfield** is a large former cotton-milling village with a sloping main street, which at weekends swarms with rucksack-clad walkers making for **Kinder Reservoir** and the high moors beyond, where the waterfall known as Kinder Downfall tumbles off the edge. Crafts- and tea-shops indicate Hayfield's day-trip popularity – Manchester and Stockport are not so very far away – but it is not conspicuously over-touristy in tone.

Crossing through New Mills, you reach **Lyme Hall and Lyme Park** (park open all year, daily 8am to dusk; hall open Easter to end Sept, Tue, Wed, Thur and Sat 2 to 4; Sun, Bank Hol Mon and some Sats 2 to 5). One of the finest English examples of Palladian architecture, the Hall is set in a deer park with rare trees and shrubs, near Disley on the edge of Stockport. Views contrast strangely: on one side the park is beautifully fringed by a moorland ridge, while eastern slopes look over the tower-blocks of Stockport and Manchester.

Lyme Hall, home of the Legh family until it was given to the National Trust in 1947, is an Elizabethan structure remodelled in 1725 by the Italian architect Giacomo Leoni, author of one of the two principal textbooks on the architecture of Palladio. He transformed the earlier, L-shaped structure into a three-storey Italianate building around a courtyard, with classical proportions, a raised floor, windows and also added the baroque ceilings. Grinling Gibbons was responsible for the limewood carving in the Saloon (originally installed in the New Parlour): his virtuoso work includes exquisitely delicate representations of music, art, poetry and the four seasons. Lewis Wyatt made further changes in 1813 to 1814, notably the remodelling of the library with a large compass-bay window. Much survives internally of the Elizabethan building, including a panelled long gallery, and items of the Leghs' furniture, clocks and glassware are on display.

THE GOYT VALLEY AND MACCLESFIELD

Not as majestic in scale as the Derwent Valley reservoirs, nevertheless the Goyt Valley reservoirs, conifer plantations and picnic sites are pleasant places to stop. On the edge of the Cheshire Plain and very much a north Midlands town in

ACCESS FOR THE MASSES: THE BIRTH

"DEAR LAND of Moors, with Hope uncrown'd
Men wait thy freedom yet
On craggy brows, beloved, renowned,
Vile trespass boards are set."
G.H.B. Ward of the Clarion Ramblers Club from Sheffield 1921.
Ward's verse epitomised the sentiment of the pre-National Park era. More than anywhere else in Britain, northern England had from the late nineteenth century a strong network of enthusiastic ramblers' clubs. The Peak District was particularly in demand, ringed by large industrial towns – a half of the population of England living within 60 miles of Buxton – it filled up on Sundays with mill- and steel-workers escaping from the grime and smoke of the cities for the freedom of the hills. But access was severely limited: much of the High Peak was carefully guarded grouse moor or owned by water authorities. Some footpaths existed, but not enough for the 10,000 ramblers who arrived each weekend; several pre-1914 footpath signposts erected by the Peak and Northern Footpaths Society survive today (look out for the one at Grindleford Bridge).

Game-keepers posted on the moors kept watch for those who defiantly ignored 'trespassers will be prosecuted' signs, and physical confrontations were not uncommon. Injunctions were served on persistent trespassers to prevent them returning, and in 1923 the Manchester Evening Chronicle carried an advertisement with photographs of ramblers and an offer of a £5 reward to anyone suppplying names and addresses.

The emergence of the socialist movement in the inter-war years provided a catalyst in the cause of increased public access

character, **Macclesfield** was once famed for its silk production. Although a few Georgian town houses and a handful of working silk mills survive from the late sixteenth- and seventeenth-century heyday, the town is only patchily interesting at first sight.

But a sight essential to an understanding of the town's history is **The Silk Museum and Paradise Mill** (Museum open Tue to Sat, 11 to 5; Bank Hol Mon and Sun 1 to 5. Mill open Tue to Sun, 1 to 5. Both closed New Year's Day, Good Fri, and 24 to 26 Dec. Joint admission available for both.) Make the museum your first visit. It is in the town centre, and housed in a former Sunday School that itself looks like a mill.

OF NATIONAL PARKS

to the countryside. In 1926 the first of the annual rallies in Winnats Pass was held and attended by thousands; they called for free access to open country and the formation of National Parks.

Matters came to a head on May 24th 1932 when four hundred ramblers, having publicised their intentions, set out from Hayfield on a deliberate mass trespass on to Kinder Scout. They walked up William Clough to find a group of game-keepers waiting; a skirmish ensued and five ramblers were arrested and imprisoned at Derby Assizes. As a result of these events the issue of public access became a matter of national policy. The Access to the Mountains Bill 1939 was rendered impotent by parliamentary amendments, but in 1945 John Dower published a seminal report calling for the formation of National Parks, and the Hobhouse Report recommended the establishment of the Peak National Park. The National Parks and Access to the Countryside Act was passed in 1949, setting up not only the machinery for the formation of the Parks, but also the survey and definitive mapping of public rights of way.

In 1951 the Peak became one of the first four National Parks; two years later, the first access agreement was signed, whereby a landowner allowed access on to open land (except during the grouse-shooting season, although rights of way crossing this are unaffected). Sixty per cent of such agreements are in the Peak, a total of 76 square miles.

An audio-visual show introduces the story of silk, its production and the people who worked on its manufacture. Upstairs an exhibition illustrates the story of manufactured silk, the looms and life in the silk town.

The visit to Paradise Mill consists of a guided tour of what was a working handloom-mill up to 1981, operating up to then in a unique time-warp. The looms were installed in 1912, many other machines are over a century old and even the office furniture is of an antique variety. You are shown silkworm cocoons, unwoven silk and then the spinning and weaving processes, followed by a look at how plates were made for the manufacture of weaving patterns.

Signposted from the A537 on the east side of Macclesfield, **Tegg's Nose Country Park** is a popular starting-point for walks. The 'Nose' is a fine viewpoint above an old gritstone quarry.

WILDBOARCLOUGH AND SURROUNDINGS

This south-western corner of the National Park is primarily an area to explore on foot, although there are one or two lovely viewpoints from the road, such as from the Cat and Fiddle Inn high up on the A537 which looks over to Shutlingsloe, and the panorama over the Roaches from Roach End, east of Danebridge. Eastwards, lonely pastures merge into moorlands, and three counties – Cheshire, Staffordshire and Derbyshire – meet at two stone bridges and a confluence of streams at **Three Shires Head**, off the road. The River Dane flows swiftly south-west, its power once harnessed by a number of mills.

WHERE TO STAY

ASHBOURNE

Stanshope Hall
Stanshope, Nr Ashbourne
DE6 2AD
TEL (033527) 278
Lovely views can be enjoyed from this well-proportioned stone house that stands on a hill above a minor road. Original furnishings and a good home-cooked dinner make this a good base for the area.
£ *All year exc Chr; 3 rooms*

Callow Hall
Mappleton Road, Ashbourne
DE6 2AA

TEL (0335) 43403

A family-run, grand old house with an excellent restaurant. Bedrooms are quite luxurious. Service is attentive.

£££ *All year exc Chr and 2 weeks Feb; restaurant closed Sun evening; 12 rooms; Access, Amex, Diners, Visa*

BASLOW

Cavendish Hotel

Baslow DE4 1SP

TEL (0246) 582311

The hotel is close to Chatsworth House and guests may walk through the fields to visit the estate. Bedrooms and public rooms are of the highest standard, and all tastefully decorated and extremely comfortable.

£££ *All year; 24 rooms; Access, Amex, Diners, Visa*

BIGGIN

Biggin Hall

Biggin, Buxton SK17 0DH

TEL (0298) 84451

A lovely old listed building which has been sensitively converted into a cosy, welcoming hotel. Log fires and comfortable old sofas make it a perfect place to relax after a day's walking.

£ *All year; 15 rooms; Access, Visa*

BOTTOMHOUSE

Pethills Bank Cottage

Bottomhouse, Nr Leek ST13 7PF

TEL (0538) 304277

A compact cottage high up on the moors. Essentially a B&B, although dinner can be provided by arrangement. All your needs have been thought of in the well-equipped bedrooms.

£ *All year, exc Chr; 3 rooms*

BUTTERTON

Black Lion Inn

Butterton, Nr Leek ST13 7ST

TEL (0538) 304232

In the centre of a peaceful, fairly isolated village, this pub/hotel dates from the eighteenth century. A cosy bar, pretty bedrooms and good food make it an excellent base.

£ *All year; rest open Fri, Sat eve and Sun lunch but bar food available every day; 3 rooms*

GLOSSOP

The Wind in the Willows

Derbyshire Level, Glossop SK13 9PT

TEL (0457) 868001 Fax (0457) 853354

A comfortable Victorian house decorated in period style, it is well-placed for exploring the northern stretches of the Peak District.

£££ *All year, rest closed Chr and New Year; 8 rooms; Access, Amex, Visa*

GREAT HUCKLOW

Hucklow Hall

Great Hucklow, Tideswell, Buxton SK17 8RG

TEL (0298) 871175

Hidden away in an isolated village, you will need directions to find the Hall. Guests are made to feel relaxed and at home; bedrooms are spacious and the three rooms share two bathrooms.

£ *Mar to Nov; 3 rooms*

GREAT LONGSTONE

Croft Country House Hotel

Great Longstone, Nr Bakewell DE4 1TF

TEL (0629) 640278
In the middle of the village with four acres of secluded garden, the house has some very original features. Neat, pretty bedrooms and spacious public rooms make this a pleasant place to stop.
££ *Mar to early Jan; 9 rooms; Access, Visa*

HATHERSAGE

Highlow Hall

Hathersage, Nr Sheffield S30 1AZ
TEL (0433) 650393
A lovely old house with wonderful views. Bedrooms are homely and quite old-fashioned and the atmosphere here is very relaxed; a good base for walkers.
£ *Mar to Dec; 6 rooms*

MATLOCK

Riber Hall

Matlock DE4 5JU
TEL (0629) 582795
A grand old hall up on the hill near the village of Tansley. The public rooms have some fine features and the bedrooms, across the courtyard, are comfortable and well-equipped.
££ *All year; 11 rooms; Access, Amex, Diners, Visa*

MATLOCK BATH

Hodgkinson's

150 South Parade, Matlock Bath DE4 3NR
TEL (0629) 582170

A very original restaurant-with-rooms right in the centre of Matlock Bath. Public rooms and bedrooms are decorated with flair and taste and the food is an equally high standard.
£ *All year, rest closed Sun eve; 6 rooms; Access, Amex, Visa*

ROWSLEY

Peacock Hotel

Rowsley, Matlock DE4 2EB
TEL (0629) 733518
A traditional hotel in the heart of the village. It provides comfortable accommodation (although some rooms are quite old-fashioned) good food and a welcoming atmosphere.
££ *All year; 14 rooms; Access, Amex, Diners, Visa*

WINSTER

The Dower House

Main Street, Winster DE4 2DH
TEL (0629) 650213
An attractive stone house at the end of the main street. The bedrooms are pretty and spotlessly clean. B&B only but there are plenty of places to eat nearby.
£ *Mar to Oct; 3 rooms*

WHERE TO EAT

BAKEWELL

Biph's
Bath Street
TEL (0629) 812687
Busy restaurant with cheaper bistro 'The Biphery' next door where they offer a reasonably priced main dish with a glass of wine. Decorated in olde worlde Tudor style. Set and à la carte menus include dishes such as stuffed quail and strawberry sablé at the upper end of the range. Champagne breakfasts on Sundays.
Rest Wed to Sat, 12–2, 7–10, bistro all week 12–2, 7–10; Access, Amex, Visa

Green Apple
Diamond Court, Water Street
TEL (0629) 814404
One of Bakewell's most enterprising restaurants. Take-aways and cheap lunches, with more elaborate and expensive dinners; European cooking has some Middle Eastern influences. No smoking.
Open all week in summer 12–2, Wed to Sat 7–9.30 (winter Mon to Sat 12–2, Thur to Sat 7–9.30; Access, Diners, Visa

BASLOW

Fischer's at Baslow Hall
Calver Road, Baslow
TEL (0246) 583259
An imposing house in large gardens. Three elegant dining-rooms offer consistently rewarding cooking of fashionable ingredients with classical leanings: calf's liver with ginger, and roast partridge with pasta and crunchy red cabbage. Prices to match.
Mon D to Sun L 12–1.30, 7–9.30; Access, Amex, Visa

BOLLINGTON

Mauro's
88 Palmerston Street
TEL (0625) 573898
Family-run restaurant with kitchen on view to diners. Anglo-Italian staple dishes with daily specials. Excellent trolleys of antipasti and desserts. Special children's rates at Sunday lunch.
Tue to Fri and Sun 12–2, Tue to Sat 7–10; Access, Amex, Visa

WATERHOUSES

Old Beams
Waterhouses
TEL (0538) 308254
Once an old inn, this charming restaurant has rooms in an annexe overlooking the river. Luxury dishes include crab soufflé with lobster sauce, a trio of game or a rendezvous of fish. Highly rated wine list with a good choice of half bottles.
Tue to Fri 12–2, 7–10, Sat 7–10, Sun 12–2; Amex, Amex, Diners, Visa

WALKING

This chapter includes
- a summary of walking, for all levels of ability, available across Yorkshire and the Peak District
- suggestions for long-distance paths, two-day or longer walks, short strolls and lesser-known paths and trails
- twelve circular walks in the Peak District, Yorkshire Dales and North York Moors

WALKING

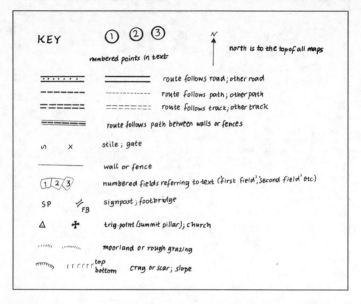

KEY

① ② ③
numbered points in text

N ↑ north is to the top of all maps

••••••• ══════ route follows road; other road

------- ----------- route follows path; other path

═══════ ════════ route follows track; other track

▬▬▬▬▬ route follows path between walls or fences

s   x   stile; gate

_____ wall or fence

1 2 3   numbered fields referring to text ('first field', 'second field' etc)

SP   ⫽FB   signpost; footbridge

△   ✝   trig. point (summit pillar); church

⁔⁔⁔   moorland or rough grazing

⌇⌇⌇   ⌇⌇⌇top/bottom   crag or scar; slope

TIME

We give approximate timings for an average walker, excluding stops.

DIFFICULTY

In the text, the walks are graded as follows, taking into account conditions underfoot, any steep slopes and length. Grading sometimes straddles two categories.

1 Very easy Mostly on the level; suitable for anyone who can manage a few miles, eg families with small children. Wear stout shoes or wellingtons.

2 Easy Within the capabilities of most occasional walkers; be prepared for stiles, gentle slopes and occasional roughish terrain. Wear stout shoes or wellingtons.

3 Middling Suitable for moderately keen ramblers: no major ascents. Walking boots strongly advisable.

4 Energetic Within the capabilities of a reasonably experienced walker, but be

prepared for some sizeable ascents and descents. Walking boots and suitable clothing essential.

5 Demanding For fit and reasonably experienced walkers only, and not to be attempted in poor weather. Expect major hill or mountain ascents. Walking boots and suitable clothing essential.

How to head half right, quarter right, sharp right

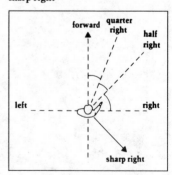

THE AREA covered by this book encompasses some of the most rewarding and best-known walking territory in Britain. The three National Parks – the North York Moors, the Yorkshire Dales and the Peak District - harbour the cream of it, but the southern Pennines in the vicinities of Hebden Bridge and Haworth have plenty to offer too. Guided walks and waymarked paths occur in profusion to tempt even the most casual rambler, while at the other end of the scale you can attempt challenge walks and long-distance back-packing routes.

Two long-distance routes of great scenic distinction cross the region.

The Pennine Way The hugely popular 270-mile route along the backbone of England begins at Edale in the Peak District and ends at Kirk Yetholm in the Scottish Borders. It divides at the start – the tough, monotonous main route and the much more eventful alternative route (p.243). The two routes unite at Kinder Downfall and head north over impressively desolate hill country – but all of the northern part of the Peak is tough-going, especially after rain when the peaty paths can become quagmires.

There are numerous guides to the Pennine Way, including the Ordnance Survey National Trail Guides, covering the path in two volumes (OS maps, directions and explanations of points of interest), and the idiosyncratic guides of the late Alfred Wainwright (hand-drawn maps, handwritten text and much gentle humour; published by Michael Joseph). Book accommodation in advance, and don't underestimate the physical demand the route makes.

The Coast-to-Coast Walk Alfred Wainwright pioneered this 190-mile route from St Bees on the Cumbrian coast to Robin Hood's Bay on the North York Moors seaboard. It has now become an official long-distance path, but waymarking for the time being is only occasional and it is quite easy to lose the route without Wainwright's guidebook.

Maps

If you're devising your own walks, carry an Ordnance Survey (OS) map. The 1:50,000 Landranger sheets (about $1^1/_4$ inches to the mile) show footpaths and are handy for where the route-finding isn't too complicated. The 1:25,000 (about $2^1/_2$ inches to the mile) Pathfinder series are clearer and more detailed, and show field boundaries in addition to rights of way; extra-large sheets, called Outdoor Leisure maps, are available for some areas, including the Yorkshire Dales (four sheets), the North York Moors (two), the South Pennines (one) and the Peak District (two). For the Yorkshire Dales and certain other parts of the Pennines there's the additional option of purchasing Arthur Gemmell's Stile Maps: these cover small areas but are inexpensive, very well researched and clearly drawn, with comments on route-finding, recommended walks and points of interest.

In this chapter we have included twelve circular walks in the Peak District, Yorkshire Dales and North York Moors, suitable for differing levels of walking ability. The key on page 238 explains the grading for these walks and how to read the hand-drawn maps that accompany them.

THE PEAK DISTRICT

The Peak's abrupt changes of landscape – from the gritstone edges of its western and eastern margins to lush farmlands and wooded river valleys, and from the quiet pastures of the White Peak plateau to the descents into crag-lined dales – make it an outstanding walking region. At the gentle end of the scale, there are strolls along level paths in the dales, along disused railway-tracks which have been opened to walkers and cyclists (much of the routes are even suitable for wheelchair-users), on dry-stone-walled tracks across unspoilt farmland typical of the limestone country, and along the spectacular eastern edges where you get grandstand views across the Hope and Derwent Valleys. More energetic walks include excursions around the western peripheries and over the great moorland tracts of the High Peak as well as sections of the Pennine Way.

Ready-made trails

Gritstone Trail This takes in the best of the complicated western gritstone edges. It starts from Lyme Park on the fringes of Stockport, and heads south via Kerridge Hill and Tegg's Nose to join up with the 92-mile Staffordshire Way at Rushton Spencer. Head for Mow Cop, a folly above the Cheshire Plain.

Monsal Trail The undoubted pearl of the old railway-track routes, the trail runs from Wye Dale, east of Buxton, to Coombs Road Viaduct, south of Bakewell. It follows part of the former Buxton-to-Matlock line, which enthusiasts are trying hard to re-open as a nostalgia rail attraction (it won't mean the end of the path, which will continue alongside). Chee Dale and Miller's Dale provide the scenic highlights – in places you are diverted on to the river path where the railway tunnels have been closed – passing the magnificent cliff scenery of Chee Tor, the old textile-mills at Cressbrook and Litton Mill, and crossing the finely sited Monsal Viaduct. Our circular walk described on p.246 includes the Chee Dale section of this.

Tissington Trail This is along the track-bed of the old Ashbourne-to-Buxton line, which merges with the High Peak Trail at Parsley Hay, north of Hartington. From Ashbourne the trail passes close to Thorpe, Tissington, Alsop and Hartington before joining the High Peak Trail and ending north of Hurdlow. Parking and picnic sites on the way.

High Peak Trail From Parsley Hay, this old railway-track route traverses empty country, with some good distant views. The final section from Middleton Top to High Peak Junction has numerous features of interest within a few miles – two engine-houses that used to provide haulage for engines climbing the inclines, Black Rocks, and fine views towards Matlock, High Peak Junction and the Cromford Canal.

Sett Valley Trail A 2½ mile railway-track walk from Hayfield to New Mills.

Roystone Grange Archaeological Trail A 4-mile way-marked walk starting from Minninglow car park on the High Peak Trail. Leaflets available from Roystone Grange Farm, which the route passes.

Torrs Riverside Park A gorge beneath the nineteenth-century mills and bridges of New Mills.

The White Peak

Most of the dales which have public access are easily managed, with level paths along the valley floor; making these part of circular walks usually involves a climb up on to the plateau. The high land above the dales is quite different in character and route-finding can be quite intricate: typically you will find yourself on walled tracks or crossing grassy fields where the path is not particularly well-defined, and looking out for well-camouflaged stone steps across the dry-stone walls.

Dove Dale The perennial favourite, the dale is worth seeing in spite of the crowds (avoid weekends if you can). The main car park is between Ilam and Thorpe, but there is a smaller one at Milldale. High-level views can be enjoyed from Thorpe Cloud and Bunster Hill at the south end of Dove Dale. The level track along the valley poses no problems, and you can extend walks northwards to take in Biggin Dale, Wolfscote Dale and Hartington; alternatively try our walk on p.129.

Manifold Valley An old railway-track along the valley has been turned into a farm road, open as a public bridleway only, which is ideal for prams and wheelchairs; there are car parks in the dale. Less tame are round walks from Wetton or Grindon, taking in Thor's Cave, the highlight of the dale.

Monsal Dale (between Buxton and Bakewell) There is a large car park on the A6 which gives access to the south side of the dale; a gentle path along the dale leads to the viaduct below Monsal Head where you can pick up the Monsal Trail.

Lathkill Dale Most easily reached from Over Haddon, the wooded valley and relics of old mines can be seen from a track; at the western end of the dale, the woods end and the landscape assumes a more rugged appearance. A good half-day circular walk can be taken from Youlgreave, dropping into Bradford Dale and continuing along Lathkill Dale, then south into Cales Dale where the Limestone Way makes a bee-line south-east towards Youlgreave.

Stanton Moor: Nine Ladies Stone Circle From Birchover village, drive east, and fork right beyond the end of the village; park by the Stanton Moor signpost. Follow the track by the signpost, take the first fork right to reach a stile and National Trust sign for Stanton Moor Edge; the path continues, alongside a fence on the left, with impressive views across Darley Dale; after half a mile, cross the stile at the memorial tower and you'll soon reach the Nine Ladies Stone Circle (p.218). The moor also has a number of curiously shaped rock outcrops: to reach the Cork Stone, take the track from the Stanton Moor signpost mentioned above, fork left, up a rise, then bear left at a cross-junction of wide paths; the stone is soon found on the right – honeycombed and overhanging, with staples placed in it to enable access to the top.

Chatsworth Estate There's free access to much of the area on the west side of the River Derwent. Paths here offer exquisite views of parkland and woodland. A stroll by the river will give you the idea: start from Calton Lees car park on the B6012 north of Beeley and follow the river north for a mile until you're level with Chatsworth House; here you can divert to the house, or bear left into Edensor village.

Around Hollinsclough The reef-knoll limestone hills of the area west of Longnor make up a complicated area of country with steep-sided hills and intimate valleys; there aren't any major objectives but it repays an exploration on foot. The area immediately north of Longnor, though attractive in the same way, has an unfortunate dearth of footpaths.

The Dark Peak

The west

Head for **The Roaches**, one of the most arresting landscape features of the Peak, a three-mile ridge west of the A53. Walking along the tops is much easier than it looks, and good round walks can be enjoyed by taking in the Dane Valley and the hidden gorge known as Lud's Church. Further north, the area around **Three Shires Head** is laced with good paths.

Several short walks up to hill-tops give splendid panoramas, particularly westwards. From Wildboarclough you can make the 800-foot ascent of **Shutlingsloe**, a pointed summit with a view stretching to Tittesworth Reservoir and Mow Cop. **The Cloud**, between Rushton Spencer and Congleton, **Tegg's Nose** and **Kerridge Hill** - both near Macclesfield – and **Shining Tor** above the Goyt Valley (see our walk on p.253) are among the best walks. The going underfoot is generally quite fair and gradients are steady rather than testing.

The north

Opportunities for walking here are dominated by the Pennine Way and long, arduous yomps over the moor, but the High Peak isn't unceasingly tough. The **upper Derwent reservoirs** offer easy strolls through woods and along tracks and reservoir roads (closed to traffic but open to pedestrians), and more ambitious walks up to Win Hill and over to the strange landform of Alport Castles above Alport Dale. The ridge from **Mam Tor** (see walk on p.249) to Hollins Cross and Lose Hill is traversed by a gentle (though often wind-blown) path – one of the most exhilarating walks of its kind in the Peak; it can be approached from Castleton, Edale or the car park at the foot of Mam Tor.

Kinder Scout, the highest land in the Peak, is crossed by the Pennine Way: this long-distance route's opening stage is a no-nonsense climb up, followed by a demanding slog over flat bog-lands – up peat hags and down into splits in the terrain known as groughs. Much preferable to all except masochists for this section is the **Pennine Way Alternative Route**

which heads east from Edale, up an old packhorse route called Jacob's Ladder and then follows the edge of the moor via a series of striking rock outcrops, with splendid views in clear weather. Hayfield village provides another starting-point for walks on to this high land; the route climbing William Clough (the historic route of the 1932 mass trespass – p.230), skirting the edge of the moor and passing Kinder Downfall is recommended.

The east

The eastern edges harbour a number of rambles with sudden and spectacular views, and great diversity. Good starting-points are found east of Curbar, by **Curbar and Baslow Edges**, at **Birch Edge** car park by the Robin Hood Inn (see walk on p.245), and the **Longshaw Estate** car park where you can walk up to Carl Wark hill-fort or along Burbage Rocks. **Stanage Edge**, the highest part of the edge, can be approached by car from below, north of Hathersage. Varied circuits can be made in the vicinity of Curbar and Hathersage by walking along the leafy River Derwent, then ascending to the gritstone edges.

See also

Holiday Which? Good Walks Guide
Walks 73 (Ingersley Vale and Kerridge Hill), 75 (Lyme Park and the Macclesfield Canal), 76 (Ladybower Reservoir), 77 (Wolfscote Dale and Biggin Dale), 78 (High Tor and the Heights of Abraham), 79 (Edensor and the Chatsworth Estate), 80 (The River Derwent and Padley Chapel), 81 (Lose Hill, Winnats Pass and Castleton), 82 (Monsal Dale and Miller's Dale), 83 (Wool Packs, Fox Holes and Edale), 84 (Dove Dale and Milldale), 103 (Lud's Church and the Dane Valley)

Holiday Which? Town and Country Walks Guide
Walks 9 (Three Shires Head and Shutlingsloe), 25 (Bradford Dale and Lathkill Dale), 26 (Around Cromford), 27 (The River Derwent and Froggatt Edge), 28 (Kinder Downfall), 103 (The Manifold Valley), 130 (Burbage Rocks and Carl Wark)

Birchen Edge and Wellington's Monument

A short exploration of the gritstone edges on the eastern fringes of the Peak, with striking panoramas from dark crags above lush scenery around the Chatsworth estates. Wild and windswept, but the going is easy on well-trodden paths and tracks with straightforward route-finding.
Length 4 miles (6.5km), 2 hours
Difficulty 2

Start Birchen Edge public car park by Robin Hood Inn, on B6050 at junction with A619 between Bakewell and Chesterfield
Refreshments Robin Hood's Inn, at start

WALK DIRECTIONS
① Turn left out of car park, up B6050 for 70 yards. Just after house on left, take path on left, leading to stile and Eastern Moors Estate sign: follow the path ahead (with wall on left and birch trees on right). ② After 200 yards, the trees start to thin out: take a short, steep

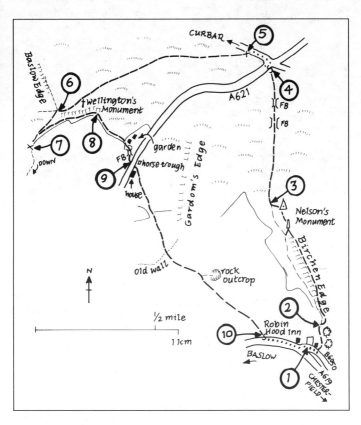

245

path on your right, up to top of Birchen Edge and continue along the edge (if it is too windy, you can continue along the bottom of the edge, diverting up to the right when level with the monument). At monument (a prominent stone pinnacle), carry on a short distance to trig point (summit pillar), where a narrow path on the left leads down. ③ At the bottom, turn right on to broad path (can be boggy), which heads roughly towards distant – but prominent – main road.

④ Cross ladder-stile giving on to main road and take minor road ahead (signposted Curbar). ⑤ After 150 yards, take gate on left (with Eastern Moors Estate sign), giving on to track. Proceed, later past Wellington Monument. ⑥ 150 yards after the monument, turn left at path junction, descending (soon ignore minor right fork). ⑦ On reaching gate, where path beyond becomes enclosed, do not pass through but turn sharp left to walk alongside fence and tumbledown wall on right just above the cultivated land.

⑧ Where the wall bends right, turn right with it; go down to stile by summer-house in garden and take short enclosed path over footbridge and round to the right to gate on to road ⑨. Cross to low step opposite, beside stone horse-trough. The path rises to cross wall at top of shoulder of hill (ignore left fork to rock outcrop) where continue on the main path down to road ⑩. Turn left on the road, and take the first turning left for the Robin Hood Inn and car park.

Monk's Dale and Chee Dale

Classic limestone scenery of the White Peak along the bottom of Monk's Dale, an important nature reserve due to its rich flora, with a spectacular finale section along the Monsal Trail in Chee Dale. The latter includes a remarkable path along the River Wye, beneath great cliffs – making use of easy stepping-stones – and through disused railway tunnels. The shorter version of the walk skips some field-crossing (where the route is not immediately obvious) and omits Chee Dale,

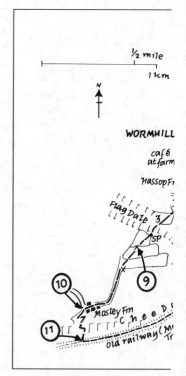

although you can easily detour into it when you rejoin the Monsal Trail near the end of the walk. The path along Monk's Dale is rocky and uneven: progress is quite slow and boots are advisable.

Length *Full walk* 7 miles (11km), 3½ hours; *Short walk* 5 miles (8km), 2½ hours

Difficulty *Full walk* 4; *Short walk* 3

Start Miller's Dale car park (east of Buxton; signposted from B6049), at old station

Refreshments Pub at Miller's Dale, near start of walk; café in farm at Wormhill (all day Sunday, and Saturday afternoons in April to September)

WALK DIRECTIONS

① Start on the old railway-track behind the old station, and turn left, across railway bridge; the hamlet of Miller's Dale is seen below on your left. **②** When level with the end of the hamlet, take path on left signposted Miller's Dale, dropping to cross bridge and reach road opposite pub. Turn left to reach T-junction, where take path opposite, to left of church. This path rises to emerge into the open by nature reserve sign for Monk's Dale. **③** Go forward, alongside wall on right on path that drops into Monk's Dale, soon over footbridge and along bottom of dale for 1½ miles. After nature

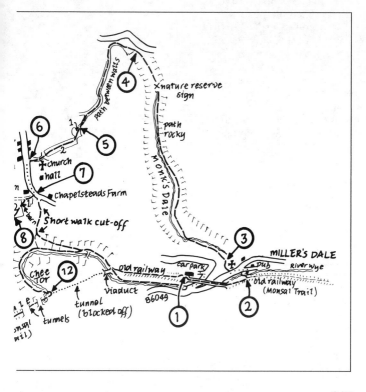

reserve sign at gate, you soon emerge into pasture ④, with wall and road just ahead: here bear left uphill, soon joining wall/fence at top of bank on your left, and follow it to reach gate, beyond which a rising path leads between walls. As path levels out, it veers right and passes through gate at fork of walled tracks, where you take the left fork. ⑤ At end of walled section, enter field and go diagonally left to small gate in corner. Enter a long strip-shaped field, with buildings of Wormhill visible ahead: walk along length of field to find signposted gate at end, where go left on short walled track, then right at track T-junction. Proceed past churchyard to road ⑥. Turn left on the road.

Carry on to just where road bends left ⑦. *For short walk* turn right opposite pond and, just after 30mph derestriction sign, on to track signposted Chee Dale and Blackwell; this soon narrows and emerges above Chee Dale: fork left and drop gently down to bridge (do not cross): here keep left on Monsal Trail, back to start (or detour in other direction along Monsal Trail to see the most dramatic section of the dale).

For full walk turn right immediately after Wormhill sign (facing other way) through gap-stile and proceed to left of farmhouse, at back of which a gate on the left gives access to a walled area with a small gate by a signpost on the far side: enter field (signposted Flag Dale) and go diagonally right to next small gate (to right of barn); maintain diagonal direction in second field to leave by far corner ⑧,

and again in third field (to find stile in middle of wall at bottom edge of field). A path leads down to bottom of Flag Dale: here you can see the continuation steeply up other side of dale, to signpost by stile, where the route continues in the signposted direction up the middle of a field. ⑨ Leave the field by a gate to the left of the only power-post in the field (80 yards to left of top corner). Cross next field to leave near power-post and in final field go diagonally right to gate in corner, then left on track between walls. At barn, track bends right and continues,

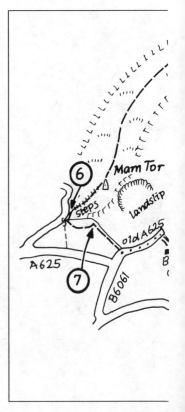

through farmyard (may be muddy), where keep to main track.

⑩ Beyond the farm, as the track (now a surfaced road) bends right, go left down a wide grass track, initially between walls, zigzagging right, left and right to reach old railway bridge at bottom of dale **⑪**. Take steps up on to old railway (Monsal Trail) and turn left along it. **⑫** After two tunnels, you are diverted to the right in front of third tunnel: drop to river, turn right under railway bridge and go over footbridge, then along stepping stones. Path keeps along the

river all the way: at viaduct, you can either go up steps and keep left for a quick return to the Miller's Dale station or keep to the river (more scenic) to road, then left to reach car park.

Castleton and Mam Tor

Starting from one of the Peak's most remarkable villages, the walk heads over farmland and ascends steeply 400 feet on to the great ridge which dominates the Hope Valley – a fine 360-degree panorama for a mile is the

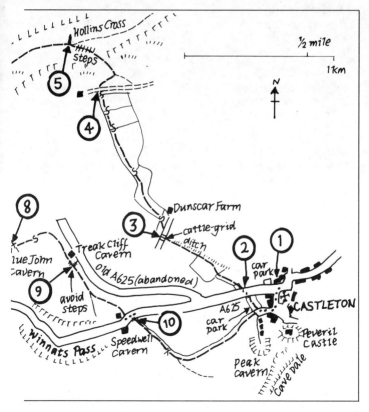

reward, culminating at the ancient fort site on Mam Tor. The route then drops down past show caves and the entrance of Winnat's Pass before returning to Castleton.

Length 5 miles (8km), 3 hours
Difficulty 2–3
Start Castleton village, on the A625 at the centre of the Peak National Park. Car park and roadside parking in village
Refreshments Pubs, shops and cafés in Castleton; the show caves passed later in the walk each sell a limited range of snacks

WALK DIRECTIONS
① Take the road opposite the Bull's Head tavern in the village centre, signposted Peveril Castle and leading past the George Inn and the Youth Hostel on your right, just after which turn right (signposted Peak Cavern). Just after crossing the river, turn right (left turn goes to Peak Cavern – it's worth the short detour to see the huge cave entrance) on track through the Peak Cavern car park. ② Turn left at the main road, then immediately right on to signposted path between walls to enter field: keep left along left edge of field, at end of which cross stile and proceed along right edge of the next two fields, soon with brook on right.
③ Emerge on to farm road at cattle-grid, turn right to cross the brook and immediately left through gate to enter field: the next section is marked by yellow painted fence-posts – cross first field diagonally to stile beside gate, follow right

edge of second field to far right-hand corner, keep left in third field (signposted Edale) and follow left edge of three more fields to emerge on to track with house away to your left at the limit of the cultivated land ④. Cross stile opposite and climb path diagonally right up moorland hill, soon joining wider path at T-junction, leading up left, soon up steps, to top of ridge at Hollins Cross ⑤. Turn left along ridge to Mam Tor, the summit has a trig point (summit pillar), continuing on far side down steps.
⑥ As soon as path joins road, turn sharp left down steps to signposted stile. Turn left on path (marked with posts), signposted Blue John, proceeding close by fence/wall on left and soon ⑦ bending right to drop to gate on to road. Turn left on road, then right on access road to entrance of Blue John Cavern. ⑧ Turn left at the cavern building, over ladder-stile beside gate. Carry on ahead (no defined path), on level, soon over stile in fence, then on defined path contouring around to right to reach Treak Cliff Cavern building, on far side of which turn left on concrete path.
⑨ As this path turns left down a final flight of steps to the road, fork right on to level path across grass alongside ruinous wall on left (ignore right fork which climbs hill). At wall corner, cross the wall by unobtrusive steps and go forward to stone building with flagpole to emerge on to road opposite Speedwell Cavern, with Winnats Pass on your

right. Turn left along the road for 50 yards then ⑩ take signposted gate on right. Follow path alongside wall on left: after the next gate, this bends left and gradually drops (ignore ascending right fork) to enter Castleton. Proceed on back road into village centre.

Hall Dale and Dove Dale

A delectable transition from the rolling plateau into secretive Hall Dale, which leads down into Dove Dale. After detour to see the dale's famous rock formations you continue to Milldale, then along a gently rising stone-walled track to Alstonefield. Route-finding is generally easy, although the initial stages were not signposted or waymarked when the walk was checked.

Length 4 miles, plus 1½ miles for recommended detour to Reynard's Cave in Dove Dale (6.5km plus 2km), 2 to 3 hours

Difficulty 2

Start Alstonefield, in the south part of the Peak; signposted car park in village

Refreshments Pub in Alstonefield; shop (serving hot and cold drinks) at Milldale.

WALK DIRECTIONS

① Turn right out of village car park and right after 30 yards at T-junction, past telephone box; turn left at T-junction in front of memorial hall, signposted Dovedale and immediately ② take track on left, which soon runs between walls. Where the track bends right, take gate ahead into field, follow right edge alongside wall; ③ at end of field, keep right into small enclosed area, still keeping beside right-hand wall to take gate and proceed downhill alongside wall on right to road ④. Take signposted ascending track opposite.

⑤ Reach road at hamlet of Stanshope – keep left and immediately left again on track between walls, signposted Milldale. After 100 yards, cross stile on right, signposted Dove Dale: head diagonally across field in signposted direction to stile in left-hand wall; carry on in same direction in next field to stile and proceed towards valley of Hall Dale which you see directly ahead. The route goes down the centre of the dale and drops to Dove Dale ⑥: here the route continues to the left along Dove Dale (but you can detour right to see the most famous section of the gorge – as far as Reynard's Cave, a natural arch, is recommended). There is a path on the near side of the river which is less crowded at peak times than the more level path on the other side, and later rises a little to get fine views – (if you wish to cross the river, turn right as you reach Dove Dale, to take a footbridge at Ilam Rock, the first big outcrop).

⑦ At the hamlet of Milldale, turn left and immediately right, passing in front of the shop and ignoring path on left signposted Alstonefield by lamp-post; follow the lane (which becomes unsurfaced) to Alstonefield – ⑧ ignore a minor left turn before you reach Alstonefield church; after the church this becomes a road, bending right to reach pub in village centre.

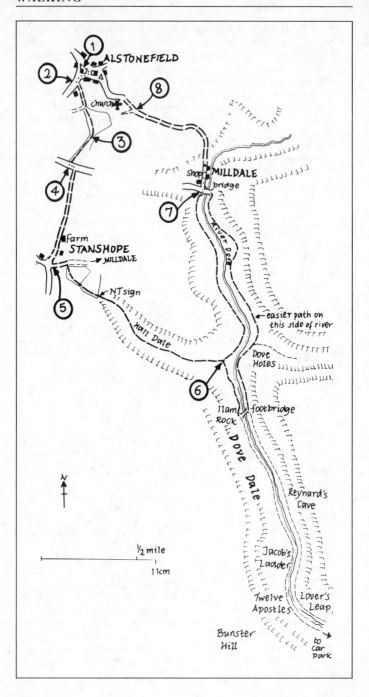

The Goyt Valley and Shining Tor

A ramble of two distinct halves: a mild and sheltered start along Fernilee Reservoir at the foot of the conifer plantations of Goyt Forest, then after a long, gentle climb a three-mile section along the ridge that forms the Derbyshire/Cheshire border, with views over the Cheshire Plain into north Wales on one side and over the Buxton area on the other. In all it gives an excellent idea of the stark whaleback wastes of the Dark Peak, with a typical gritstone outcrop at Windgather Rocks, a favourite with rock-climbers. The moorland section of the walk is easily followed, as there is a well-trodden path with a wall and signposts. If you don't have time for the full walk, park at Pym Chair and follow the path along the ridge to Shining Tor and back – this gives all the views with little climbing. Total ascent 900 feet.

Length 8$\frac{1}{2}$ miles (13.5km), 4$\frac{1}{2}$ hours

Difficulty 3–4 (4 if windy or after rain)

Start Goyt Valley (NNW of Buxton) car park on west side of Errwood Reservoir: approach from the west via Jenkin Chapel, as one-way systems restrict access via other roads

WALK DIRECTIONS

① From car park take road signposted Buxton and toilets, heading for reservoir dam.

After 70 yards, just before dam, turn left on to signposted grassy path; ② after 50 yards turn right at next signpost. The path drops just to left of grassy slope of dam and continues just above the water's edge: continue to the end of the reservoir (halfway along, the path bends left to join a forest track – keep right along this). ③ At end of reservoir, emerge from forest by stile beside gate and turn right on surfaced road; just where stone parapet of dam begins, turn left on semi-metalled track. ④ After $\frac{1}{2}$ mile, this bends left in front of Knipe Farm and drops to cross stream, then bends right, passing just to left of house and then bending sharp left. ⑤ Soon pass Overton Hall Farm on your right (ignore right turn at beginning of buildings and keep to right fork at the end of them). The track ascends to cattle-grid (and bends right) ⑥: here, take signposted path ahead, climbing across open land and passing through small group of trees, with forest fence quite close to the left. At top, path drops to wall: ignore ladder-stile to left (leading to enclosed path) but ⑦ take stile ahead into field and go forward to farm visible ahead (soon walking alongside wall on left). ⑧ Immediately before the farmhouse itself, take gate entrance on left and ascend alongside right-hand wall to Windgather Rocks. The path continues to ladder-stile, then proceeds closely parallel to road, joining it near Pym Chair viewpoint ⑨. Continue forward along road, left at

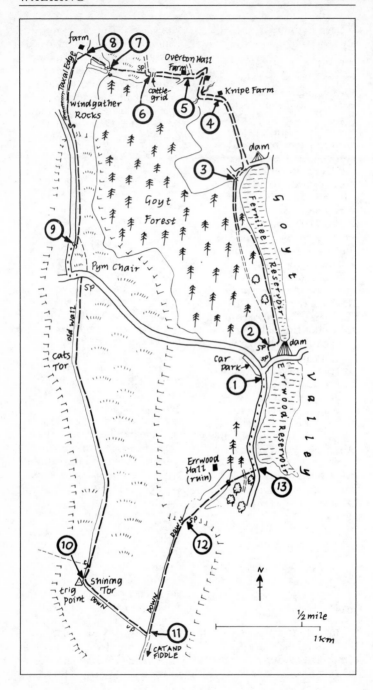

254

T-junction and right after 150 yards on path signposted Shining Tor: this goes along spine of ridge, with old wall on right, for $1^1/_2$ miles to summit of Shining Tor (where wall reaches a corner and bends left and there is a trig point/summit pillar over the right-hand wall) **⑩** : turn left, signposted Cat and Fiddle, alongside wall on right, dropping and then gently rising. **⑪** At top of rise, go over stile by gate, and turn left (signposted Errwood), making a gradual descent to the reservoir, alongside wall on left. **⑫** Halfway down, by a stile on your left, the path deflects slightly right as signposted, leaving the wall, to ladder-stile, then down path slightly right and across track, through woods to road **⑬** . Turn left along the road to return to the start.

YORKSHIRE DALES

With such a wealth of scenic diversity and 1100 miles of footpaths and bridleways, it is no surprise that walkers of all levels of ability and experience frequent the Dales for much of the year. Medium to energetic rambles that lead over pastures, limestone pavements, hillsides and moors are abundant, and in the western side of the National Park there are opportunities for challenging walks in the Howgills and the Three Peaks. The most enjoyable easy routes tend to be along rivers, green lanes (wide, grassy or stony tracks between dry-stone walls, many constructed as packhorse or drovers' roads) and over low-lying pastures with distant views. The National Park Authority publishes a series of individual walk pamphlets detailing short routes of up to half a day's duration.

Route-finding across pastures and moorland can be quite tricky, even for the experienced walker. Typically you will be looking for walls and ladder-stiles (wooden-ladder type constructions, placed like an inverted V over walls). The path itself may be invisible and on the moors you may have even less to go on.

In addition to OS maps, Arthur Gemmell's Stile Maps (covering much of the Dales in small, inexpensive sheets) are invaluable as there are often indications about route-finding, missing bridges, permissive paths and so on. For details of guided walks, contact any tourist office or National Park Information Centre.

Long-distance paths

The Pennine Way (see also p.239). Some 60 miles of the Way crosses the National Park south to north, and many who have completed the entire walk will claim that the Dales section from Gargrave to Tan Hill is the finest. The four or five days this entails gives a cross-section of all that is best in the Yorkshire Dales. Linear day walks are problematic in that transport back has to be arranged, but two strenuous samples of the Pennine Way offer ample rewards for the hassle: Malham to Horton-in-Ribblesdale (by way of Malham Tarn, Fountains Fell and Pen-y-ghent) and Hardraw to Keld (climbing Great Shunner Fell from Wensleydale to enter upper Swaledale). Easy highlights of these are from Malham to Malham Tarn, and from Thwaite to Keld.

The Coast-to-Coast Walk (p.239) crosses the northern dales. The 35 miles from Kirkby Stephen to Richmond can be comfortably undertaken in three days, with stop-overs at Keld and Reeth. Part of the route is at high level, above Swaledale, across the old lead-mines at Gunnerside Gill.

The Dales Way An 81-mile route which keeps to a low level, from Ilkley to Bowness-on-Windermere, taking in the length of Wharfedale and passing through Dentdale and Sedbergh before ending on the east side of the Lake District. A useful guidebook is by Colin Speakman, with clear maps by Arthur Gemmell; signposting is quite thorough.

The Ribble Way 72 miles from Longton in Lancashire to Gayle Moor north of Horton in Ribblesdale; leaflets from Lancashire County Council Planning Department, Preston, Lancashire.

The Yoredale Way Follows the course of the River Ure from York to its source near Kirkby Stephen, by way of Boroughbridge, Ripon, Middleham, Wensleydale, Hardraw and the upper Eden Valley for 100 miles. A booklet by Ken Piggin (Dalesman Publications) describes the route.

The southern Dales

Wharfedale is particularly rich in outstanding walks. Around Bolton Abbey there are gentle strolls by the Wharfe, with the woodlands and nature trail (free leaflet from car park kiosks) around the Strid being the scenic high-spot. Rather more demanding are paths up on to nearby Barden Fell (where there is freedom to roam except in the grouse-shooting season; dogs are not allowed), culminating at a superb vantage-point from crags on Simon's Seat – not as difficult to climb as it looks from a distance. The river can be followed all the way to Grassington, and again from Kettlewell to the top of the valley and into Langstrothdale. Paths and green lanes at the side of the dale give plenty of scope for round walks – as well as the route we have described in detail below from Kettlewell, there is fine walking into Littondale (notably from Kettlewell to Arncliffe, then back over the top to Starbotton, with a finale along the Wharfe); up the path into Dowber Gill east from Kettlewell (a there-and-back walk); and along an outstanding path on a grassy terrace between Cray and Yockenthwaite that looks down Wharfedale.

Nidderdale How Stean Gorge and the hill-top village of Middlesmoor make worthwhile places to aim for, and it is possible to include them in a short round walk from Lofthouse. A path runs along the River Nidd almost as far as Scarhouse Reservoir, but more dramatic is the high-level track which heads along the north side of the dale – if you want to avoid the steep climb up to it, you can drive along the road which leaves Lofthouse to the north-east and start walking from the top.

Malhamdale The limestone scenery is at its most striking here, and the route linking Janet's Foss, Gordale Scar and Malham Cove must be the most interesting four miles in the Dales. Route-finding as far as Gordale Scar is easy: a path along the beck in Malham village is signposted and much-trodden. A path leads up Gordale Scar towards Malham Tarn, but it involves a hazardous scramble and notices dissuade you from attempting it; it is better to retrace your steps to the road and trace your route across fields (for which you will need a map) to the top of Malham Cove – where you will find a remarkable area of limestone pavement, and from which the Pennine Way drops towards Malham. A path from the top of Malham Cove to Malham Tarn takes in more limestone scars, pavements and a dry valley. The tarn itself has a level, waterside path and a boardwalk trail.

Ribblesdale and the Three Peaks The tough, but extremely popular, 22-mile Three Peaks challenge walk involves climbing Pen-y-ghent, Whernside and Ingleborough in a day. It is generally done in eight hours, but anyone who completes the route within twelve qualifies for membership of the Three Peaks of Yorkshire Club of the Pen-y-ghent café at Horton-in-Ribblesdale. For those who want to take a more leisurely approach, we have described the ascents of Pen-y-ghent and Whernside in full in this chapter.

Ingleborough, a fascinating mountain peppered with scars, caves and potholes, can be climbed from Ingleton – a gentle path for most of the way before the final slog to the top, continuing past the entrances to Gaping Gill and Ingleborough

Cave (p.53), to Clapham, where regular bus services take you back to Ingleton. The final stage of the walk takes in part of the Reginald Farrer Trail, a 2¹/₂-mile route from Clapham past an ornamental lake, woodlands and farmland. A more remarkable trail is the Ingleton Waterfalls Walk (p.54), easily followed but not on the gentlest of paths, with rocky and uneven surfaces to contend with; the glen is one of the glories of the Dales.

Walks in Ribblesdale are inevitably associated with the Three Peaks, but near Settle there are several excellent and less demanding routes that include the walk described in this chapter, and the ramble from Stainforth via Catrigg Force (waterfall) to Langcliffe, and back along the river, passing Stainforth Force near the end.

The northern Dales

Wensleydale Aysgarth Falls are best seen with rest of the world on the heavily tramped footpath from the car parks. A good prelude to a visit to Hardraw Force is to take paths from Hawes to Sedbusk, then cross a series of tiny fields to Hardraw, before viewing the waterfall and returning along the Pennine Way. Semerwater lies in lovely country just off the main dale, but it is quite difficult to find a worthwhile circular route that doesn't involve a lot of lane-walking. A useful feature for walkers hereabouts is a Roman road (an unmade track) – noticeable on OS maps for its straightness – which leads from Bainbridge south-westwards and gives fine views; it is best walked from the south-west, as you will be descending gradually into Wensleydale with the view before you. The hills forming Wensleydale's northern side are wild and rather bleak.

Around Sedbergh The Howgills offer superb fell-walking of a character more associated with the Lake District than the Dales – deep valleys, high ridges and plunging slopes; the eastern buttresses of the Lakeland fells themselves form part of the huge views. Most of the top-level routes demand stamina, experience and a compass, with The Calf (2,220 feet) the highest point and the obvious destination for the energetic. More convenient for a couple of hours is the ascent of Winder (1,551 feet, but you start at nearly 800 feet) from Sedbergh: take Joss Lane by the toilets near the tourist information centre, follow the road-markings and park before the road narrows; this later becomes a track and then a path leading to Settlebeck Gill at the foot of the hill. Easiest of all, but giving a taste of the range, is the stroll up to Cautley Spout waterfall (p.55).

Dentdale has numerous paths, none more satisfying than the old packhorse track that winds around the hillside on the south of the dale; this can be reached by taking a very steep unmade lane alongside Flinter Gill from Dent. There is also the Sedgwick Trail (leaflet from National Park centres), which takes a look at the geology of the area.

SwaledaleThis is a popular walking area in the Dales, and it is easy to see why. The steep-sided dale between Muker and Keld has a very special charm, with deciduous trees and the fine Kisdon Force waterfall (visible only from the west side); you can walk up one side of the river and return on the other, or venture on to higher paths – including the Pennine Way and the old coffin-bearers' route over Kisdon Hill. Further east, Gunnerside Gill has a path along the bottom to the old lead-mines.

Reeth makes a good centre for strolls along the Swale or for more ambitious walks on to Fremington Edge in Arkengarthdale, from where you can see the western edges of the North York Moors. Further east still, Richmond Castle looks at its best from Hudswell Woods, above the south banks of the Swale; the woodland paths are especially pretty in spring and autumn. Longer routes can be devised by taking in Whitcliffe Scar, where a path high above the valley runs along a dramatic cliff past Willance's Leap monument; this can also be reached from the Richmond-to-Marske road (just west of a prominent mast by the road; start from a side-turn on the south side).

Upper Teesdale For a sampler of the rugged northern Pennines, the Pennine Way neatly links up the famous waterfalls of the dale – High Force, Low Force and Cauldron Snout – as well as taking in a scenic riverside section beneath Cronkley Scar. A nature trail from Bowlees Visitor Centre near Low Force leads up to Gibson's Cave, another waterfall (allow 10-15 minutes each way). At Barnard Castle, wooded paths along the Tees closely resemble those at Richmond (see above); in all it is possible to walk close above the river for $1\frac{1}{2}$ miles until you are diverted up on to farmland.

See also

Holiday Which? Good Walks Guide
Walks 147 (Hardraw Force), 148 (Upper Swaledale and Kisdon Hill), 149 (Simon's Seat), 150 (Mastiles Lane and Kilnsey Moor), 151 (Arncliffe and Moor End Fell), 152 (Gordale Scar

and Malham Cove), 153 (Ingleborough and Gaping Gill), 154 (Upper Nidderdale)

Holiday Which? Town and Country Walks Guide
Walks 24 (Dentdale), 44 (Cauldron Snout and Cow Green reservoir), 45 (Barnard Castle and Teesdale), 47 (High Force), 125 (Richmond and the Swale), 126 (Northern Wharfedale), 127 (Swaledale and Arkengarthdale), 128 (Catrigg Force and Langcliffe)

Pen-y-ghent

The lowest of the Three Peaks, involving a mild scramble – the rockiest and steepest feature on the Pennine Way's 270 miles – to reach its flat summit. In addition to the vast panorama over the central and southern dales, the route passes close to two fine pothole entrances – Hunt Pot and Hull Pot – before taking a stone-walled green lane back down to Horton. The paths are well-defined to a point of serious erosion, although much repair work has been done.
Length 5 miles (8km) 2¹/₂ hours
Difficulty 4
Start Horton in Ribblesdale car park (B6479 north of Settle)
Refreshments Café and pub at start

WALK DIRECTIONS
① Turn right out of car park on main road, past information centre; 80 yards later, turn left on to track signposted Pennine Way. At fork, bear right (signposted Three Peaks Walk).
② Emerge at farms and buildings, turn right on surfaced road, then immediately left over

footbridge and turn left on other side to follow road past primary school. ③ At beginning of hamlet of Brackenbottom take signposted gate on left, through enclosure to gate beside stile; the route up Pen-y-Ghent is obvious:

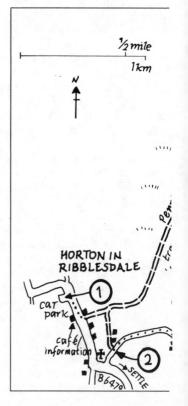

proceed along wall on left; after ladder-stile with signpost pointing back to Brackenbottom, you are at foot of final part of the ascent – the route leads up to left and needs care on loose rocks.

④ At trig point (summit pillar) at top, go left over ladder-stile and take Pennine Way (signposted PW Horton), which is obvious all the way back: it drops and later reaches ladder-stile (just after, look for Hunt Pot, a few yards off the path to the left). ⑤ After next ladder-stile you soon continue (to the left) between walls (a 300-yard detour to right brings you to the spectacular entrance to Hull Pot). At fork reached near start, keep right to enter village.

Whernside

Yorkshire's highest mountain (2,415 feet) has an enthralling ridge section to compensate for an uneventful final ascent; from the top you look far into Cumbria and over the Settle-Carlisle railway line and the huge Ribblehead Viaduct. The opening stages follow the railway before crossing it at an aqueduct below Force

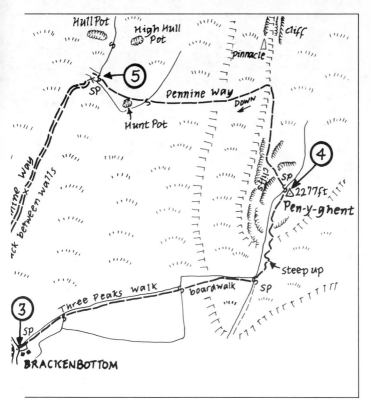

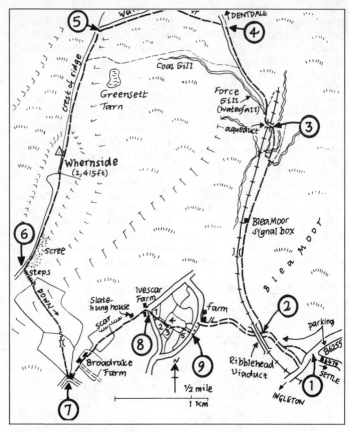

Gill waterfall. Total ascent is 1,500 feet; one steep descent, over loose rocks, then down steps.

Length 7 miles (11km) 3½ hours

Difficulty 4

Start Ribblehead (junction of B6479 and B6255 near Ribblehead Viaduct); extensive roadside parking (if full, park on track towards viaduct from Station Inn nearby)

Refreshments Snack van (daily; weekends in winter if fair weather) and pub at start

WALK DIRECTIONS
① Take signposted path for Whernside opposite B6479 at road junction, heading towards left end of viaduct, soon joining stony track. ② Just before the track bends left to pass under viaduct, branch off right on to grassy path that continues with wall and railway on left. After ½ mile, pass Blea Moor signal box; ¼ mile later keep left, to lower of two paths, where stony stream bed appears. ③ Soon after, cross railway at aqueduct, and on other side almost immediately fork left at signpost, with wall now on left. ④ After ½ mile cross stile signposted

262

Whernside. Path later bears slightly left on reaching wall and ascends to the main ridge of Whernside ⑤, along which turn left to the summit (with wall on right all the way).

After summit, path continues along high ridge which after ¹/₂ mile drops abruptly (take care on loose stones); ⑥ at the end of this section, where ridge path is grassy again, turn left to begin main ascent, down steps. At bottom, cross ladder-stile: the path heads over two large fields to stile in right-hand corner of second field, by barn ⑦. Beyond this stile, go forward on enclosed track 20 yards only, then left through signposted gate; cross field to gate by farm ahead, go in front of farm and into field. Follow left edge of two fields then maintain direction across next two fields towards slate-hung house; pass just to right of it and go forward to farm.

⑧ Just after farmhouse, take right fork of surfaced farm roads and just after last barn take stile on left into field. Head across to ladder-stile; follow left edge of second field to stile at end, and left edge of third field for short distance to next stile; bear half right in fourth field towards middle of viaduct to find stile into fifth field where follow left edge to road ⑨. Left on road. At beginning of farm soon reached, go right on track (over bridge), which bends right at end of farm and passes under viaduct to reach starting-place.

Gunnerside Gill and Upper Swaledale

Gunnerside Gill displays spectacular relics of the lead-mining industry – spoil heaps, mine buildings and miners' tracks, set in a deep secluded dale. This walk heads along its floor for most of the first two miles before taking a gentle track over the exposed moorland tops, giving distant views. The second half consists of a route along a grassy terrace beneath crags and above crooked hawthorn trees, offering some of the very finest of all views over Upper Swaledale. Paths and tracks are mostly well-defined, although towards the end you will be relying more on nearby landscape features to guide you.

Length 8¹/₂ miles (13.5km) 4¹/₂ hours
Difficulty 3–4
Start Gunnerside village, Swaledale
Refreshments Pub at start

WALK DIRECTIONS
① From road-bridge in village centre, take path upstream, on right side of river, signposted Gunnerside Gill. This diverts to right at gate in front of converted chapel, then after short enclosed section bends left to continue along bottom of valley, close to river. ② After one mile, pass ruins of crushing-house, the first obvious relic of many remains of the old lead industry which you will now encounter; beyond it, a stile is crossed and the path rises a little. ¹/₂ mile later Botcher Gill (a side gorge) is seen across the valley to the left; ¹/₄ mile further, pass through mine ruins (buttresses of crushing-house and a mine

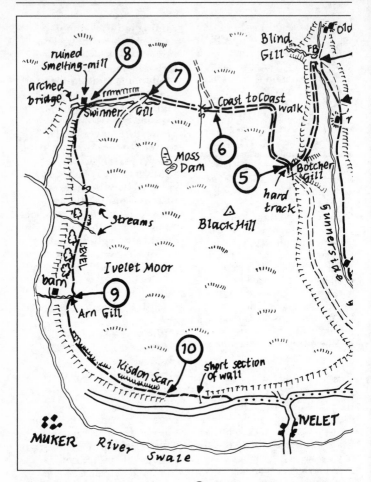

building), and after 200 yards
③ turn left at staggered cross-
junction of paths by cairns (piles
of stones). Path drops gently
down to river, which follow
until ④ crossing footbridge and
turn sharp left on rising grassy
track (doubling back above the
valley).

⑤ At top of Botcher Gill,
where there is a gate a short
distance to your left, join hard
track and turn right on it. This
later bends right and then left,
crossing the open moor.

⑥ Keep straight on at major
track junction where another
track goes off to right; 80 yards
later you pass through gate
beside stile. ⑦ Where Swinner
Gill (a side gorge above
Swaledale) appears below, leave
the track for a signposted path
on the right, which drops down
the right-hand side of the gill.
⑧ Just before ruin of smelting-
mill, cross the stream on your
left and take defined narrow
path that leads towards
Swaledale and soon bends left

264

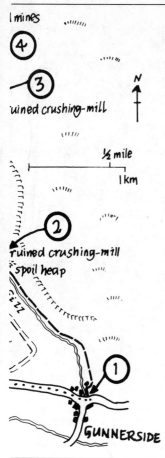

around the contour of the hill as the dale is revealed. Path is intermittently defined but reasonably clear at first: keep level, later dropping slightly to gate beside ladder-stile in wall; route can be seen ahead, on level grass terrace beneath crags that have been prominent for some time.

Cross two streams in quick succession. ⑨ ¹/₂ mile further, cross Arn Gill (where there is a semi-ruined stone building down to your right); on other side, path is indistinct – go

slightly right without losing height and the route soon becomes self-evident, with crags close up on left to guide you for most of next mile, accompanied by occasional abrupt drops on your right. Road down to right later comes into view; ⑩ after end of Kisdon Scar on left, go forward (no path) over open land and descend gently to road (which is unfenced, so it doesn't matter where you reach it). Left on road, left again at next road junction to return to Gunnerside.

Cam Head and Upper Wharfedale

Changes in altitude are the key to the scenic variety of this walk: a gentle amble along the dale, a steady climb up a classic walled track, followed by a lengthy descent, with Wharfedale stretching before you. Route-finding is about as simple as you'll find anywhere in the Dales.
Length 5 miles (8km) 2¹/₂ hours
Difficulty 2–3
Start Car park at edge of Kettlewell village, Wharfedale, by double-arched bridge over River Wharfe
Refreshments Pubs and shops in Kettlewell; pub in Starbotton

WALK DIRECTIONS
① Walk out of village and cross the double-arched bridge over the Wharfe (not to be confused with the smaller bridge over the brook in the centre of the village) and take gate on right by National Trust sign for

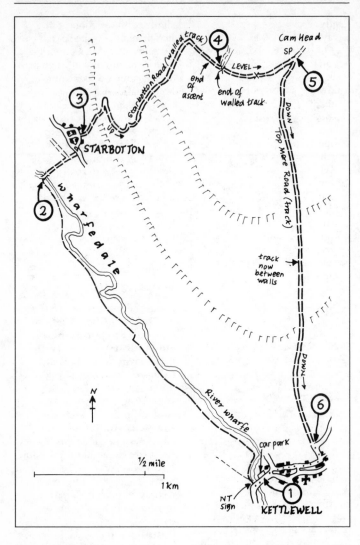

Upper Wharfedale. Immediately fork right, signposted Buckden and Starbotton, to join river; follow path 1½ miles, close to the Wharfe (usually with one field between you and the river, but sometimes alongside it); route is obvious. ② Cross footbridge (signposted Starbotton),

follow track to village, ignoring left turn just before you reach village. Left on road, and after 150 yards turn right opposite telephone and postbox, on road leading to junction ③: take track between walls, opposite, signposted Cam Head. This rises, steeply at first, then more gently, and bends several times, always between walls.

④ After one mile, walled section ends at highest point on walk: take gate ahead and follow level track through pasture. Pass through gate beside stile and ⑤ 300 yards later turn sharp right, signposted Kettlewell, on track which descends in a straight line to Kettlewell and later becomes a track between walls. ⑥ Keep forward on joining corner of road, keep right at next road junction to enter centre of village. Pass to right of Post Office, bear left by Racehorses Hotel, over beck, to starting-point.

Victoria Cave and Warrendale Knotts

A tour of some typical karst scenery features – limestone scars, cliffs, cave entrances and screes. In addition to the interest of the scene close at hand, there are wonderful views nearly all the way – at first towards Ingleborough and Pen-y-ghent, then later over Settle and the great massif of the Forest of Bowland in Lancashire. Paths are not particularly clear on the ground, but there are plenty of features to guide you.
Length 4 miles (6.5km) 2 hours
Difficulty 2–3
Start Market square, Settle town centre
Refreshments Full range in Settle

WALK DIRECTIONS
① Standing in the market square with the Royal Oak Hotel behind you, take the road along the left side of the square, past National Westminster Bank on left, then up Constitution Hill (road with 1:7 sign). Soon keep straight on at junction where left turn goes into small estate called Townhead; the road bends left, and ② 50 yards later, fork right on to rising stony track between walls, (with pasture on left and woods on right). Shortly reach gate and continue with wall on left in this and second field. ③ Midway through the second field, take gate on left and follow wide grassy track between walls: keep along left-hand wall where walls taper outwards.

Carry on to end of field (ignoring ladder-stile on left midway along) to stile into fourth field, where you no longer have a wall as a guide. Go forward, slightly uphill, to wall ahead and find gate just below and to left of nearest woodland ④. In fifth field, follow right edge alongside woodland wall; in sixth field, go forward, aiming immediately below woodland ahead, then walking alongside or close to woodland wall. At end of wood, go half right to gate on to corner of road, where ⑤ turn right on surfaced track (quality later deteriorates).

⑥ After ½ mile, pass barn on right and continue on the track to take gate at foot of impressive cliff, immediately crossing ladder-stile up on right (signposted Stockdale Lane). This path proceeds with wall on right and crags and hillside on

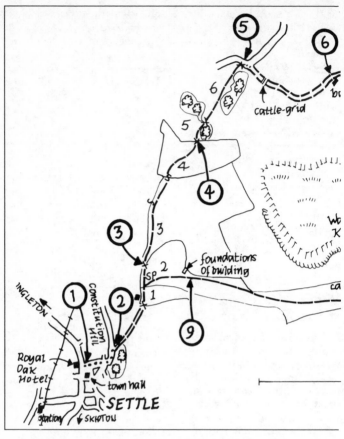

left. ⑦ Shortly after next stile, look for path on left which leads up to the two entrances to Victoria Cave (do not venture in); return to main path which after next stile drops to wall on right; where wall reaches a corner, carry on along level, over grass towards right end of rocks and scree; you are later rejoined by wall on right and path (now well-defined) drops abruptly. You now have the crags on Warrendale Knotts on your right and Attermire Scar on your left, with a dry valley in between. ⑧ At end of

Warrendale Knotts, at bottom of slope, immediately take gateway in wall on right and follow left edge of two fields; at end of second field (level with small cave to right beneath Warrendale Knotts) bear half right across field (either of two paths); beyond skyline, wall to right comes visible, with Warrendale Knotts beyond it – the paths join it and it is followed for most of next ½ mile. ⑨ By the time the wall ends at a corner, Settle has now come into view and you drop directly ahead to join signpost

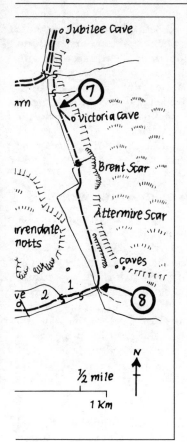

and traversing wall at point reached earlier: turn left to return to start.

NORTH YORK MOORS

The dual character of the best parts of the National Park – the fertile, green dales and the bleak, open moors – makes for some strongly contrasting walking. It can be surprisingly remote in character, but the terrain, even on the moorland tops, isn't particularly tough-going, with a network of gentle tracks and paths criss-crossing the area. The climate is distinctly drier than in the Pennines.

Rights of way across fields and moorlands are sometimes invisible on the ground, making route-finding occasionally tricky, especially where rights of way (printed in green on Outdoor Leisure 1:25,000 maps) are not overprinted on to a broken black line; the green refers to a legal right of way – the black to the existence of a defined path). Distinct focal points to aim for are few and far between on the moors, with no peaks, and views unchanging for mile after mile. But with careful planning you can pack in plenty of variety – perhaps an ascent from a dale up on to the moor, along a moorland track and into another dale. Every walker should sample some of the Cleveland Way, but there are a number of other worthwhile walking areas in the National Park.

For details of guided walks, contact any tourist office or the National Park centre at Helmsley.

Long-distance paths and ready-made walks

The Cleveland Way (waymarked by acorn motifs). By skirting three sides of the National Park this 93-mile route from Helmsley to the cliffs near Filey takes in much of the best walking in the region, with huge views from the edges of the Cleveland Hills for much of the way. It is not particularly demanding, consisting of well-defined tracks and paths across rolling pastures and moors, through forests and with a magnificent finale along sea-cliffs; for much of the way you are relatively unhampered by stiles and gates and progress can be swift. Wind can make the going cold and tiring however, and it is advisable to take light waterproofs (cagoules and over-trousers are ideal), a hat and pullover on all but the warmest summer days.

From Helmsley, the Cleveland Way heads across Duncombe Park, crosses Rye Dale near Rievaulx Abbey and encounters the first of many huge views off the edge at Sutton Bank. It then skirts the top of the Hambleton Hills, looking across to the Pennines all the way, to Osmotherley, past the Captain Cook Monument and Roseberry Topping. A descent takes you out of the National Park and through forest and farmland to the seaside resort of Saltburn, from where the coast is followed all the way to Filey (technically the Way stops a mile or so short of Filey, but it's more satisfying to carry on past the promontory of Filey Brigg and into Filey).

The path is an excellent source of day walks. However, these tend to be more of the there-and-back type rather than circular, as most of interest is concentrated along the Cleveland Way itself, and the hinterland is often undramatic and monotonous – typically flat moors or huge forestry plantations. Inland sections particularly worth walking include: Sutton Bank, a level walk along the top of an inland cliff from the A61 car park, either south to the White Horse hill figure or northwards as far as you like – Gormire Lake below makes a worthwhile objective if you want a circular route; Hasty Bank to Carlton Bank, from the B1257 car park between Great Broughton and Chop Gate, is a fine walk along a dramatic edge; Roseberry Topping, near Great Ayton, is reached by a level walk along the top, then a short climb on to the hill itself for a spectacular panorama over industrial Teesside.

At the coast, you're generally best off restricting yourself to there-and-back walks: much of the landscape immediately inland is rather dull farmland and consequently worthwhile round walks are rare. But you do have the option of walking one way and using the bus to get back between Scarborough, Robin Hood's Bay, Whitby, Sandsend, Runswick Bay and Staithes (frequent services on weekdays, but on Sundays it is advisable to check times before venturing out). Be prepared for some sizeable ascents and descents into the coastal villages and towns; but otherwise the coast path is often pretty much on the level.

Among the finest sections of the coastal path are: Skinningrove to Staithes (four miles), ending at a picturesque fishing-village – the path only follows the cliff-edge for part of the way however; Staithes to Sandsend (eight miles), taking in Runswick Bay and continuing if desired two-and-a-half miles along the beach to Whitby; Whitby to Robin Hood's Bay (six miles), spoilt a little by a holiday camp near Whitby but soon getting splendid views; Robin Hood's Bay to Scarborough (13 miles), taking in the highest sea-cliffs on the English east coast – an old railway-track, now a footpath, provides an inland alternative from Ravenscar to Robin Hood's Bay (hence an easily followed circular walk). For an energetic two-day walk which really gets the best of this coast, walk from Scarborough to Staithes, staying at Robin Hood's Bay or Whitby.

The Missing Link This unofficial 50-mile route was devised by ramblers to make the Cleveland Way into a circuit by using existing public rights of way and forestry paths across the south of the National Park. It runs from Crook Ness, on the coast north of Scarborough, to Helmsley via Levisham, Lastingham and Hutton-le-Hole; for full information and a mapped route see *Walking the Cleveland Way and the Missing Link* by Malcolm Boyes (Cicerone Press).

The Lyke Wake Walk is a 40-mile route which originally connected ancient burial grounds, and was immortalised by the 'Lyke Wake Dirge'. Today it is a popular challenge walk, completed within a day. The scenery is desolate and exposed, and the path is so eroded that tourist authorities deliberately do not promote it. The route begins at Osmotherley, continues over the edge of the Hambleton Hills and over peat bogs to Ellerbeck, then over Fylingdales Moor to finish at the coast at Ravenscar.

The Derwent Way The last section of this 90-mile route from Barmby-on-the-Marsh in Humberside crosses the North York Moors by following the Derwent from East Ayton, past Hackness and Langdale End, to finish at Lilla Howe on Fylingdales Moor.

The Coast-to-Coast Walk The last sections are across the moors, ending at Robin Hood's Bay (p.239).

The Rosedale Circuit A 37-mile challenge walk, making a circuit around one of the finest parts of the National Park; details from information centres.

Waymarked routes The National Park publishes about forty leaflets giving details of short and easily managed waymarked walks; these are available from information centres. The routes are mostly between one and three miles. Starting-points include Glaisdale, Lealholm, Roseberry, Rosedale, Egton Bridge, Castleton, Pickering, Grosmont, Goathland, Staithes, Sandsend, Robin Hood's Bay, Thornton Dale and Helmsley. At Ravenscar, the old alum quarries and lias fossil beds provide the focus for a $4^1/2$ mile geological trail.

Forest walks The Forestry Commission areas on the east side of the National Park contain numerous self-guided trails with coloured marker- posts showing the way. Dalby Forest in particular is laced with routes; a map of these is obtainable from the visitor centre at Low Dalby.

Other walks

Rosedale and **Farndale** both offer varied walking in the dales themselves and along the track-bed of the old Rosedale Mineral Railway, which now makes an almost too easy walker's route at high level across the moors. The most popular walk in Farndale is from Low Mill, along the river to Church Houses. **Rye Dale** is best approached via field paths from Old Byland if you want the experience of walking to Rievaulx Abbey; there's a magical moment as the dale is suddenly revealed.

The **Hole of Horcum**, a great hollow below the A169, provides a focal point for walks along the steep-sided dale of Levisham Beck and in the vicinity of Blakey Topping and the Bridestones (p.114). Much of the eastern moor is taken up with conifer plantations – occasional viewpoints break the monotony of the forest itself. The side valleys leading south from Esk Dale have just enough paths to make up one or two good walks; of these, Glaisdale provides one of the most varied short circuits. An abandoned railway-track parallel to the North York Moors Railway from Grosmont to Goathland is now the absorbing Rail Trail (p.113), giving views of the steam trains and the valley, and you can continue to Mallyan Spout waterfall before returning by train. Beyond Mallyan Spout, the riverside path snakes along a romantic wooded gorge.

See also

Holiday Which? Good Walks Guide
Walks 155 (Sutton Bank and Gormire Lake), 156 (Ryedale and Rievaulx Abbey), 157 (Crosscliff and the Bridestones), 158 (Roseberry Topping), 159 (North York Moors Railway and Mallyan Spout), 160 (Robin Hood's Bay)

Holiday Which? Town and Country Walks Guide
Walks 120 (Rosedale), 121 (Hutton-le-Hole and Lastingham), 122 (Hole of Horcum and Levisham), 123 (Farndale), 124 (Cold Moor and White Hill)

Glaisdale

A quintessential dale-and-moor walk in the heart of the National Park. It begins along ancient tracks and paths, following a stone causeway for some of the way over pleasant pasture, with fine middle-distance views of the steep hillsides that enclose the valley, and ends with a note of drama along a moorland track with three-way views into Glaisdale, Great Fryup Dale and Esk Dale. Field paths are not all waymarked or defined, but follow field edges; one short climb on to the moor.

Length 4^1/$_2$ miles (7km), 2^1/$_2$ hours
Difficulty 2–3
Start Mitre public house, Glaisdale village, W of Grosmont and WSW of Whitby. Glaisdale railway (BR) station ^{1}/$_2$ mile east of village
Refreshments Pub at Glaisdale

WALK DIRECTIONS
① Take the road to the left of the Mitre public house, signposted Glaisdale Dale only. As soon as you pass the church, fork right on to rising path to reach school, where follow an access road down to rejoin the dale road; cross road to gate opposite (signposted Bridleway), by Red House

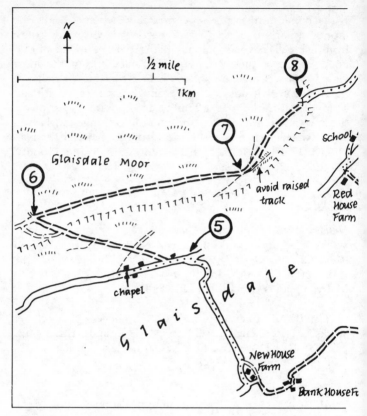

Farm, and go forward to gate giving on to wide track between hedges. ② Reach gate into field and continue forward along right edge; at end of field, enter a small enclosed area and turn right through gateway, to join descending cart track (which soon bends left).

③ Just as track is about to enter field, cross stile on right and follow enclosed path to cross footbridge. Bear half left (no defined path) diagonally up and across field, crossing a broken line of hedgerow trees and finding gate and signpost in opposite fence ④. Pass through the gate and follow cart track,

initially along top edge of field. The track snakes a little and finally reaches Bank House Farm, where turn right on farm track, which soon bends right and then left to reach road. Turn right on road. ⑤ After ¹/₂ mile, turn left at road T-junction; after 400 yards, just after chapel, take signposted bridleway on right, rising to junction with cross-track; here turn left, uphill on to Glaisdale Moor. Continue up ignoring all side turns.

⑥ At the top, turn right on track which goes along the spine of the ridge. Follow the main track all the way back: ⑦ after

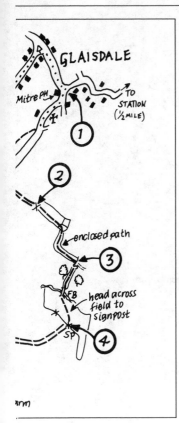

3/4 mile, bear slightly left at junction of well-defined tracks (where there is a signposted bridleway sharp right and a raised track ahead), soon ignoring minor track signposted to the left. ⑧ The track later reaches gate and becomes a surfaced lane, dropping into Glaisdale village. Turn right at T-junction at small green, along village street, to return to start.

Wade's Causeway and Mallayan Spout

A bracing start to this walk is provided by a path over moorland, looking into lonely and elemental scenery, and later crossing easy stepping-stones to join the well-preserved Roman road (Wade's Causeway). The return route skirts a few grassy fields before a final section along the beautiful gorge of West Beck, leading to crags at Mallyan Spout waterfall. The gorge path is rocky and uneven and strong footwear is recommended.
Length 4¹/2 miles (7km) 2¹/2 hours
Difficulty 3
Start Goathland church (opposite Mallyan Spout Hotel, at SW end of village), S of Grosmont and SW of Whitby. Goathland station (North Yorkshire Moors Railway) ³/4 mile away, at far end of village
Refreshments Shops, pubs and cafés in Goathland

WALK DIRECTIONS
① From road junction by church, walk away from the village along road signposted to Roman Road and Egton Bridge. After 75 yards, just after tree in walled enclosure on left, fork half left on to signposted path. This climbs gently (avoid going too far left), with the road generally in view to the right; the path soon becomes indistinct, but then (when level with last house, a red brick one, on right) is clear again, with the road about 100 yards away from you.

Soon a road junction ahead comes into view; the path bends left to run parallel and above the left-hand road turn so that the road is now about 200 yards down on your right; follow this

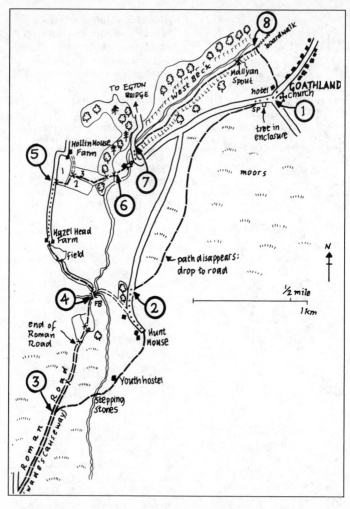

moorland path until it peters out then head down to join the road and carry on along it to reach a signpost by a small plantation of trees beside the road ②. Continue along the road (signposted Roman Road 1.5 miles via stepping-stones); at Hunt House Farm take the track ahead, to the left of the farm and soon past youth hostel on your right; the path (well

signposted) soon bends right, at end of fence on right, to cross stepping stones; on far side of river the path climbs steeply up to join the Roman Road (also known as Wade's Causeway), a broad stone track ③. Turn right along the Roman Road (you can detour ½ mile to the left along it if you want to walk it in its entirety).

At next gate but one, the Roman Road ends: continue into the field ahead, walking along right edge, to cross stile beside gate, then turn left as waymarked on cart-track which descends. ④ At river, pass through gate on right, then immediately cross footbridge, after which a short path takes you on to an enclosed bridleway (marked with blue arrows; ignore cattle-grid into field on left just before this begins). Proceed on this path, leading up and eventually entering field where go forward along left edge, to pass through yard of Hazel Head Farm, and then proceed along farm road.

⑤ After ¼ mile (where wall begins close beside left edge of road) take signposted gate on right into field (immediately ignore ladder-stile on right) and go downhill away from road along right edge. Enter second field by gate, turn left along top edge to gate into third field, where turn right down right edge to trees at bottom of field; keep slightly left here, finding path (initially with fence on left) leading down through gate and woods. ⑥ At bottom, enter field, go forward along left edge to next gate and follow enclosed path past house on left, over footbridge and up short path to join track; continue up this track to reach road. Left on the road (downhill).

⑦ Immediately before river-bridge, turn right on riverside path. After ¾ mile, pass Mallyan Spout, a tall waterfall gushing down from a tiny tributary on your right; ⑧ shortly after, reach signpost at path junction and turn right to ascend to Goathland, emerging at road by the Mallyan Spout Hotel.

WALKING OUTSIDE THE NATIONAL PARKS

The South Pennines

The early industrial flavour of the area – canals, mills and Pennine villages – combined with the unexpected peace of stone-walled pastures and moorland tops make the South Pennines a worthwhile area to explore on foot.

Around Hebden Bridge This varied area possesses a number of enjoyable walks. Easiest of all is the stroll along the **Rochdale Canal**, which snakes along Calderdale past mill-chimneys and back-to-back terraces; the railway provides a way to get back to your starting-point – for example from Mytholmroyd to Hebden Bridge. An outstanding short walk can be had by walking up from Hebden Bridge to the hill-top village of Heptonstall, along the path that skirts the rim of the **Colden Clough** gorge, and finally dropping to join the canal which leads back to the start.

To the north, **Hardcastle Crags** are unimpressive rocks in themselves but give their name to a justifiably popular beauty spot, the sylvan gorge of Hebden Water; access is easiest from a car park at New Bridge. Paths at various levels head along the gorge for about two miles until the end of the woods, where you can continue along a water-board road towards the Walshaw Dean reservoirs. South of Hebden Bridge the network of public rights of way is remarkably dense, but be prepared for some patient map-reading – much is unwaymarked.

Cragg Vale offers some lush scenery, and armed with a 1:25,000 Outdoor Leisure map for the South Pennines you can find plenty of alternatives to the valley road. A car park at nearby Withens Clough Reservoir is the starting-point for the shortest walks up to **Stoodley Pike**, where the Calderdale Way and Pennine Way meet and where a finely sited memorial tower overlooks the hills around Todmorden. **Luddenden Dean**, east of Hebden Bridge, has rural charm and some characteristic stone-built villages and old mills; the best walks here take in the valley floor with some moorland for contrast.

Around Haworth This area is much frequented by walkers and Brontë admirers alike. There is a pleasant walk (signposted from the village) westwards over Penistone Hill Country Park to the famous Brontë Waterfalls. The falls themselves are rather an anti-climax, but the moorland scene is an appealing one, and you can wander on along the valley of South Dean Beck to Top Withens, the derelict farmstead believed to have been Emily Brontë's setting for *Wuthering Heights*. The nine-mile **Brontë Way** is a linear route from Haworth to Wycoller (the hall of which was the model for Ferndean Manor in *Jane Eyre*), taking in sites associated with the Brontës; return is possible by bus via Keighley. Haworth information centre stocks leaflets detailing the route.

The east coast

A path follows the low-lying coast from Filey to Hull with scarcely a break. But the views are unchanging and it's mostly dull compared to the majesty of the sea-cliffs further north. The one moment of glory is at **Flamborough Head** where cliffs are indented and echo to the cries of thousands of kittiwakes. A fine round walk can be taken by starting from Flamborough village, heading south to the coast, then east to the Head itself, and finally north-west (the most scenic part of the route) to North Landing before diverting inland.

The Yorkshire Wolds and Howardian Hills

The Wolds Walkers here are almost entirely dependent on the Wolds Way, which forms a 79-mile route from Hessle Haven near the Humber Bridge to Filey Brigg on the east coast, where it joins the end of the Cleveland Way. The footpath network is remarkably meagre and there are virtually no round walks that do not entail using roads. Most of the area is intensively farmed, but the Wolds Way takes in some pleasant sections along dry valleys and along easily managed chalky tracks (with something of the character of the Lincolnshire Wolds), backed by distant views of the Vale of Pickering and the North York Moors; signposting and waymarking is very thorough, making the route-finding straightforward. The start of the route is of interest for the views of the impressive Humber Bridge, and the section from Fridaythorpe to the abandoned medieval village of Wharram Percy epitomises the best of the Wolds scenery. South of Malton, not on the Wolds Way, there is a path along the River Derwent, ideal for gentle strolls in the vicinity of Kirkham Priory.

The Howardian Hills The area is laced with paths, some little-used. It is scenically mild, with forest and farmland, but the villages make attractive focal points for walks. The vicinity of Castle Howard has enough for a half-day's walk of considerable interest, with views of the house itself, its parkland and estates and a path along the northern escarpment of the area which overlooks the Vale of Pickering and the southern fringes of the North York Moors.

See also

Holiday Which? Good Walks Guide
Walks 146 (Castle Howard Estate), 161 (Hebden Dale and Hardcastle Crags)

Holiday Which? Town and Country Walks Guide
Walks 119 (The River Derwent and Kirkham Priory), 129 (York), 131 (Anston Brook and Chesterfield Canal), 132 (Cragg Vale and Stoodley Pike), 133 (Heptonstall and the Colden Clough), 134 (Luddenden Dean)

PRACTICAL INFORMATION

The main sources of information for this area are:

The Yorkshire and Humberside Tourist Board, 312 Tadcaster Road, York, North Yorkshire YO2 2HF Tel. (0904) 707961 Fax (0904) 701414

The Peak National Park Office, Aldern House, Baslow Road, Bakewell DE4 1AE Tel. (0629) 814321

Peak District National Park Information Centres at Bakewell Tel. (0629), Edale Tel. (0433) 70207 and Castleton Tel. (0433) 20679

Yorkshire Dales National Park Information Centres at Aysgarth Falls Tel.(09693) 424, Clapham Tel.(04685) 419, Colvend Tel.(0756) 752748, Hawes Tel.(07293) 363, Sedbergh Tel.(0587) 20125

North York Moors National Park Information Centre, The Old Vicarage, Bondgate, Helmsley Tel.(0439) 70657

Other Tourist Information Numbers

* Operates a seasonal service (April/May to September/October)

Ashbourne, Tel. (0335) 43666
Bakewell, Tel. (0629) 813227
Barnsley, Tel. (0226) 206757
* Bedale, Tel. (0677) 24604
* Bentham, Tel. (052 42) 62549
Beverley, Tel. (0482) 867430
* Boroughbridge, Tel. (0423) 323373
Bradford, Tel. (0274) 753678
Bridlington, Tel. (0262) 673474/606383
Buxton, Tel. (0298) 25106
* Danby, Tel. (0287) 660654
Doncaster, Tel. (0302) 734309
* Easingwold, Tel. (0347) 21530
* Filey, Tel. (0723) 512204
Glossop, Tel. (0457) 855920
Goole, Tel. (0405) 762187
* Grassington, Tel. (0756) 752774
* Great Ayton, Tel. (0642) 722385
Guisborough, Tel. (0287) 633801
Halifax, Tel. (0422) 368725
Harrogate, Tel. (0423) 525666
Hartshead Moor, Tel. (0274) 869167
* Hawes, (0969) 667450
Haworth, Tel. (0535) 642329
Hebden Bridge, Tel. (0422) 843831
Helmsley, Tel. (0439) 70173
Holmfirth, Tel. (0484) 687603/684992
* Hornsea, Tel. (0964) 536404
Horton-in-Ribblesdale, Tel. (072 96) 333
Huddersfield, Tel. (0484) 430808

Hull, Tel. (0482) 223559
Humber Bridge, Tel. (0482) 640852
Ilkley, Tel. (0943) 602319
* Ingleton, Tel. (05242) 41049
* Knaresborough, Tel. (0423) 866886
Leeds, Tel. (0532) 462454/462455
Leyburn, Tel. (0969) 23069/22773
* Malton, Tel. (0653) 600048
Matlock Bath, Tel. (0629) 55082
Northallerton, Tel. (0609) 776864
Otley, Tel. (0943) 465151
* Pateley Bridge, Tel. (0423) 711147
Pickering, Tel. (0751) 73791
Richmond, Tel. (0748) 850252
* Ripon, Tel. (0765) 4625
Rotherham, Tel. (0709) 823611
Scarborough, Tel. (0723) 373333
* Scotch Corner, Tel. (0325) 377677
Selby, Tel. (0757) 703263
Settle, Tel. (072 92) 5192
Sheffield, Tel. (0742) 734671/734672
Skipton, Tel. (0756) 792809
* Sutton Bank, Tel. (0845) 597426
Todmorden, Tel. (0706) 818181
Wakefield, Tel. (0924) 295000/295001
Wetherby, Tel. (0937) 62706
Whitby, Tel. (0947) 602674
York, Tel. (0904) 621756
York Accommodation, Tel. (0904) 620576

Accommodation

At the end of each chapter in this book we recommmend hotels and B&Bs that have been inspected by *Holiday Which?* researchers. The local tourist boards have comprehensive lists of accommodation available in their areas including all hotels, B&Bs, guesthouses, private rooms and self- catering accommodation. Some of the listings have been inspected by tourist board inspectors and the commended and highly commended gradings are given for a good standard of decoration, furnishings and comfort.

Campsites

The National Parks' offices and the Yorkshire and Humberside Tourist Board publish up-to-date information on caravan and camping sites in the area.

Markets and millshops

Bustling under striped awnings in the open air, or filling the cathedral-like vaults of Victorian halls, West Yorkshire's markets provide an insight into the history and character of the county's people and towns. Arrive in workaday places like South Elmsall or Ossett on market day and you will not need directions to the crowded, patter-filled rows of stalls.

Almost every town in the region has at least a weekly market, with the majority open two or more days a week, generally from about 9 a.m. to late afternoon. Days can change so check with local tourist offices which will also have information on specialist markets. You can take your pick from large, covered market halls, open stalls in traditional market squares, or rural markets in country districts.

Leeds Market (open weekdays) is by far the largest in West Yorkshire, with hundreds of stalls inside a listed Victorian hall, writhing with wrought-iron dragons and exotic curlicues. The badinage is marvellous; Yorkshiremen and women abandon their terse reputation, willing you to buy something (all cheap, some bargains, some dross). Dewsbury (mainly Wed, Fri, Sat), Huddersfield (weekdays), and Wakefield (Mon, Fri, Sat) have similar bazaars in their own, smaller Victorian Aladdin's Cave buildings; all three are particularly strong on clothes, fabrics and wool, on which their past wealth has depended. Bradford has three covered markets (open Mon to Sat), Victorian Rawson being the most characterful. Look around for delicatessens started by the city's Eastern European exiles.

Northern cuisine for the tough-stomached can be studied at tripe stalls, still a feature of many markets: Batley (Fri) has several to choose from among its 100 or so traders, as do Todmorden (weekdays) and Dewsbury, where Gothard's tripe stall also offers an oily by-product called neat's-foot which allegedly heals bruises, alleviates rheumatism and helps to soften leather. Heckmondwike (Tue and Sat) has a fine cooked ham and potted meat stall, just down the street from a good range of Indian saris.

If the setting means more to you than bargain-hunting, visit Otley (Fri and Sat), Halifax, in the Piece Hall (Thur, Fri, Sat), and Pontefract (Sat, crafts on Wed) where the stalls spread out from the eighteenth-century Buttercross and Moot Hall.

West Yorkshire's markets are particularly vigorous and in places constitute a whole economy, separate from the usual retail domination of supermarkets and shops. But stallholders thrive in the rest of Yorkshire and the huge markets in Barnsley (Wed, Fri, Sat; second-hand on Tue) and Doncaster (Tue, Fri, Sat; antiques and bric-à-brac Wed) tempt many West Yorkshire shoppers across the South Yorkshire boundary. The charm of ancient market squares in Ripon (Thur and Sat), Settle (Tue) and Skipton (every day except Sun and Tue, with stalls picturesquely leading up to the castle entrance) exercise a similar lure. So does Beverley (Sat) in the old East Riding, with its two squares actually called Saturday Market and Wednesday Market. Goods match the outstanding setting here.

Bargains are not the only appeal of West Yorkshire's other notable hunting ground for the thrifty: the network of mill shops. Textiles are not what they were in the nineteenth and early twentieth century, when West Yorkshire clothed much of the world; but the county's high quality firms have weathered successive recessions by keeping up standards unmatched by mass-produced foreign competitors.

Mill shops display a fascinating range of clothing made from the washing, combing, carding, spinning and weaving of wool. Most larger mills have a shop attached, frequently specialising in seconds (faults are almost invisible) and other bargains. One of the largest and most interesting, even if you are not remotely intending to buy anything, is Lister's, incorporated into the vast bulk of Manningham Mills in Bradford. Velvet seconds are available here by the yard, and it is a delight to stroke the swatches, savour the colours and contemplate the continuing skills of West Yorkshire's most famous trade.

Early Closing Days (EC) and Market Days (M)

Ashbourne, (EC) Wed (M) Thur, Sat

Bakewell, (EC) Thur (M) Mon

Barnsley, (EC) Thur (M) Tue, Wed, Fri, Sat

Batley, (EC) Tue (M) Fri, Sat

Bawtry, (EC) Thur (M) Sun

Bentham, (EC) Thur (M) Wed

Beverley, (EC) Thur (M) Sat

Bingley, (EC) Tue (M) Wed, Fri

Boroughbridge, (EC) Thur (M) Mon

Bradford, (EC) Wed (M) Mon, Tue, Thur–Sat

Bridlington, (M) Wed, Sat

Brigg, (EC) Wed (M) Thur, Sat

Buxton, (EC) Wed (M) Tue, Sat

Castleford, (EC) Wed (M) Mon–Sat

Castleton, (M) Wed

Doncaster, (EC) Thur (M) Tue, Fri, Sat

Driffield, (EC) Wed (M) Thur, Sat

Easingwold, (EC) Wed (M) Fri

Glossop, (EC) Tue (EC) Thur–Sat

Goole, (M) Wed, Fri, Sat

Grassington, (EC) Thur

Great Ayton, (EC) Wed

Halifax, (M) Fri, Sat

Harrogate, (EC) Wed (M) Mon–Sat

Hatfield, (EC) Thur

Hawes, (EC) Wed (M) Tue

Helmsley, (EC) Wed (M) Thur

Hemsworth, (EC) Wed (M) Tue, Fri, Sat

Holmfirth, (EC) Tue (M) Thur, Sat

Huddersfield, (EC) Wed (M) Mon, Thur

Hull, (M) Thur–Sat

Ilkley, (EC) Wed

Keighley, (EC) Tue

Kirkbymoorside, (EC) Thur (M) Wed

Knaresborough, (EC) Thur (M) Wed

Leeds, (EC) Wed (M) Tue, Fri, Sat

Malton, (EC) Thur (M) Sat

Masham, (EC) Thur (M) Wed, Sat

Matlock, (EC) Thur (M) Tue, Fri

Meltham, (EC) Wed

Middleham, (EC) Wed

Middlesbrough, (M) Mon–Sat

Mirfield, (EC) Tue

New Mills, (EC) Wed (M) Fri, Sat

Northallerton, (M) Wed, Sat

Ossett, (EC) Tue, Wed (M) Tue, Fri

Otley, (EC) Wed (M) Fri, Sat

Pickering, (EC) Wed (M) Mon

Pocklington, (EC) Wed (M) Tue

Pontefract, (EC) Thur (M) Wed, Sat

Richmond, (EC) Wed (M) Thur, Sat

Ripon, (EC) Wed (M) Thur

Rotherham, (EC) Thur (M) Mon, Fri, Sat

Scarborough, (M) Mon–Sat

Selby, (EC) Thur (M) Mon

Settle, (EC) Wed (M) Tue

Sheffield, (EC) Thur (M) Mon–Wed, Fri, Sat

Skipton, (EC) Tue (M) Mon, Wed, Fri, Sat

Thirsk, (EC) Wed, (M) Mon, Sat

Thorne, (EC) Thur (M) Tue, Fri, Sat

Wakefield, (M) Mon–Sat

Wetherby, (EC) Wed (M) Thur

Whitby, (EC) Wed (M) Sat

Wirksworth, (EC) Wed (M) Tue

York, (EC) Wed (M) Mon–Sat

Market and early closing days are subject to alteration at short notice and readers are advised to check such details when finalising their arrangements. Wherever possible the Tourist Information Centres will be pleased to assist with enquiries.

Entertainment
Cinemas

Barnsley	Metro Cinema, Shrewsbury Road, Penistone, (0226) 762004
	Odeon Cinema, 62/68 Eldon Street, (0226) 205494
Beverley	Playhouse Cinema, Market Place, (0482) 881315
Bradford	Odeon Cinema, Princes Way, (0274) 722442
Chesterfield	Regal Cinema, Cavendish Street, (0246) 220876
Doncaster	Cannon Cinema, Cleveland Street, (0302) 366241/367934
	Odeon Cinema, Hallgate, (0302) 344626/342523
Filey	Grand Cinema, Union Street Tel. (0723) 512129
Goole	Carlton Cinema, Boothferry Road, (0405) 762570
Halifax	Cannon Cinema, Wards End, (0422) 346429/352000
Harrogate	Odeon Cinema, East Parade, (0423) 521590/503626
Hebden Bridge	Hebden Bridge Cinema, New Road, (0422) 842807
Huddersfield	Cannon Cinema, Queensgate, (0484) 530874
	Empire Cinema Club, John William Street, (0484) 540978
Hull	Cannon Cinema, 9A Anlaby Road, (0482) 224981/224733
	Odeon Cinema, Kingston Park, Kingston Street, (0482) 586420/586419
Keighley	The Picture House, North Street, (0535) 602561
Leeds	Cannon Cinema, Vicar Lane, (0532) 451013
	Odeon Cinema, The Headrow, (0532) 436230
Malton	Palace Cinema, Chantry Lane, (0653)600008
Matlock	The Ritz Cinema, Causeway Lane, (0629) 582121
Middlesbrough	Odeon Cinema, Corporation Road, (0642) 242888
Northallerton	Lyric Cinema, High St, North End, (0609) 772019
Pickering	Castle Cinema, Burgate, (0751) 72622
Pocklington	Ritz Cinema, Market Place, (0759) 303420
Ripley	Hippodrome Cinema, High Street, (0773) 746559
Sheffield	Odeon Cinema, 1 Burgess Street, (0742) 767962
Shipley	Unit 4 Cinema, Bradford Road, (0274) 583429
Skipton	Plaza Cinema, Sackville Street, (0756) 793417
Wakefield	Cannon Cinema, Kirkdale, (0924) 365236
	Cannon Cinema, Kirkgate, (0924) 373400/365236
York	Odeon Cinema, Blossom Street, (0904) 623040/623287
	York Film Theatre, 156b Haxby Road, (0904) 612940

Theatres and Concert Halls

Bingley	Bingley Little Theatre, Main Street, (0274) 564049/567983
Bradford	Alhambra Theatre, Morley Street, (0274) 752000/757777
	Bradford Playhouse, Chapel Street, (0274) 720329
Bridlington	Spa Theatre, South Marine Drive, (0262) 678258
Buxton	Opera House, Water Street, (0298) 72190
	Pavilion Gardens, St John's Road, (0298) 23114
Chesterfield	Pomegranate Theatre, Corporation Street, (0246) 232901
	The Winding Wheel, Holywell Street, (0246) 220876
Doncaster	Doncaster Civic Theatre, Waterdale, (0302) 342349
Guiseley	Guiseley Theatre, The Green, (0943) 76686
Halifax	Halifax Playhouse, King Cross Street, (0422) 365998
Huddersfield	Venn Street Arts Centre, Venn Street, (0484) 422903
Hull	New Theatre, Kingston Square, (0482) 226655/25994'
Harrogate	Harrogate Theatre, Oxford Street, (0423) 502116
Ilkley	The Playhouse, Weston Road, (0943) 609539
Keighley	Keighley Playhouse, Devonshire Street, (0532) 604764
Leeds	Astoria, Roundhay Road, (0532) 490362
	City Varieties Music Hall, The Headrow, (0532) 430808
	Grand Theatre, 46 New Briggate, (0532) 459351

	Leeds Playhouse, Pennington Street, (0532) 442145
	Opera North, 46 Briggate, (0532) 445326
	The West Yorkshire Playhouse, Quarry Hill Mount, (0532) 442111
Pickering	Kirk Theatre, Hungate, (0751) 74833
Richmond	Georgian Theatre Royal, Victoria Road, (0748) 2472
Rotherham	Rotherham Civic Theatre, Catherine Street, (0709) 823640
Scarborough	Opera House, St Thomas Street, (0723) 369999
	Spa Theatre, The Spa, (0723) 365068
	Stephen Joseph Theatre in the Round, Valley Bridge, (0723) 370541
Sheffield	Crucible/Lyceum Theatre, 55 Norfolk Street, (0742) 769922
	Lantern Theatre, Kenwood Park Road, (0742) 551776
	South Yorkshire Opera, 1 Broad Lane, (0742) 75489
Wakefield	Theatre Royal & Opera House, Drury Lane, (0924) 366556
Whitby	Spa Theatre, Westcliffe, (0947) 604855
York	Grand Opera House, Cumberland Street, (0904) 654654
	Theatre Royal, St Leonards Place, (0904) 623568

Public golf courses

Barnsley, Wombwell Hillies Golf Club (9), Tel. (0226) 754433
Barnsley, Barnsley Golf Club (18), Tel. (0226) 382856
Derby, Allestree Park Golf Club (18), Tel. (0332) 550616
Derby, Derby Golf Club (18), Tel. (0332) 766323
Huddersfield, Bradley Park Golf Club (18), Tel. (0484) 539988
Ilkeston, Ilkeston Golf Club (9), Tel. (0602) 307704
Leeds, Temple Newsam Golf Club (2 x 18), Tel. (0532) 645624
Leeds, Gotts Park Golf Club (18), Tel. (0532) 636600
Leeds, Roundhay Golf Club (9), Tel. (0532) 662695
Pontefract, Pontefract Municipal Course (9), Tel. (0977) 702799
Rotherham, Grange Park Golf Club (18), Tel. (0709) 559497
Sheffield, Concord Park Golf Club (18), Tel. (0742) 570111
Sheffield, Tinsley Park Golf Club (18), Tel. (0742) 560237
Sheffield, Beauchief Golf Club (18), Tel. (0742) 620648
Wakefield, City Of Wakefield Golf Club (18(, Tel. (0924) 255104
Whitwood, Whitwood Golf Club (9), Tel. (0977) 512835

Railway stations (enquiries)

Barnsley (0226) 200148
Bradford (0532) 448133
Doncaster (0302) 340222/344031
Huddersfield (0532) 448133
Hull (0482) 26033
Leeds (0532) 448133
Middlesborough (0325) 355111

Rotherham (Brinsworth) (0709) 360472
Scarborough (0482) 26033
Settle (07292) 3536
Sheffield (0742) 726411
Skipton (0756) 2543
Wakefield (0532) 448133
York (0904) 642155

Regional offices for general enquiries

North East: Main Headquarters Building, York YO1 1HT, (0904) 653022
Midlands: Midland House, Nelson Street, Derby DE1 2SA, (0332) 42442

Private railways

Keighley & Worth Valley Railway, (0535) 645214
North Yorkshire Moors Railway, (0751) 72508

By coach

National Express operates from London, tel. 071-730 0202, the Midlands, tel. 021-622 4373, and the north, tel. Preston (0772) 51177, running a fast service between major towns. Bookings can be made at the above office numbers or in local travel agencies. Tourist Information offices have details of the extensive network of local bus and coach services.

INDEX